THE TAROT ACCORDING TO YOU

A WORKBOOK

NANCY GAREN

A FIRESIDE BOOK
PUBLISHED BY SIMON & SCHUSTER
NEW YORK   LONDON   TORONTO   SYDNEY   SINGAPORE

FIRESIDE
Rockefeller Center
1230 Avenue of the Americas
New York, NY 10020

FIRESIDE and colophon are registered trademarks
of Simon & Schuster, Inc.

Manufactured in the United States of America

1   3   5   7   9   10   8   6   4   2

ISBN 0-684-85044-3

The author gratefully acknowledges permission from the following sources to reprint material in their control:

Beyond Words Publishing, Inc., (800-284-9673), for the poem "Autobiography in Five Short Chapters" from *There's a Hole in My Sidewalk* by Portia Nelson, copyright © 1993 Portia Nelson.

Dell, a division of Bantam, Doubleday, Dell Publishing Group, Inc., for an excerpt from *Evergreen* by Belva Plain, copyright © 1987, and for two excerpts from *Illusions* by Richard Bach, copyright © 1998.

Health Communications, Inc., for "The Rules for Being Human" by Cherie Carter-Scott from *Chicken Soup for the Soul* by Jack Canfield and Mark Victor Hansen, copyright © 1995.

ACKNOWLEDGMENTS

With love to my mom, Donna Del Re,
whose sagacious editing made this book possible;
my sister Patti Strong who supported me during the mean times;
Jean-Charles Beytrison for his "practical" input and humorous insights;
and to all the people who liked my first book and wanted me to write another.

CONTENTS

PART 1

When the student is ready, the teacher appears.

Chinese proverb

◆   WHAT IS THE TAROT?   ◆

The Tarot, or Royal Road, as the ancients referred to it, is a method for discerning the essential truths of life.

It is widely believed that Egyptian Masons developed Tarot cards (which were originally tablets) as a means of charting their spiritual, psychological and physiological discoveries. Over the centuries, as various countries and cultures translated these tablets, many new Tarot decks (and interpretations) came into being. Each one, due to distinctions in religion, philosophy and belief system, differed from the other.

In essence, Tarot cards are stories conveyed in pictures. Think of them as a symbolic history of events, which, when properly interpreted, can be used to foretell or guide an individual's future. But of themselves, they have no inherent powers. What makes the Tarot accurate, unique and profound is *you*!

◆   WHAT ARE THE ADVANTAGES OF
DOING A TAROT WORKBOOK?   ◆

I believe that the only way to really understand the Tarot is to live it experientially. Other people's interpretations (including mine) simply aren't enough. As insightful as they seem, until you experience a card personally, it will never be exactly right.

One of the most enlightening and transformational journeys I ever undertook was when I decided to travel the "Royal Road" and make my own Tarot deck.

Much more than the mere mechanical production of a set of cards, journaling about my Tarot experience on a day-to-day basis increased my awareness in every area of my life: work, love, the people I was involved with and what I was doing on the planet in the first place. It was as if I had tapped into an Akashic record that allowed me to peek between the veils of secrecy and understand the inner workings of God, his works and his children.

When I was working with a Court card, I found that I *knew* what it felt like to be a different astrological sign than I am because I literally experienced it as if I *were* that sign.

As I explored the Suits (Wands, Cups, Swords and Pentacles) I realized firsthand the essence of their meaning, from the beginning or inception of an idea (Wands) to the completion and/or manifestation of that idea (Pentacles).

When my card was a Major Arcana, I always felt that a power greater than myself was steering my course and that I was gaining insights that not only helped me move beyond my personal limitations, but deal with the world more effectively.

In short, living the Tarot made such a difference in my life and my ability to accurately read for others that I couldn't wait to share the process with you.

Through *The Tarot According to You,* you will be able to re-create the same enlightening journey that I embarked upon, and I believe that as *you* walk the Royal Road, your increased perceptions, clarity and confidence will not only provide a means of guidance for your future, but a life-changing transformation as well.

How is this possible? It's as simple as pulling a card and then jotting down your observations and experiences. I've established some guidelines to help you get started, but believe me, like the river, it flows by itself!

Another advantage of this process is that you learn by doing. You are actually creating new pathways and you're teaching yourself as you go along. But don't worry, you are not alone in this. God, your Higher Self, Higher Power, Guardian Angel or whatever you choose to call It will be right there beside you. You may not be aware of it now, but I promise you that by the time you've completed this workbook, Its loving presence will make Itself known. In *The Tarot According to You* you will have answers that are tailored to your life, interpretations that address your needs and insights that speak to your soul.

If you ever wished that you could really learn the Tarot, do readings for yourself and others or be more in touch with your inner guidance, this book is for you.

CHAPTER 1

The Basics

 ## TRADITIONALLY SPEAKING

If you haven't already done so, the first thing you will need to do is buy yourself a deck of Tarot cards. My suggestion is to go to a store that sells several selections and look at them all. There is such a wide variety of cards on the market today, I'm sure you will find one that you feel comfortable with. My favorites are the Rider-Waite, Cosmic, Connolly and Palladini decks, but it really doesn't matter what cards you choose; all that matters is that you like them because all Tarot decks share a common theme. Each consists of seventy-eight cards depicting life experiences from the mundane to the sublime, and each contains three sections: twenty-two Major Arcana, forty Minor (or Lesser) Arcana and sixteen Court Arcana.

The Major Arcana are the strongest cards in the deck. They signify soul growth and herald *major* lessons and opportunities designed to put us on the right path and help us to evolve. When a Major Arcana appears in a reading, we become conscious of something that was previously unknown or face challenges emanating from beyond our personal sphere of influence or control.

The Minor Arcana is comprised of four suits: Wands, Cups, Swords and Pentacles. These cards deal with our human aspirations, planes of expression and the *minor* (or more mundane) aspects of life:

The Wands (or Rods) represent ideas, growth, creativity and expansion. When a Wand appears in a reading, one is motivated by what inspires and what one can begin or create. Concepts, enterprise and things usually take precedence over people and/or social amenities. The element associated with the suit of Wands is fire.

The Cups refer to emotions, pleasure seeking, intuition and spiritual awareness. When a Cup appears in a reading, one becomes more conscious of his/her emotional needs and the spiritual/metaphysical realm. People, feelings and emotional fulfillment become more important than things or mental pursuits. The element associated with the suit of Cups is water.

The Swords signify discernment, struggle, sorrow or sickness. When a Sword appears, striving to achieve one's goals generally overshadows one's inner world or more pleasurable activities, and physical requirements (health, stamina, acumen, etc.) become paramount. The element associated with the suit of Swords is air.

The Pentacles (or Coins) deal with tangibles and issues involving money, manifestation, values or power. When a Pentacle appears, the material aspects of life are emphasized and one is more concerned with rewards, utilizing one's abilities or how one is demonstrating one's power. The element associated with the suit of Pentacles is earth.

The Court Arcana contain four Kings, four Queens, four Knights and four Pages (or Princes and Princesses). These cards, with the exception of the Knights, are represented by the twelve astrological signs of the zodiac and aspects associated with the type of person their suit represents.

Traditionally, the Kings and Queens are adults and the Pages are youths or children. Although most Tarot cards depict the Court Arcana as males or females, I experience them as people who are active or passive or expressing masculine or feminine aspects of their psyche.

The Knights indicate movement, sudden changes and situations that are coming into or going out of one's life. Therefore, they are not given any astrological significance.

◆ THE MEANING OF THE NUMBERS ◆

The numbers on Tarot cards refer to stages of development based upon the principles of numerology. There are nine "root" numbers, which, put simply, represent the following:

1. Beginnings
2. Assimilation
3. Expression
4. Solidification
5. Change
6. Adjustment
7. Inner work
8. Outer reward
9. Completion

There are also two master numbers (11 and 22). Although they have the same basic meaning as their "root" number (2 and 4), master numbers aspire to qualities that are often loftier than, or superior to, one's current level of understanding.

In this book, *all* numbers except the 11 and 22 are read as a single-digit number.

Numbers 1 through 22 in the Major Arcana refer to one's evolutionary process from the beginning, or original thought (The Magician, number 1), to enlightenment, or material mastery (The Fool, number 22).* These numbers provide insights into the purpose and impelling force of each Major Arcana experience and point to the opportunities that, if followed, bring success, self-realization and reward.

The sequence, Ace (1) through 10, on the Lesser Arcana pertain to a beginning (Ace), a completion (9) and a cyclical rebeginning (10). Included in these numbers are a positive, constructive application and a negative challenge.

◆ THE SIGNIFICANCE OF THE SIGNS AND PLANETS ◆

When I was learning the Tarot, it seemed that every book I read had a different slant on the astrological associations to the cards. For instance, one respected author would write that the sign associated with the Queen of Swords is Virgo, while another would say it's Libra. This was quite confusing to me, and until I actually experienced the

---

*Note: In most Tarot books, The Fool is interpreted as a "0." Because of the way I experience it, I prefer to think of it as the master number 22.

cards myself, I didn't know who to believe. As it turned out, to me, The Queen of Swords felt like a Virgo. And although some Tarot books combine the signs and planets, I believe the signs fit the Court Arcana because they represent personalities, and the planets belong with the Major Arcana because they rule the signs and other significant aspects of our lives. I also felt that two planets best described the Major Arcana instead of just one. Therefore, this book will contain *my* take on the Court cards and the Major Arcana; however, *your* interpretation may differ.

In case you're not familiar with astrology, I've listed some of the basic characteristics of the astrological signs you'll be seeing in the Court Arcana as well as the ten planets I'll be using in conjunction with the Major Arcana.

The Astrological Signs Associated with the Court Cards are as follows:

Sign	Personality	House	Deals With	Symbol
Aries March 21–April 19	Bold Forceful Direct	1st	Beginnings Physical Self Outlook on the world	♈
Taurus April 20–May 20	Practical Persistent Patient	2nd	Finances Possessions Security	♉
Gemini May 21–June 20	Versatile Mental Clever	3rd	Communications Relatives Short journeys	♊
Cancer June 21–July 22	Sensitive Intuitive Changeable	4th	Home environment Endings Mother	♋
Leo July 23–August 22	Affectionate Adventurous Creative	5th	Love affairs Pleasurable pursuits Children	♌

Virgo
August 23–September 22

Analytical
Cautious
Reserved

6th

Work
Service
Health

♍

Libra
September 23–October 22

Balanced
Just
Harmonious

7th

Marriage
Partnerships
Dealings with the public

♎

Scorpio
October 23–November 21

Secretive
Intense
Shrewd

8th

Death
Occult experiences
Legacies

♏

Sagittarius
November 22–December 21

Independent
Philosophical
Sportive

9th

Higher learning
Vision
Long journeys

♐

Capricorn
December 22–January 19

Pragmatic
Conventional
Responsible

10th

Profession
Worldly attainments
Father

♑

Aquarius
January 20–February 18

Sociable
Progressive
Humanitarian

11th

Aspirations
Associates
Friends

♒

Pisces
February 19–March 20

Mystical
Imaginative
Impressionable

12th

Institutions
The psychic realm
Karma and
    self-undoing

♓

Planets Associated with the Major Arcana

Planet	Deals With
Sun	Identity, manner of expression, direction of energy
Moon	Moods, feelings, responses to life
Mercury	Thinking, perspective, communication

Planets Associated with the Major Arcana (*cont.*)

Planet	Deals With
Venus	Attraction, love, beauty
Mars	Action, conflict, accidents, impatience
Jupiter	Luck, success, enlargement, improvement
Saturn	Tribulations, blocks, lessons, delays
Uranus	Changes, testing, upheavals
Neptune	Idealism, confusion, illusion, dissolve
Pluto	Letting go, transformation, rebirth

◆ UNDERSTANDING THE SYMBOLS ◆

Symbols are a means of communicating information without a language barrier. We dream in symbols and most of us think in symbols. For instance, if I say "a rose has thorns" most of you will picture a rose rather than the sentence structure.

In like manner, the pictures on Tarot cards are a means of conveying a thought without the use of words. They speak to our hearts as well as our minds.

Most of the symbols below were from the Rider-Waite Tarot deck. Some of the definitions are universal concepts; many are my own. Needless to say, they are not the only interpretations possible. As you work with your cards, you will undoubtedly come up with valuable insights and, hopefully, the following symbol descriptions will inspire you to keep exploring.

ANDROGYNOUS: Blending of male and female energy. *See* Male and Female.

ANGEL/CHERUB: Important message or dream. Connection between man and God, heaven and earth. Spiritual activation, development, go-between. Guardian angel.

ANKH: Egyptian symbol of life everlasting. Spiritual power. Drawing on ancient wisdom and Akashic records.

APPLES: Knowledge of good and evil, right and wrong. Temptation.

ARMOR: Feeling impervious to danger or needing to protect one's self.

ARMS: What one is reaching for, blocking, holding on to, or surrendering. *Also see* Hand.

ASTROLOGICAL SYMBOLS: Tools, talents, gifts, various approaches to life.

AURA/HALO: Enlightened thinking.

BANDAGE: Feeling wounded. Hurt. Defensive. Desire to protect or be noticed.

BANNER: Accomplishing a feat.

BED: Transition from body to spirit. A message asking us: are we awake or asleep? The bed we've made for ourselves. The need for nurturing, relaxation, or letting go.

BEGGAR: Spiritually or materially impoverished. Needy.

BIRDS: Ability to soar above one's current problems or beliefs.

BLEEDING: A painful or draining experience.

BONDS/BLINDFOLD: Feeling restricted, limited, "tied up." Not seeing alternatives.

BOAT/SHIP: Ability to navigate the ups and downs of life; deal with our emotions. Flowing with or against the tide. Material treasures.

BOOK: The "book of life." The search for God or purpose. A message to be open to new information and experiences.

BRIDGE: Making a transition. Bridging states of consciousness or emotions.

BUTTERFLY: Transformation.

CASTLE/HOUSE: Our dreams. What we aspire to, what we are in the process of becoming or manifesting. Various aspects of the self. *Also see* Window.

CAT: Clairvoyant abilities or paranormal experiences. An actual cat.

CHAINS: Something that is imprisoning or enslaving one. *Also see* Bonds.

CHILD: Undeveloped potential. Recognizing one's childlike qualities and positive aspects of self. Birth of a new self. An actual child or birth.

CITY: Commerce. Trade. Dealings in the world. What we've made of our lives or are striving for.

CIRCLE: Wholeness. Completeness. God. Eternity.

CLOAK/CURTAIN/MASK: Something yet to be revealed.

CLOUD: Force of the divine. Growing spiritual awareness. Jagged: strife, conflict, "stormy weather," literally or figuratively.

COFFIN: Buried parts of self. Atonement.

COLORS:

Red: Energy, desire, passion.

Pink: Love. Concord. Unification of one's earthly desires with the will of the Divine.

Yellow: Intellect. Objective mind. The search for fulfillment.

Orange: Blending of intellect and passion. Development. Self-control.

Green: Healing. Growth. Nature. Money.

Blue: Reflection. Perseverance. Poise.

Purple: Self-confidence. Spiritual thinking or application.

Brown: Material thinking or application.

White: Divine protection. Spiritual power. Positive thinking. Yang/male energy.

Gray: Making a transition from one state to another. "Gray area."

Black: Unknowns. Unconscious aspects of self. Negative thinking. Yin/female energy.

CONCRETE: Making something real, actual or solid.

CRAYFISH: Fear of the unknown. A negative aspect of self. A problem that will soon surface. *Also see* Fish.

CROSS: Cross to bear. Sacrifice. Block. Lack of self-love or spiritual understanding. A message to awaken to one's inner truths.

CROWN: Who or what is ruling our lives. Crown chakra.

CUP: Symbol of fulfillment, who or what will bring it and how one feels about it. Note position, placement and what the cup is filled with for clues.

DEATH: End of an era, situation or part of self.

DEVIL: Race-conscious beliefs. Materialistic viewpoint. Negative thinking or energy. Earthbound spirit. Worshiping the wrong things.

DOG: Elevated part of the self. *Faith*ful companion. An actual dog. *Also see* Wolf.

DOORWAY/OPENING/ARCH/KEY: Opportunity. Discovery. Access.

DOVE: Spiritual awakening. A message from above. The Holy Spirit. God's grace.

EAGLE: Spiritual ascension. Freedom from limitations or bondage.

ELEMENTS:

Fire: Masculine. Spirit. Lion. East. Intuit. Create. Initiate. Inspire.

Water: Feminine. Spirit. Eagle. West. Sense. Respond. Nurture. Feel.

Air: Masculine. Body. Man. North. Reason. Alert. Carry on. Do.

Earth: Feminine. Body. Bull. South. Imbue. Possess. Reap. Be.

EYE: "I" see. "I" know. "I" understand. "I" am. Eyes closed: a message to look inward for answers.

FACE: Facing life. Facing up to situations. How we identify ourselves.

FAMILY: Harmonious integration of all parts of the self. Cooperative unions.

FEATHER: A gift from above. "A feather in your cap." A message to lighten up.

FEET/LEGS: Understanding. Foundation. Ability to move forward in life.

FEMALE: Passive. Receptive. Gentle. Intuitive mind. Opening. In. Later. Stay.

FIRE: Illumination. Purification.

FISH/DOLPHINS: Plumbing our spiritual depths. Emerging awareness. A message to meditate or use our intuition. Manna.

FLAG: A message of warning or surrender.

FLOWERS: How we make use of our potential. Our mental "garden." Seeds we've sown in life. The "flowering" of our abilities.

FRUIT: Reaping the fruits of our labor. *Also see* Apples and Pomegranate.

GARDEN: The manifestations of our conscious and subconscious mind.

HAND: Hand of God. Offerings. Means of expressing ourselves. Ways of dealing with experiences.

> *Up:* Look to God.
>
> *Extended:* Something offered to you or to be given by you.
>
> *Left:* Receives.
>
> *Right:* Gives.
>
> *Holding something:* Grasp the opportunity.

HANGING/FALLING: A message to surrender, release negative thoughts, look at things differently or reverse one's thinking.

HEART: Opening of the heart chakra. Ability to love and be loved. Embracing life.

HORNS: A choice, decision or dilemma.

HORSE: Movement. Freedom. Expanded sense of self. A message or messenger from God. Facing left: something coming in. Facing right: something going out.

KING: Awareness of self and worth. Giving. *Also see* Male.

LAME: Crippled by fear or doubt.

LEMNISCATE (HORIZONTAL 8): Balancing energies. Unlimited potential.

LIGHT/LAMP: Lighting the way. Enlightened state of consciousness. Wisdom. Clarity.

LIGHTENING: A rude awakening. A bolt from above. Seeing the truth.

LILIES: Purified desires. Rebirth into higher states of consciousness.

LION: Animal nature. Sexual self. Masculine energy. Courage. Meeting one's fears. Owning one's power.

MALE: Active. Creative. Strong. Reasoning mind. Penetrating. Out. Now. Go.

MAN: *See* Male.

MONK/PRIEST: Spiritual initiation. A message to seek answers from within; to recognize the Divine in *all* things.

MOON: Facing our illusions. Hidden perils or unconscious aspects of self. Crescent: not seeing the whole picture; a message to follow the light of the soul.

MOUNTAIN: Attainment. Enlightening experience. Triple peaks: unity of mind, body and soul. *Also see* Pyramid.

NAKED: The "naked truth." The "bare" facts. Vulnerability. Something exposed.

OLD MAN: Wisdom gained through experience. *Also see* Male.

PATH: Goal. Direction in life. Paths we choose: inner or outer, toward or away, up or down, etc.

PENTACLE: Symbol of material power and how one uses or abuses it.

PEOPLE: Various aspects of self. Sitting, lying, dancing, working: the "position" one is taking or needs *to* take (point of view, attitude, implementation, etc.). *Also see* Male and Female.

PILLARS: Support system. Beliefs. Inner truths. *Also see* Tower.

PLATFORM/BENCH: Rising to the occasion. Stepping up in the world. Becoming bigger than we are. Higher awareness. Working at our trade.

POMEGRANATE: Abundant possibilities. United parts of the self. *Also see* Fruit.

PYRAMID: Secret treasures. Accomplishment at great effort. *Also see* Mountain.

QUEEN: Awareness of others and one's inner guidance. Receiving. *Also see* Female.

RAIN: Tears. Sorrow. Release.

RAINBOW: A bridge between heaven and earth. God's reminder of His love for us.

ROCKS: Grounding.

ROSES: Desires. Passions. Red: Physical. White: Spiritual.

SAILS: Who or what is guiding or pushing one.

SCALES: Balance. Justice. Objectivity. Impartiality. Karmic or man-made laws. Time.

SKY: A message to look up or beyond limitations.

SNOW/ICE: Crystallized thoughts, frozen emotions. A message to let go, "melt," change.

SPHINX: Mysteries revealed. Choice between "aliveness" or "deadness."

SQUARE: The physical world. The four elements. Limitations or stepping stones.

STAR: The call of destiny. Guiding light. Inner truth. Hope. "Wishing upon a star."
> *Five-pointed star (pentagram):* The five senses. The five parts of the body.
> *Eight-pointed star:* Cosmic order.
> *Upside-down star:* Misuse of energy and power. Negative influence.

STREAM: Flow of consciousness.

SUN: Facing ourselves. Our potential in the outer world. *Also see* Face.

SWORD: Symbol of action or reaction. The two-edged blade can cut either way.

TENT: Temporary situation or perception of self.

THRONE: Who or what one gives power or sovereignty to.

TOWER: Self-imposed limitations. Twin towers: one's male and female counterparts. *Also see* Male and Female, Pillars.

TREE: "Tree of knowledge." Stages of growth and development.
> *Roots:* Strong, "down to earth," "deeply rooted."
> *Trunk:* Rising above "base" emotions, earthly pulls, ego.
> *Limbs:* Capacity to reach out to the world or support life.
> *Leaves:* The flowering of one's talents, gifts and abilities.

TRIANGLE: Trinity of mind, body, spirit. Pointed up: female. Pointed down: male.

TRUMPET: A message to pay attention; listen, "hear the call."

VINES: Growth. *Also see* Tree.

WALL: Something to surmount. Who or what is blocking one.

WAND: Symbol of energy and how one directs it.

WATER/SEA: Emotional or subconscious state. Note condition of water: calm, tumultuous, stagnant, choppy, etc. *Also see* Stream.

WHEEL/ROTA: How we move through life. Ups and downs. Karma. Cyclical return. Spinning chakras. The Royal Road.

WINDOW: A "window of opportunity." Looking into, or outside of, ourselves. What is our current perspective? How clear are we?

WINGS: Ability to transcend difficulties.

WOLF: Lower self. *Also see* Dog.

WOMAN: *See* Female.

WORLD: Material manifestation. Earthly values.

WREATH: Something completed. A cause to celebrate.

YOUTH: Becoming aware. Growing up. Learning. Trying.

ZERO: *See* Circle.

◆

CHAPTER 2

How to Use This Book

◆ BEGINNING YOUR JOURNEY:
IT'S AS EASY AS 1, 2, 3! ◆

All right. You've got your cards, you've read all the fundamental stuff and now you want to get on with it! Well okay!

1. Shuffle the deck and silently ask: "What's coming up for me this week?" When you feel the cards are shuffled enough, take the top card off the deck and place it face up before you. Then go to chapter 5 in the back of the book and write down the name of your card on the page that says "Your Card for the Week."

2. At the end of the week (or sooner if the spirit moves you), turn to Chapter 4, "Walking the Royal Road," and find the pages that correspond to your card. After reading the information I've provided, record what you have experienced and observed. I've included specific categories from my book *Tarot Made Easy*, so if you prefer, you can just underline the relevant parts.

   Note: If you're already familiar with the Tarot and have some working knowledge of what the cards represent, you can expedite this procedure by doing a card a day. However, your range of experiences would obviously be less.

3. The final step in the process will be to compare your experiential observations to the pictures on your Tarot card and notice whether or not anything stands out about it

that you weren't aware of before. You may also want to jot down any words, images or symbols you feel the card *should* have included; or your creative genius emerges and you decide to create your own deck of cards!

Don't feel shy about using your own designs; modern symbols are just as acceptable as the traditional ones. If you flew to Hawaii, for instance, you could draw an airplane. If you purchased a new car, you could just write "bought a car."

Once you've finished exploring your first week (or day), put that card back in the deck and shuffle the cards for the next week (or day). Ask the same question (What's coming up for me this week/day?) and then repeat steps 2 and 3. Continue in this manner, pulling a new card each week (or day), until all seventy-eight cards have been experienced.

During the time it takes to complete this workbook, it's likely that you'll have a few repetitive cards, especially if you're experiencing a prolonged situation of any kind. If this happens and a card you've already had comes up again, make a note of it in Chapter 5 on "Your Card for the Week" page, then shuffle once more, take another card from the deck and record it. Your notes will be for the new card, but by keeping a record of both, you'll be able to see how the second card you drew related to, or clarified, the original.

You'll notice that the cards don't repeat themselves too often. When they do, it's usually because you've overlooked some important aspect, or a similar situation occurs in a slightly different way.

Don't concern yourself with how long it's going to take to finish all of your cards; the journey is just as important as the destination, and the insights you'll gain and the accuracy of your readings will be well worth the time you put into it. If you want to skip a day, week, month or year for that matter, that's okay too. You can always pick up where you left off later.

◆ # PERSONALIZING YOUR EXPERIENCE ◆

At the beginning of the Major Arcana and each of the four suits (pages 00, 00, 00, 00, 00), you'll find a question and answer sheet that you can use in addition to and in conjunction with your weekly observations. I included this query sheet because when I was studying the Tarot, I had a lot of questions besides "What's coming up for me this week?" (as I'm sure you will) that took longer than a week to be answered as I had to wait for the events to happen (or not happen). I found that by pulling a card for each specific question and keeping a record of the question, card and answer on my query sheet, it not only sped up the process of learning the Tarot (because I was able to utilize more cards), it also augmented my weekly cards by adding perspectives that weren't readily apparent. As time went on and I continued to review my query sheets, a definite pattern emerged in the way the cards answered me. A case in point: almost invariably, if I asked a question about money or material matters, a Pentacle would turn up. When I asked about love, an emotional issue or something very important, more often than not I'd get a Cup or a Major Arcana.

You'll find that the more questions you ask, the greater your understanding will be. So by all means, when you have a question, pull a card. You don't have to wait until you've completed the workbook. As time goes on, and your query-sheet questions are being answered, you'll be amazed at the way all of the seemingly unrelated and/or synchronistic events came together.

For those of you who *hate* journaling, you can omit the weekly process altogether and just use the query sheet to record your questions and cards, then when your answers come, you can transfer them from your query sheet to the corresponding card pages. I didn't do it this way but it's *your* book and you can use it whichever way works the best for you!

Following each query sheet are your Tarot card pages. This will be *The Tarot According to You*! Think of it as your road map and reference book for the future. The categories therein pose *suggested* interpretations in the form of questions with ample space for you to personalize the information to fit your experience.

These categories are as follows:

FOCUS:
This represents the general atmosphere: the events, highlights or conditions that capsulize the overall thrust of your experience.

DESIRES:
Covers the things you want, wish or yearn for.

LOVE:
Defines your personal relationships: whether you are married or single, in a committed relationship or unattached. Your feelings, your experiences or your thoughts about love and relationships can be expressed here.

OTHERS:

Deals with people who have an effect on you. It covers your friends, business associates (or people you do business with), spiritual mentors or anyone else you come in contact with who influences your life in some way.

HOME:

Relates to your dwelling or property. It also includes things that come into your home such as mail, news, visitors or callers, etc.

TRAVEL:

Represents comings or goings, influences surrounding travel, that which is in transit (through the air, media, internet, and so forth) or traveling to you, weather conditions and trips of all kinds, be they short, long or only in your mind.

WORK:

Covers your job, career or place you find yourself operating in most frequently, be it at home or in the field. This could also represent housework, schooling, hobbies or projects. Whatever you are industriously applying yourself toward, or that *feels* like work, goes here.

BODY/MIND:

This grouping deals with your health and well-being. It comprises the mental, physical and emotional aspects of your life: your feelings, attitudes, bodily needs or wants and anything else related to your corporal self.

SPIRIT:

This category relates to things of the spirit: intuition, dreams, ESP experiences and so forth. It also represents tangible pleasures (gardening, watching a good movie with your sweetheart, having a BBQ, etc.), gifts that are given or received and events that make you feel lucky, grateful or blessed. Anything that brings happiness, gives you enjoyment, lifts your spirits or enlightens you can be noted here.

RELATIVES:

Deals with your immediate family (including your pets), your in-laws and those who are so close you think of them as family, such as dear friends or ex-spouses.

FINANCES:

Covers everything relating to money and finance.

PROBLEMS:

Relates to trouble spots, problems and disappointments; events that discourage you or cause you to be anxious, worried or depressed and how/if you deal with them.

GUIDANCE:

This is a very significant topic because it concerns the advice you receive (intuitively or externally) that, when followed, works to your benefit, or what you come to understand about your experience that makes your way easier.

SUCCESS:

This category is not limited to worldly or material success. It also includes inner rewards; personal achievements or accomplishments; and who, what or where your success comes from.

ACTION:

Describes the action(s) you take, decisions you make or the difficulties you must overcome in order to achieve your goals or accomplish your objectives.

This blank line is for you. It's for anything you want to add to your list of experiences. It's the last "category" and you can call it anything you choose. If you'd like to include an "outcome," name it that.

When considering the interpretations I've provided, ask yourself:
- Does the information apply?
- *How* does it specifically pertain to me?
- What could I add that wasn't said?

If the categories or definitions *don't* add to your understanding or fit your experience, *IGNORE* them! The only thing that counts is what was going on with *you*. For instance:

MENTALLY

- What direction were your thoughts taking? Were you contemplating the future or the past; the positive aspects of your life or the negatives; what you could do or what you couldn't?
- Were you studying or going through any specialized training? If so, what kind? Vocational? Scholastic? Psychological? Spiritual?

- Were you alert and aware or were you tiptoeing through life, distracted or unmindful?
- Were your perceptions clear or did you feel lost and confused?
- What did you want?

PHYSICALLY

- Were you healthy or ill? If you were ailing, what kind of problems were you having? Could you see any correlation between your illness and what you were thinking or doing?
- Did you develop a sudden interest in exercise or nutrition? If so, what was it?
- Did you have bursts of energy that caused you to be more productive than usual or were you tired and listless?
- Was it a time of relief and healing or of burdens and pressure?
- Were there any deaths or miraculous recoveries?
- What were you experiencing sexually?
- What did you do?

EMOTIONALLY

- What type of relationships did you have? Romantic? Platonic? Teacher/student? Were they nurturing and supportive or painful and depressing? Did you *want* a relationship?
- How did you feel when you were with your husband/wife/lover?
- What were you feeling about yourself?
- What, if any, impact did your environment have on you?
- How were you responding to the world in general? Did you feel compassionate and understanding or indifferent and disinterested? Were you loving and responsive or angry and resentful?
- Were you experiencing a time of harmony and contentment or dissatisfaction and chaos?
- What did you feel?

SPIRITUALLY

- What effect were the events in your life having upon you? Did they lead you to seek spiritual guidance or deeper understanding? Were you receiving benefit from any religious groups, metaphysical teachings or "new age" establishments?
- How were you relating to your position in the universe? Did you feel as if you were being tested or did you feel blessed and rewarded? Was it a time of good fortune and faith in your future or of bad luck and feelings of hopelessness?

- Were there any uplifting, transcending or enlightening revelations? If so, did they come about as the result of another person or was your guidance of an indirect nature as in dreams, visions, insights or intuitive impressions?
- Did anyone (or anything) profoundly affect the way you felt about yourself or how you viewed your reality?
- Did you receive guidance that changed the way you perceived yourself or your world?
- Did you have any mystical experiences?
- Was there a sudden manifestation of psychic, clairvoyant or ESP abilities?
- What inspired you?
- What did you believe?

MATERIALLY

- Did you enjoy your work and get along with your boss or employees? Were you looking for a job or a different career? Did you want to start your own business?
- Was your income satisfactory? Did you make the kind of money you wanted? Did you earn the income you felt you deserved? Did you feel capable of achieving wealth?
- How did you make your money?
- Did you feel like a lucky person or that you were more fortunate than others?
- Were you feeling successful?
- Did you aspire to a position of power, authority or fame?
- What were your accomplishments?
- Were you happy with your home life? Did you look forward to being with your family? Did you spend your weekends with your children? Did your husband/wife/significant other understand you? Did you move, buy new furniture or redecorate your house?
- Did you take a vacation? Were your travels enjoyable? Where did you go? What were the weather conditions like?
- Did you buy or sell a vehicle? Was there anything unusual about your means of transportation?
- Did you do anything out of the ordinary?
- Did you have what you wanted?

IF YOUR CARD WAS A MAJOR ARCANA

- Were there any "major" changes or developments? If so, were you personally responsible for them or did you feel that they happened *to* you?
- Did you become aware of something you didn't see before?
- Did anything alter your course? If so, how or in what capacity?

- Were there any superior accomplishments, achievements, breakthroughs or transformational experiences?
- Did you feel compelled to mature or evolve?
- Was the impact of this card more strongly felt than other cards?
- Did more than one planet fit your experience? Did any?

IF YOUR CARD WAS A COURT ARCANA (King, Queen, Knight, Page)

- Was the astrological sign or month significant in any way?
- Did the traditional interpretation or ethnic coloring apply?
- Did you come into contact with anyone who shaped your life or altered your thinking?
- Did you find that you experienced yourself or your perceptions differently?
- Were there any sudden beginnings or endings when your card was a Knight?
- Were children, lovers or problems accentuated when your card was a Page?

IF YOUR CARD WAS A MINOR ARCANA (Ace-10)

- Was the season noteworthy when you experienced an Ace? Did it mark a new phase or signal a new direction? Did anything "spring" up or "fall" into place?
- Were any new projects contemplated or ideas cultivated when your card was a Wand?
- Were you more aware of your emotional and/or spiritual needs when your card was a Cup?
- Did you act and accomplish goals when your card was a Sword or were there conflicts and health problems?
- Did business, material concerns, accumulation or finances occupy your thoughts when your card was a Pentacle?
- Was there a culmination or rebeginning when your card was a 10?

For more examples of the types of questions your cards can address, see "Doing Readings," pages 00–00.

The main and most important thing to keep in mind is that this is a book about *your* Tarot experience. It's about *your* life, *your* revelations and *your* "ah ha's." It's *not* about strict adherence to Tarot traditions, answering every question or trying to make information that doesn't fit, fit. The *only* thing that matters is what's meaningful to *you*. My suggestions are *only meant as a guide,* and although they are designed to assist your understanding and help you organize your thoughts, your experience could be *completely different* and my interpretations may not apply at all!

Once you have experienced all of the cards, you will be qualified to do meaningful, accurate readings for yourself and others, and it's my belief that you will attract the people who need to hear what you have to say. The only difference between reading for yourself or reading for another may be the semantics; i.e., if your notes say you bought a car, the person you're reading for might buy a truck, bike or an RV. However, in most cases, your interpretation will be right on the money.

CHAPTER 3

Making the Most of Your Cards

♦ DOING READINGS ♦

If you're like me, chances are you'll ultimately want to create your own Tarot card spreads, but in the interim, the most commonly used is the Keltic (or Celtic) Cross. In case you're not familiar with it, the layout and significance of the card positions is as follows:

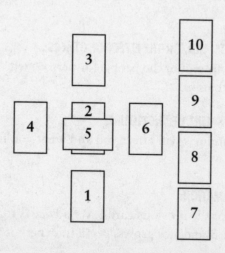

CARD 1, THE BASIS OF THE MATTER:

Indicates that which brought you to the point where you are now.

CARD 2, WHERE YOU ARE NOW:

Represents you in the present and the circumstances that motivate your question or concern.

CARD 3, HOPES OR FEARS:

Describes the inner workings of your mind as a result of your past and present and is oftentimes the determining factor in the outcome of your reading.

CARD 4, PRESENT AND PASSING:

Covers not only your recent past, but long-term blocks or influences, and although its effect may still be felt, its influence is passing away.

CARD 5, FORCES FOR OR AGAINST YOU:

Indicates the conditions surrounding your question. If the card is positive, they will be working in your favor. If it's negative, opposing.

CARD 6, THE NEAR FUTURE:

Shows how you've emerged from your recent past as well as any new factors that come into play.

CARD 7, HOW THE NEAR FUTURE WILL EVOLVE:

Reveals the way you've responded to the sixth card and how or in what way the future is evolving.

CARD 8, NEW TURN OF EVENTS AND/OR THE EFFECT OF OTHERS:

Indicates new developments and/or the people (or person) who will alter your course or shed new light on your situation.

CARD 9, YOU IN THE ENVIRONMENT OF THE FUTURE:

Reveals how your surroundings will affect you and what you'll think or feel in times to come.

CARD 10, OUTCOME OR SUMMATION:

Is the outworking of all of the previous cards. My advice is to start with a basic layout such as this, and as your confidence grows, begin to experiment with the more complicated ones. I've devoted an entire chapter to spreads in my book *Tarot Made Easy,* and there are several other books on the subject if you need to know more.

YOUR QUESTIONS

It's important to formulate your questions as clearly as you can. If you ask one thing but think another, the cards may answer your underlying thought. More often than not, a misunderstood answer is the result of an ambiguous question. When in doubt, think of the situation you *want* to happen and then word your question accordingly.

It also helps to put a time limit on questions, such as: "What's going to come up between now and January?" or "Will I sell my house before this time next year?"

One thing I *never* ask is *ever* (such as will I *ever* fall in love, etc.). The cards seem to know you're going to ask the question again and they will only focus on your current situation (or fear).

MAJOR ARCANA CARDS ANSWER QUESTIONS SUCH AS:
- What are the forces working for or against me?
- What is the purpose of my experience?
- What major lesson am I learning?
- What is the highest path for me to pursue?
- What am I destined to learn, become or do?
- Where will I find my opportunities?
- What stumbling blocks or karmic lessons do I need to resolve?
- What major changes can I expect?

COURT ARCANA CARDS ARE GREAT FOR ANSWERING QUESTIONS SUCH AS:
- What kind of job am I best suited for?
- What career would bring happiness and success?
- What type of person will I meet or marry?
- How do others perceive me?
- What is the thrust of my experience?
- What life lesson am I learning?
- What health problems do I need to look out for?

ALL CARDS *CAN* ADDRESS QUERIES SUCH AS:
- What does he/she want?
- Will I be lucky?

- What's coming up in my love life?
- Will I fall in love or get married?
- Will we stay together?
- How will I feel about him/her?
- What's my financial outlook?
- Will I make a lot of money?
- Will I be successful?
- What will be my best achievement?
- What guidance should I follow?
- What action should I take?
- What would make me happy?
- What did the dream I had mean?
- Will I travel?
- What will be so about travel plans?
- What will the weather be like?
- What should I focus on now?
- Will I get the job?
- How will I feel if I work there?
- How will my health be?
- What's bothering him/her?
- What fun things are coming into my life?
- Will I sell my house or move?
- Will I have a family?
- Will I get along with my family, relatives, in-laws?
- How will I get along with others?
- What will my social life be like?
- Will he/she support my goals?
- What's coming up next?

YES OR NO ANSWERS

The more readings you do, the easier it will be for you to discern which cards mean yes and which mean no. I've found that Aces almost always indicate a yes answer:

The Ace of Wands: The answer is yes, but you must be willing to apply yourself.

The Ace of Cups: The answer is yes, but you must first believe it's possible.

The Ace of Swords: The answer is yes, despite all apparent odds.

The Ace of Pentacles: The answer is yes, but it will take time.

If the card is:

A King: The answer is yes, but you must go after it.

A Queen: The answer is not yet, but it will come to you.

A Page: The answer is no, probably not.

TELLING TIME

It's difficult for even the most advanced student of the Tarot to pinpoint exactly when an event will happen, but I've found that certain guidelines seem to work:

1. Aces signify the season:

   Ace of Wands: Autumn

   Ace of Cups: Summer

   Ace of Swords: Winter

   Ace of Pentacles: Spring

2. The Minor Arcana (two–ten) represent the number of days or weeks it might take for an outcome to occur.

3. The Court Arcana (Kings, Queens and Pages) predict the months associated with the astrological sign and the type of person or activity that will be involved.

4. Major Arcana cards foretell an event that will probably supersede one's current plans or present way of thinking, the duration of which will depend on how quickly one masters the lesson(s) or grasps the opportunities presented.

REVERSING THE CARDS

Personally, I don't use the "reversed" and "upright" method when I do readings because I've found that, to some degree, *all* of the information applies; however, there are a few things you might want to consider.

For example, "good" cards that come up in the reversed position can signal that the energy may be frustrated or blocked and/or that the emphasis tends to be on the "negative" aspects of that card rather than the positive. In some cases (depending on the card) the information in one or several of the categories is either mitigated or transposed. "Bad" cards when reversed tend to be less severe.

If a Court Arcana comes up in the reversed position, it warns that the person in question is more likely to express the less desirable characteristics of that astrological sign.

When a Major Arcana is upside-down, it can signify that the message and purpose of the experience (described in the guidance category) and the opportunities suggested (in the success category) are either not understood or not being utilized.

As you become more familiar with your cards, you'll be able to discern the subtle nuances between cards that are upright or reversed, and you can choose the method that works the best for you.

SOME FINAL THOUGHTS

- If, after having completed the workbook, you haven't experienced an event you want your cards to answer (like getting married, having a child or changing your career, etc.), *choose* a card you feel would represent that situation or ask your cards to tell you which card *would* predict that event.
- If a card falls out of the deck, turns sideways or attracts your attention as you are shuffling, it is not a coincidence; it's *your* card.
- If you *think* something is important, it *is*.
- If you wonder if an intuitive thought is your guidance, it *is*.
- *Everything* is relative.
- The answers you seek are within you.
- Trust yourself.

PART 2

What I hear, I may forget. What I see, I may remember. What I do, I understand. What I understand, I master. What I master, I enjoy.

Confucius

CHAPTER 4

Walking the Royal Road

THE
MAJOR
ARCANA

YOUR QUERY SHEET

You can use this query sheet in addition to your weekly notes for questions you may have during the course of your workbook experience and in times to come.

Date:	Card:	Your Questions and Answers:
		Q:
		A:
		Q:
		A:
		Q:
		A:
		Q:
		A:
		Q:
		A:
		Q:
		A:
		Q:
		A:
		Q:
		A:
		Q:
		A:
		Q:
		A:
		Q:
		A:
		Q:
		A:
		Q:
		A:
		Q:
		A:
		Q:
		A:
		Q:
		A:
		Q:
		A:

THE MAGICIAN

MAJOR ARCANA cards signify soul growth and herald lessons and opportunities designed to put us on the right path and help us to evolve. When a Major Arcana appears, we become conscious of something that was previously unknown or face challenges emanating from beyond our personal sphere of influence or control.

PLANETARY INFLUENCE

Mercury: Reasoning ability. Intellectual prowess. Perceptions. Formulating thoughts. Conveying ideas. Communications of all kinds.

Sun: Identity. Manner of expression. Direction of energy. Health and vigor. Willpower. Decision making. Beliefs about one's abilities. People in positions of authority or authority issues. Positive thinking. Encounters with men (or masculine, active energy).

NUMEROLOGICAL ASSOCIATION

The number 1 indicates fresh starts, invention, creativity, originality, independence, force and will. During the influence of the number 1, ideas, opportunities and new projects begin to flourish, and although one may know *what* one needs to do, it may take courage or daring to follow through.

Why do you think a Major Arcana showed up in your life at this time?

• **What stood out the most in your experience of this card?**

In addition to your recollection, here are some other possibilities you might want to consider:

FOCUS   Was your focus on love, finances, your home or the future? Were there any *major* changes, new beginnings or fresh starts?

DESIRES   Did you want to *do, be* or accomplish something? What was your most fervent wish?

LOVE   Was there a positive change in your love life? Did an aura of romance prevail, bringing a great new love or strengthening an old one? Did you have the kind of relationship you wanted? If not, did you still want it?

OTHERS   Did you believe that *you* controlled your destiny or did you feel that it was in the hands of others? If you were struggling to assert yourself or your work, did that condition change? Did any new partnerships begin?

HOME   Were there any discussions about real estate, rent or money? If you were trying to sell your house, was an offer accepted? Did it get sold?

TRAVEL   Did you travel or talk about an upcoming trip? Were any decisions made? Did you (or another) have to postpone a vacation or cut it short?

Was the work you were doing original or creative? Did you wish it were? Did you have faith in yourself or your project? If you were trying to begin a new enterprise, were you successful? If you were looking for a job, did you find one?

WORK

Were you in a positive frame of mind? Did you feel more motivated and goal-oriented? Do you think you were too headstrong or impatient? Were you experiencing any stress or finding it difficult to obtain the right medication or treatment? Did you have to get a blood test or take a medical exam?

BODY/MIND

Did something lucky, visual, creative or metaphysical cause your spirits to soar?

SPIRIT

Did a relative call asking for help or advice? Were there any changes in your existing plans or relationship?

RELATIVES

Were you financially sound? Was there a considerable increase in your salary or income? Did you conduct business over the phone? Were your transactions successful?

FINANCES

Did you have trouble maintaining a consistent attitude? Did you think that you were applying yourself to the best of your ability? Were you worried about a lover, your finances or the sale of your home? Did you feel that you were doing all of the giving in a relationship or that what you had to offer was unappreciated or taken for granted?

PROBLEMS

GUIDANCE

The impelling force of the number 1 is toward *creation.*

What were you creating in your world? Did someone or something encourage your creativity? Did a new potential emerge? Was a situation presented that, if acted upon, could be the answer to your dreams?

SUCCESS

Opportunities for a number 1 come through purposeful intention, leadership and innovative thinking.

Did you realize that your attention on something kept the energy flowing or made it happen? Did you have a new idea or method of doing something that could assure a successful future? Did you attain that which you asked for, wanted or envisioned?

ACTION

Did the results you hoped to achieve depend on your willingness to do what it took to get what you wanted? Did you decide on a goal or make any long-range plans concerning a project already started? Were you willing to promote yourself or your ideas? Was there something you felt you simply *must* do or say?

• **In light of your experience, what do you believe The Magician signified?**

• **What did you learn from it?**

- **If you drew The Magician in response to a question you asked, in what way did this card answer it?**

- **Now, take another look at your card. Is there anything that stands out about it you didn't notice before?**

- **If you were to make your own Tarot card, what words, pictures or symbols would you put on it?**

SOMETHING TO REFLECT UPON

Everyone has a power spot, a place where they feel empowered and insights come more readily. It could be by the sea, in the mountains, the garden or even floating in the pool. Think about your favorite place and if you can, take this book and go there now. If you can't physically go, then visit that place in your mind . . . pretend that you *are* there . . . feel the sensations . . . take in the landscape . . . imagine all of the sights, sounds or smells you'd be aware of if you were actually there. Then close your eyes, focus your thoughts and voice whatever it is that you need or want. Don't just think it, literally *say it out loud*. . . . Notice the feelings you experience as the words leave your mouth . . . the elation in your heart . . . the smile on your face . . . and imagine now that your words are going out into the universe and into every corner of the world. . . . Now, open your eyes and know with absolute certainty that as surely as the sun comes up in the morning, your wish *will* come back to you as an established, material fact.

Thou shalt decree a thing, and it shall be established unto thee.
                                                                JOB 22:28

THE HIGH PRIESTESS

MAJOR ARCANA cards signify soul growth and herald lessons and opportunities designed to put us on the right path and help us to evolve. When a Major Arcana appears, we become conscious of something that was previously unknown or face challenges emanating from beyond our personal sphere of influence or control.

PLANETARY INFLUENCE

Moon: Feelings about one's self. Responses to life. Instability. Changeability. Cycles and rhythms. Intuition. Psychic sensitivity. Tendency toward negative thinking. Encounters with women (or feminine, passive energy).

Mercury: Reasoning ability. Intellectual prowess. Perceptions. Formulating thoughts. Conveying ideas. Communications of all kinds.

NUMEROLOGICAL ASSOCIATION

The number 2 connotes assimilation, balancing polarities and dealing with unknowns. When the number 2 is present, partial success can be realized but one may also find oneself having to repeat previous lessons or experiences in order to eliminate flaws or continue to progress. Reunions, reconciliations and an element of surprise could also be indicated.

Why do you think a Major Arcana showed up in your life at this time?

• **What stood out the most in your experience of this card?**

In addition to your recollection, here are some other possibilities you might want to consider:

FOCUS Were communications, negotiations, public relations or finances emphasized? Were you waiting for something important to be decided or take place? Do you think you were learning a lesson about patience, moderation or speaking up for yourself?

Did you wish your talents would be recognized or that you could utilize an idea, skill or philosophy? Did you want/need a partner or helpmate?

DESIRES

Were your relationships romantic or platonic? Were you open to the advances of others or cool and nonresponsive? Were you willing to *feel* your feelings or did you prefer to avoid emotional entanglements? Were you at a crossroad with anyone? Did you wonder if you and another were going to come together or split apart? Did you need more time to make up your mind or for the answer to be revealed?

LOVE

Were your ideas, requests or presentations well received? How did you conduct yourself with your business associates or behave with others? Did you stay in touch with your friends or did you neglect them?

OTHERS

Were you anxious about a call or caller? Was there a decision to make concerning a communication device? Did you think you needed to clean up your surroundings or put your house in order? Were you planning a trip or move? Did you have a pleasing surprise?

HOME

Were travel plans discussed or arranged? Did you take a quick trip or travel to a convention? Did an incident involving a car or driver sur-

TRAVEL

prise you? Were you looking forward to a vacation you would soon be taking?

WORK

Were you waiting to hear from someone about an assignment you've been working on, a project you wanted to complete or a deal you hoped to finalize? If your work or business was slow in the beginning, did it pick up greatly later on? Did you benefit through a wise career move? Were you close to realizing a very important goal?

BODY/MIND

How were you reacting to life? Were you unusually moody or remote and intellectually detached? If you were ill did you have a swift recovery? How comfortable were you with *you?*

SPIRIT

Was your intuition exceptionally strong? Were there any notable ESP or telepathic experiences?

RELATIVES

Did you feel close to your family or strangely removed? Did you feel supported or alone and on your own? Did your experiences help you understand or identify with what a loved one might be feeling or going through?

FINANCES

Were you making good money? Were you lucky in financial matters? Did you profit through communications or things involving papers? Were there any unexpected gains, opportunities or bonuses?

Were you tired of learning through the school of hard knocks, putting up with "less than" or wasting time or money? Was a demanding job depleting your energy? Were you troubled by an encounter with sexual overtones?

PROBLEMS

The impelling force of the number 2 is toward *association*.

Was it of utmost importance to make or keep a particular connection? What "associations" or analogies were you making between your inner world and your outer experience? What were the people you came in contact with teaching you about yourself? Did you just *know* the truth about things or how certain events were going to turn out? Did you trust that knowingness?

GUIDANCE

Opportunities for a number 2 come through friends, groups and communities.

What benefits, opportunities or blessings came through friends, colleagues or your connection with a community? Did being associated with a group, or represented by an organization contribute to your success? Were you (or do you think you could be) a spokesperson?

SUCCESS

Were you patient, cooperative or accepting? What steps were taken to round out your life or eliminate problem areas? How committed were you?

ACTION

- In light of your experience, what do you believe The High Priestess signified?

- What did you learn from it?

- If you drew The High Priestess in response to a question you asked, in what way did this card answer it?

- Now, take another look at your card. Is there anything that stands out about it you didn't notice before?

- If you were to make your own Tarot card, what words, pictures or symbols would you put on it?

SOMETHING TO REFLECT UPON

You may want to tape this guided meditation and play it back with your eyes closed.

Take a moment and think about a goal you really want to achieve . . . now close your eyes and picture that goal at the end of a path before you . . . picture it in vivid detail . . . begin now to notice the thoughts, feelings or fears that crop up when you think about attaining that goal . . . pay very close attention to these things and as each one surfaces, mentally record it or, if you prefer, write it down . . . continue on until every possible obstacle has been exhausted. . . .

Imagine now that you are walking down that path, and as you head toward your goal, notice how littered the path has become . . . how far away your goal looks to you now. . . .

These are the very things that, in one way or another, have *always* sabotaged you, have always come between you and having the thing you wanted most. . . . Knowing this, ask yourself, "Am I willing to pursue this anyway? What steps would it take to reach my goal?" Then, "Am I willing to do what it takes to get what I want?" If the answer is no, then it's as it should be. Do *not* make yourself wrong for your decision. If your answer is yes, then you must now make a conscious decision to achieve it . . . to see it *only* as if it were *already* an accomplished fact . . . and in the days or weeks to come, you must keep this picture to the fore, recognizing and brushing aside any negative thought or thing that comes between you and the ultimate attainment of that goal.

◆ THE EMPRESS

MAJOR ARCANA cards signify soul growth and herald lessons and opportunities designed to put us on the right path and help us to evolve. When a Major Arcana appears, we become conscious of something that was previously unknown or face challenges emanating from beyond our personal sphere of influence or control.

PLANETARY INFLUENCE

Venus: Emotional values. Social behavior. Relationships. Companionship. Attraction. Desirability. Harmony. Beauty. Touching. Nurturing. Acceptance. Appreciation.
Jupiter: New undertakings. Favor. Luck. Improvement. Opportunity. Enlargement. Long-term and future plans. Recognition. Material benefits. Generosity. Feelings of (or beliefs about) success, accomplishment and abundance.

NUMEROLOGICAL ASSOCIATION

The number 3 indicates expressing one's self, creating, externalizing and relating. With the number 3, group activities or situations involving more than one person are usually emphasized. Although the 3 brings conditions to fruition, there may also be some delay. Growth of an inner, emotional nature is also indicated.

Why do you think a Major Arcana showed up in your life at this time?

• **What stood out the most in your experience of this card?**

In addition to your recollection, here are some other possibilities you might want to consider:

FOCUS

Did you feel that there was something missing or lacking in your life? Did you want to express something but not know what? Were you feeling scattered? Did travel, connecting or emotional nurturing mean more to you? Did it seem as if you were going through a *major* reorientation period?

DESIRES

Did you want to *be* rather than *do*? What wishes, passions, needs were imperative to you?

LOVE

Were you longing for love and affection? Did you attract admirers? Were you content to be with someone just for the sake of having a relationship or were your needs different and deeper? Were you involved with (or meeting) men/women who craved a similar depth or did they tend to be more "surfacy" or shallow? Did you give any thought to what you wanted in a partner or how you could attract the type of person you wanted to have in your life? Was money a consideration? Were you having trouble sorting out your feelings?

OTHERS

Were significant contacts primarily with women (or men who were expressing more of their feminine energy)? Were you open and easygoing around others or were you intolerant and critical? Were relationships congenial or were they a strain? Did they motivate you to seek a higher truth or clarify your needs?

Was something in need of repair, improvement or expansion? Was a new or bigger home considered? If you were thinking about moving or living with someone, was the event delayed or decided against? Did you buy a potted plant or do something that brought the outside in?

HOME

Were you feeling a sense of wanderlust? Did you think about cross-country traveling or going on a short or extended (nature) trip? Did you follow your inclination to get away? If you traveled, did you have ample money to enjoy your journey?

TRAVEL

What were your feelings about the work that you were doing? Were you listening for inner cues? If you were having trouble applying yourself, did you put the work aside temporarily? When you returned to your work, did you have a new job title or resolution? Was restructuring necessary? Did you need someone else's input? What creative resources were you utilizing? Were you considering a career in the arts, self-help field or human-potential movement?

WORK

Did your back bother you? Were you feeling taut or tense? Did it occur to you that it might be your body's way of telling you that you were pushing yourself too hard or you were disregarding the pangs of your heart? Were you starting to become more aware of your physical needs, what you put into your body and how it may be affecting

BODY/MIND

you? Did you supplement your diet with vitamins? If you didn't *feel* like doing something and you did it anyway, how did it turn out?

SPIRIT

Did healing, pleasure or comfort come through social activities, travel or contact with nature? Did you feel happier when you were outdoors or in the company of others? What brought peace, inspiration or clarity of thought? What did that teach or tell you?

RELATIVES

Did you have a happy, loving family life? Were there any communication problems? Were you pregnant (or pregnant with ideas)? Did you feel more motherly (or visit your mother)?

FINANCES

Were there delays or postponements in your financial affairs? Was it to your advantage to hold off on business matters until a more propitious time, or you were sure you had what you wanted and were getting the best deal? If you had money in your pockets, did you spread the wealth or tip people well?

PROBLEMS

Were you led astray when you ignored your intuition or followed the dictates of your reasoning mind instead of your feelings? Were you depressed about love or something you couldn't make happen, synthesize or work through?

GUIDANCE

The impelling force of the number 3 is toward *self-expression.*

   Were you expressing the things you truly felt or doing what you really wanted to do? If not, what were you afraid of; what was stopping you? What were your feelings and inner promptings urging you to do? What input or feedback were you receiving from the world around you? How could you be more joyful, expressive or creative?

Opportunities for a number 3 come through creative channels, social awareness and interacting with the public.

SUCCESS

Were you enlarging your social sphere or moving in the right circles? Did you do, give, make or create something that touched the hearts or lives of others? What attainment, achievement or meeting meant the most to you? If you had plenty of money and no responsibilities, what activity, experience or adventure would you pursue?

Were you learning to trust your feelings and instincts more? What decisions did you make? What did you explore?

ACTION

- **In light of your experience, what do you believe The Empress signified?**

- **What did you learn from it?**

- **If you drew The Empress in response to a question you asked, in what way did this card answer it?**

- Now, take another look at your card. Is there anything that stands out about it you didn't notice before?

- If you were to make your own Tarot card, what words, pictures or symbols would you put on it?

SOMETHING TO REFLECT UPON

Imagine that you lived in a world without words . . . how would you express yourself? Follow your heart . . . it knows where it's going.

◆ # THE EMPEROR

MAJOR ARCANA cards signify soul growth and herald lessons and opportunities designed to put us on the right path and help us to evolve. When a Major Arcana appears, we become conscious of something that was previously unknown or face challenges emanating from beyond our personal sphere of influence or control.

PLANETARY INFLUENCE
Saturn: Structures. Stability. Discipline. Material security. Affairs that demand patience and endurance. Profound learning experiences. Maturing. Feelings of (or beliefs about) failure or powerlessness.
Jupiter: New undertakings. Favor. Luck. Improvement. Opportunity. Enlargement. Long-term and future plans. Recognition. Material benefits. Generosity. Feelings of (or beliefs about) success, accomplishment and abundance.

NUMEROLOGICAL ASSOCIATION

The number 4 connotes formation, stability and solidification. With the number 4, one's work and dreams are stressed, and although one's eyes may be on a bigger picture, or the promise of future reward, one must concentrate on what *is* and deal with the practical task(s) at hand.

Why do you think a Major Arcana showed up in your life at this time?

• **What stood out the most in your experience of this card?**

In addition to your recollection, here are some other possibilities you might want to consider:

Were there new plans, platforms or opportunities? Was a new relationship, partnership or lifestyle among them? Was something successfully launched or completed? Was it a time of conquest, solidity and material gains?

FOCUS _____

Did you want your ideas to become a tangible reality and/or achieve concrete, lasting or long-term results?

DESIRES _____

Were you in a solid relationship or marriage? Did someone want to legally cement the union? If single, did you meet/date a father figure or a woman who wielded a position of power or authority? Did it seem that the relationship you were in was bigger than both of you? Did the two of you have work to do together?

LOVE _____

OTHERS — Were significant connections or interactions primarily with men (or women who were expressing more of their masculine energy)? Did friends foster your growth? Did people of influence help your cause? Were sales people, administrators or assistants agreeable?

HOME — Did someone (or something) exert a strong influence over you? Were there discussions about tenants or realtors?

TRAVEL — Were travel plans changed or a rendezvous temporarily postponed? If so, was it due to a work schedule, legal matter or financial concern? Was a relative planning a trip back home?

WORK — Did new conditions, new avenues or a new direction emerge? Did you have discussions about contractual agreements, profit sharing, subsidies or management? Were you good at working with your hands or building things?

BODY/MIND — Were you worried about the health of a parent (or a pet)? Was there a problem with someone's teeth (yours?)? Were you concerned about a growth or tumor? Was it benign? Were you enjoying sensual pleasures? Was sex better the second time around?

SPIRIT — Did someone (or something) change the course of your experience for the better? Were you grateful for the completion (or elimination) of something that was oppressive to you?

Were you planning to visit the home of a relative? Were you invited on a trip? Was someone lying to a family member or not revealing all the facts?

RELATIVES

Did you prosper in your financial transactions? Were large sums of money exchanged or discussed? Did someone offer to subsidize you? If you lost money or received a bad check, was it recovered? Was your income such that you could afford to spend money on others, buy luxuries or pay your bills without flinching?

FINANCES

Were you troubled by tedious, repetitious or plodding work? Were you involved in a sordid relationship or an extramarital affair? Do you think your assessments were premature or inaccurate? Did something that *looked* as if it was carved in granite turn to sand? Did you have to start over, rebuild or accept it and move on? How did you handle the situation?

PROBLEMS

The impelling force of the number 4 is toward *security*.

   How were you securing your future? Were your foundations built on facts and experience? What guidance were you receiving? What was your Higher Self telling you?

GUIDANCE

Opportunities for a number 4 come through practical application, work and service.

   Did discipline, persistence and hard work pay off? Did you successfully complete a project that took a great deal of time or effort to develop? Did you prove your worth? What avenue(s) brought the greatest reward?

SUCCESS

ACTION _____   What action did you take to accomplish your goal or make your dream a reality? In what way were you a self-made man/woman?

_____

- In light of your experience, what do you believe The Emperor signified?

- What did you learn from it?

- If you drew The Emperor in response to a question you asked, in what way did this card answer it?

- Now, take another look at your card. Is there anything that stands out about it you didn't notice before?

- If you were to make your own Tarot card, what words, pictures or symbols would you put on it?

SOMETHING TO REFLECT UPON

A wise man builds a house on rock. The foolish man builds a castle on the sand.

THE HIEROPHANT

MAJOR ARCANA cards signify soul growth and herald lessons and opportunities designed to put us on the right path and help us to evolve. When a Major Arcana appears, we become conscious of something that was previously unknown or face challenges emanating from beyond our personal sphere of influence or control.

PLANETARY INFLUENCE

Saturn: Stability. Discipline. Material security. Affairs that demand patience and endurance. Profound learning experiences. Maturing. Feelings of (or beliefs about) failure or powerlessness.

Mercury: Reasoning ability. Intellectual prowess. Perceptions. Formulating thoughts. Conveying ideas. Communications of all kinds.

NUMEROLOGICAL ASSOCIATION

The number 5 indicates change, fluctuations in fate or fortune, conflict, experiential learning and the expansion of one's thinking. With the number 5, opportunities and challenges go hand in hand and one must look to both the material and spiritual realm if one is to triumph or understand.

Why do you think a Major Arcana showed up in your life at this time?

• **What stood out the most in your experience of this card?**

In addition to your recollection, here are some other possibilities you might want to consider:

Were you having trouble with administrators, organizations, conventional relationships or organized religions? Were there conflicts   **FOCUS** between you and key figures in your life? Were structures becoming unbearable?

DESIRES

Did you wish you could break free of the restricting binds that were keeping you from having what you wanted? Were you seeking guidance or understanding? Did you need to be certain about something you were doing or to know how, if, or when you should act on it?

LOVE

Did your relationship or marriage require new thinking or a new commitment? If you were not involved with anyone, were you seeking a relationship based on spiritual rather than physical values? Did you prefer abstinence to jeopardizing your relationship or marriage by having a liaison that, in your heart, you knew wasn't right? Was someone or something (your Higher Self?) teaching you to think in these terms?

OTHERS

Were you a pawn in someone's power play? Did somebody issue an ultimatum or drive a wedge between you and another? Were you forced to confront a situation you didn't want to contend with? Did you feel lost or alone even among friends?

HOME

Was there work to be done around your home? Did you want to hire a contractor? Was something that troubled you easily fixed or remedied?

Did travel become a requirement? Did you need to contact or connect with someone who was in a different state or country? Were
travel plans disorganized or changeable?

TRAVEL

Were you getting as much out of your work as you were putting in?
Was what you wanted beyond your grasp or ability? Did a business
venture fail? Were you contemplating a new direction or thinking about going into business for yourself? Do you think you were
ready to embark on something new? Were you able to find work (or
a partner) that was more aligned with who you are and what you
want?

WORK

Did you experience chest pains, shortness of breath or other respiratory problems? Were you, or someone close to you, having a rough
time with medical establishments or limited health-insurance benefits?

BODY/MIND

Did you have an insight into something that hitherto had been a mys-
tery? Did someone give you a helpful suggestion or a gift that involved paper, food or furnishings?

SPIRIT

Was there someone in your family who always had to be right? Did
you prefer to keep the peace rather than argue? How were you relating to your loved ones? Who set the tone or wielded the power? What
ethics, morals or code of conduct were impressed upon you?

RELATIVES

FINANCES

Were financial institutions giving you the runaround? Were you arguing about money or bucking a ridiculous policy? Was someone having financial problems or neglecting (refusing?) to pay you? Despite that, was your financial position stable?

PROBLEMS

In your drive to push forward, were you losing yourself? Were you faced with overwhelming adversity? Was your "I can't" really an "I won't"? Who or what helped you through the difficult times? What was your biggest challenge?

GUIDANCE

The impelling force of the number 5 is toward *freedom*.

How did the desire for liberation manifest in your world? What limiting attachments, constraints, beliefs or dogma did you need to discard?

SUCCESS

Opportunities for a number 5 come through change, progressive thinking and the establishment of something new.

Were your experiences building character by teaching you to think for yourself and to rely on your Inner Counsel? Did opportunities come through foreign countries, eastern cultures or breaking away from the beaten track? What new thing or resolve did you bring forth or establish?

ACTION

Were you prevented from advancing by circumstances beyond your control? If so, did you refuse to let it undermine your confidence? Did it motivate you to try harder?

• In light of your experience, what do you believe The Hierophant signified?

• What did you learn from it?

• If you drew The Hierophant in response to a question you asked, in what way did this card answer it?

• Now, take another look at your card. Is there anything that stands out about it you didn't notice before?

• If you were to make your own Tarot card, what words, pictures or symbols would you put on it?

SOMETHING TO REFLECT UPON

It's so easy to forget that we have an Inner Teacher we can rely on, especially when obstacles are confronting us and others are telling us what our truths should be. But we *do* have an Inner Guide and that is the *Hierophant* we must seek.

One of the ways we can become more aware of our Inner Wisdom is through reflective meditation, by sitting still and contemplating a question inwardly.

Set aside about ten minutes or so and try this process:

Find a place where you feel comfortable. If you have a meditation room, you might want to go there. Once you've settled in, close your eyes and imagine that you are in a bubble of bright white light that surrounds your entire body. Then silently ask yourSelf your question. Do not *think* about the answer or try to *reason* it out, just state the question inwardly and then observe your thoughts and impressions. If your mind wanders off the topic, repeat the question again. Don't worry if nothing comes. Like a seed growing unseen beneath the earth, your answer will eventually surface. If it doesn't arise during the meditation itself, it will come later as a sudden inspiration, a feeling to do something, or an unmistakable clarity of thought.

Be a light unto yourself.
BUDDHA'S LAST WORDS

◆ THE LOVERS

MAJOR ARCANA signify soul growth and herald lessons and opportunities designed to put us on the right path and help us to evolve. When a Major Arcana appears, we become conscious of something that was previously unknown or face challenges emanating from beyond our personal sphere of influence or control.

PLANETARY INFLUENCE

Venus: Emotional values. Social behavior. Relationships. Companionship. Attraction. Desirability. Harmony. Beauty. Touching. Nurturing. Acceptance. Appreciation.
Jupiter: New undertakings. Favor. Luck. Improvement. Opportunity. Enlargement. Long-term and future plans. Recognition. Material benefits. Generosity. Feelings of (or beliefs about) success, accomplishment and abundance.

NUMEROLOGICAL ASSOCIATION

The number 6 indicates the need to make adjustments in one's thoughts, attitudes, behavior or condition. While this may feel burdensome, the number 6 also carries with it the ability to transcend difficulties and oftentimes serendipitously. Responsibilities, family and health may also be emphasized.

Why do you think a Major Arcana showed up in your life at this time?

• **What stood out the most in your experience of this card?**

In addition to your recollection, here are some other possibilities you might want to consider:

Did your values, goals or activities change? Was there a stronger emphasis on love, social interactions, meetings or alliances? Did property matters, travel or (new) products come into view? Were you faced with important choices? Did you make any pivotal decisions? Were there unexpected gains in unexpected ways through unexpected sources?

FOCUS _____

Did you want to be in love again? Were you wondering if anything would come of a meeting with someone, trying to solve a dilemma or looking for the right way to proceed?

DESIRES _____

Were you feeling alone or trapped in a dead-end situation or marriage? Did you attract a new admirer? Were you in a position where your mind said "go" but your heart said "no" or vice versa? Did you hear from someone you formerly loved or from one who still loves you? Were there delays in manifesting your heart's desires or your plans to get together with another? What did you value most in a relationship: romance and companionship or having someone to talk to and share your interests with?

LOVE _____

OTHERS

Was your social life changing? Were you expanding your horizons? Did you look forward to meeting new people or were you afraid of making the same mistakes you made in the past? Were you comfortable around others or did you feel that you were always explaining yourself? If your sole focus was on your career, projects or studies, were you beginning to realize that it was counterproductive, that you needed more than things to fill up your life?

HOME

Did you want to improve your surroundings or beautify your home? Did you need to make repairs or purchase new products? Were you busy, productive or unusually active? If so, in what way?

TRAVEL

Were you indecisive about a trip? Did you decide not to go and then change your mind? Did you forget something and have to turn around and go back? Did you take two trips?

WORK

Were people interested in your work or what you were trying to sell? Were you working on, or offered, an artistic, creative or aesthetic assignment? Were you doing what you loved to do? Was it more important to get the job done or to do it right? Were you synthesizing information, restructuring or eliminating weak points?

BODY/MIND

Did you want to improve your appearance or augment your wardrobe? Did you have an earache or pinched nerve? Were you building a healthier body and mind? Were you more physically or sexually active? Were you acting responsibly?

Did you have an imaginary conversation or heart-to-heart talk with someone? Did you feel the presence of an angel or ask the angels to intervene in a situation that was troubling you? Did something that looked negative on the surface later prove to be a blessing? What inspired you?

SPIRIT

Were you getting along well with your family? Were there loving exchanges between you? Was anyone troubled by a property matter, financial expenditure or relationship problem? Did you feel that you were taking on too many responsibilities or burdens?

RELATIVES

Were you receiving an income through your trade or skills? Did money come through commissions, a mail-order business or a mortgage? Did you pull off a financial coup? Did you receive unexpected money? Did someone call and tell you that you would soon be getting a check? If, in the past, you felt you had been wronged or short-changed, were you recompensed or reimbursed? If you had a financial need, did the Universe fill it?

FINANCES

Did a project fail or a plan collapse? Were you upset when things didn't go the way you wanted them to and you had no control over it? Were you tempted to do something you knew you shouldn't? What was creating conflict within you?

PROBLEMS

The impelling force of the number 6 is toward *harmony*.
  Were you in harmony with yourself, the people you were involved with and the flow of life? If something you were doing didn't feel

GUIDANCE

right, did it occur to you that it probably *wasn't*? Did you wait for guidance or a clear direction? What needed to be healed or balanced? What new understanding(s) were you coming to?

SUCCESS

Opportunities for a number 6 come through helping those in need of material or spiritual assistance and expressing the art, beauty or music of life.

    Did what you were doing contribute to the betterment of another or mankind on the whole? Were you expressing the joy of living? If not, what could you have done to improve your situation?

ACTION

Did new conditions call for an adjustment in your thinking or attitude? Were you able to look beneath the surface of appearances? Did you trust your intuition even if it seemed illogical or contrary to your aims, beliefs or usual way of thinking?

• **In light of your experience, what do you believe The Lovers signified?**

• **What did you learn from it?**

- If you drew The Lovers in response to a question you asked, in what way did this card answer it?

- Now, take another look at your card. Is there anything that stands out about it you didn't notice before?

- If you were to make your own Tarot card, what words, pictures or symbols would you put on it?

SOMETHING TO REFLECT UPON

There is no such thing as a problem without a gift for you in its hands.
You seek problems because you need their gifts.
   RICHARD BACH, *Illusions—The Adventures of a Reluctant Messiah* *

◆   THE CHARIOT

MAJOR ARCANA cards signify soul growth and herald lessons and opportunities designed to put us on the right path and help us to evolve. When a Major Arcana appears, we become conscious of something that was previously unknown or face challenges emanating from beyond our personal sphere of influence or control.

*Bantam, Doubleday, Dell Publishing Group.

PLANETARY INFLUENCE

Sun: Identity. Manner of expression. Direction of energy. Health and vigor. Willpower. Decision making. Beliefs about one's abilities. People in positions of authority or authority issues. Positive thinking. Encounters with men (or masculine, active energy).

Moon: Feelings about one's self. Responses to life. Instability. Changeability. Cycles and rhythms. Intuition. Psychic sensitivity. Tendency toward negative thinking. Encounters with women (or feminine, passive energy).

NUMEROLOGICAL ASSOCIATION

The number 7 indicates a period of introspection, analysis or solitude. During the influence of the number 7, one's psychological and spiritual resources are expanded and faith in what can't be seen, but nevertheless exists, is demanded.

Why do you think a Major Arcana showed up in your life at this time?

• **What stood out the most in your experience of this card?**

In addition to your recollection, here are some other possibilities you might want to consider:

FOCUS   Were you reevaluating your current position? Were you seeking guidance on questions like: "Am I doing the right thing?" "Is this going to work?" "How should I proceed?" "Why am I being blocked?" and so forth.

DESIRES   Did you want to gain more control over the things that ran you or held you back in life?

Were you looking for love? Did love find you? Were you wondering if **LOVE**
you had enough in common with someone to have a future together?
If communication was a problem, did being more candid resolve it?
Did you have meaningful encounters or only brief involvements?

Did you enjoy flirting, popularity or the attention of others? Were **OTHERS**
you open to intimacy and responsive to friendly gestures or were you
uncomfortable, reticent or reserved?

Did you get a late-night call from an admirer? Did someone phone **HOME**
just to say they loved you? Was something finally getting done or
fixed? Did an event concerning real estate, property or a new home
take a surprising twist?

Were your thoughts on someone who was away? Did you make plans **TRAVEL**
to get together with him/her? Did absence make your heart grow
fonder or wander?

Were you wondering if you should pursue a project that didn't come **WORK**
with a guarantee? Were you driven to do it anyway? Did you enjoy
initiating new projects, musical composition or creative writing? Did
your work involve film, tape or the media?

Were you getting the feeling that you needed to practice "non- **BODY/MIND**
doing"; that being "busy" all the time or constantly striving to
achieve was taking you farther and farther off your inner path and

damaging your health? Did you feel the need to meditate, take up a Bible study or join a Science of Mind–type church?

SPIRIT

Did you enjoy taking a few personal risks?

RELATIVES

Did you want to spend more time with your family but felt that your schedule or commitments (or theirs) wouldn't permit it? Were you always rushing but never on time?

FINANCES

Were there heated debates over money? Were your arguments successful? Were you able to surmount challenges or difficulties? Were you pleased about a business matter or an increase in your salary or income?

PROBLEMS

Did you seesaw between faith and fear? Were you tired of trying to force resolves or living in your head? Were you ignoring your physical or emotional needs?

GUIDANCE

The impelling force of the number 7 is toward *wisdom*.

Were you becoming more aware of the way people, things and thoughts affect your energy; whether they lift you up or pull you down, exhilarate or frustrate, enliven or deaden? Did you make choices that made you feel happy and alive? Did you sense that there were cycles for growth and times to rest? Did you instinctively know what course was the best?

Opportunities for a number 7 come through what is *brought* to one, inner poise and the spiritual, unseen realm, rather than what is actively pursued.   **SUCCESS**

   Did you make a decision to stop fretting and start *letting?* What insights, successes or opportunities appeared *without* effort on your part and/or when you were alone?

Were there control issues you had to resolve? Once you mastered yourself, was your position stronger than you thought?   **ACTION**

• **In light of your experience, what do you believe The Chariot signified?**

• **What did you learn from it?**

• **If you drew The Chariot in response to a question you asked, in what way did this card answer it?**

• **Now, take another look at your card. Is there anything that stands out about it you didn't notice before?**

• **If you were to make your own Tarot card, what words, pictures or symbols would you put on it?**

SOMETHING TO REFLECT UPON

A friend described his inner struggles thusly:

"There are two sides to my thinking; one is positive, one is negative and they fight constantly." When asked which one wins, he replied, "The one I heed the most."

◆   # STRENGTH

MAJOR ARCANA cards signify soul growth and herald lessons and opportunities designed to put us on the right path and help us to evolve. When a Major Arcana appears, we become conscious of something that was previously unknown or face challenges emanating from beyond our personal sphere of influence or control.

PLANETARY INFLUENCE

Saturn: Structures. Stability. Discipline. Material security. Affairs that demand patience and endurance. Profound learning experiences. Maturing. Feelings of (or beliefs about) failure or powerlessness.

Sun: Identity. Manner of expression. Direction of energy. Health and vigor. Willpower. Decision making. Beliefs about one's abilities. People in positions of authority or authority issues. Positive thinking. Encounters with men (or masculine, active energy).

NUMEROLOGICAL ASSOCIATION

The number 8 connotes the potential for success, accomplishment or recognition and the capacity to achieve one's goals; but unless one seeks the Power Within, these may not be easily attained. Although a positive change of mind or status almost always accompanies the number 8, moral integrity, fortitude and emotional equilibrium will also be required.

Why do you think a Major Arcana showed up in your life at this time?

• **What stood out the most in your experience of this card?**

In addition to your recollection, here are some other possibilities you might want to consider:

Did you feel that you were dealing with karmic situations and/or elements from the past, present and future? Were you feeling challenged by someone or something? Were you learning to rely on spiritual strength rather than physical force?   **FOCUS** _____

Did you want to succeed in business, have positive experiences in love and overcome any obstacle that prevented you from attaining what you wanted? Were you praying for courage or spiritual fortitude?   **DESIRES** _____

Did you believe that if you wanted to be loved, you needed to change something or make yourself known? Did you wish you could meet or be with someone you really loved or had more in common with? Did   **LOVE** _____ you and another have a serious discussion about your relationship, marriage or getting back together again? Were you beginning to see things in a more positive light?

OTHERS

Did you take a stand for what you wanted and believed in even if it was uncomfortable? If other people's opinions were not in accord with yours, did you feel challenged by them? Were you involved with any self-help or consciousness-raising groups? Did you meet or speak with someone who left a lasting impression on you? Did cultivating more friends step up your progress or teach you to love yourself more?

HOME

Did your hobbies include spiritual studies, mystical training or philanthropic endeavors? Were you enmeshed in paperwork or a project that was complicated or time-consuming? If you were living alone, were you glad you had the freedom to do as you pleased?

TRAVEL

Was someone planning to visit you? Did he/she call and tell you so? Were there any confrontations or unpleasant discussions? Did you have a brush with an authority figure or get a traffic ticket?

WORK

Did your work combine business with spiritual development? Were you learning new things about your abilities, or how to handle people or conflict better? Did you feel that the work you were doing today bore the seeds of your tomorrows? Were you undaunted in the pursuit of your goal(s)?

Did you feel vigorous and energetic? Did time spent in meditation or spiritual contemplation rejuvenate you? If, in the past, you felt that your energy was almost depleted, were you given new strength? **BODY/MIND**

Did you receive Divine assistance? Was a Spiritual Force making its presence known in your life? Were you aware of any unusual sensations or smells (incense, flowers, perfume) that occur when an invisible teacher, guru or angel is present? Did you receive good news, praise or recognition for your work or efforts? **SPIRIT**

Were there any squabbles? If so, was the reason you argued due to a situation that stemmed from the past? Was someone trying to assert his or her authority in the wrong way? Did you feel slighted or dismissed? **RELATIVES**

Did money become an issue? Were disputes handled effectively and successfully overcome? Was a worry dispelled? Did you feel that you were fortunate in financial matters? Were you self-sufficient? Did your income accrue? What moneymaking activities or ventures were you involved in? **FINANCES**

If you were experiencing difficulties, was it because you doubted yourself, mistrusted others or harbored a grudge against someone? Did you need to establish a firmer relationship with your God? **PROBLEMS**

GUIDANCE

The impelling force of the number 8 is toward *authority*.

Were you becoming more conscious of your Inner Authority? What did that voice sound like? What "message" were you receiving? Who or what did you put your faith in or give power to? What was giving you strength?

SUCCESS

Opportunities for a number 8 come through assisting those in need of direction, worthwhile goals and large, progressive corporations.

Did you believe that your mission in life was a spiritual one and/or your work could benefit many? Did you attain or have the potential to achieve a position of influence, wealth or fame? Did success come through taking charge of a situation, aligning yourself with a corporation or heading your own company?

ACTION

Did you advance with faith believing that your prayers would be answered? Was an Inner Strength giving you the courage to do so? How were you demonstrating your authority? Did your love or acceptance make a difference?

• **In light of your experience, what do you believe Strength signified?**

• **What did you learn from it?**

- If you drew Strength in response to a question you asked, in what way did this card answer it?

- Now, take another look at your card. Is there anything that stands out about it you didn't notice before?

- If you were to make your own Tarot card, what words, pictures or symbols would you put on it?

SOMETHING TO REFLECT UPON

You may want to tape this guided meditation and play it back with your eyes closed.

Take a few deep breaths and close your eyes. . . . Imagine that a bright, white light is coming down from above and entering the top of your head . . . feel the warmth of the light as it flows down into your shoulders, your chest and arms, your stomach and into your hips, legs and feet . . . when it reaches your toes, imagine that it is encircling your entire body and then gradually coming to rest around your heart area. Feel the sensation of the light within your chest . . . if a thought enters your mind, simply brush it aside and bring your attention back to your heart area. . . .

Keep focusing on your heart until your thoughts begin to subside and you feel a sense of peace. . . .

Now take another deep breath and begin to recall the events, people or conditions you encountered during your week . . . take special note of the circumstances that upset or disturbed you and then choose the one that stands out most in your mind . . . then, just as if you were watching a videotape rewinding to the beginning of a movie, imagine that you are going back in time to the moment that preceded the event you chose . . . only this time, instead of going forward in your memory to the way the situation turned out, put your tape recorder on pause and recreate the entire event the way you *wished* it would have happened; a way that would have made you happy and left a good feeling in your heart and mind. . . . When you have finished, release the event with love and then let it go . . . let it go knowing that your love *can* heal . . . and what cannot be reconciled within you, God will do *for* you.

Our faith isn't the problem; it's the object of our faith that rewards or destroys us.
LUKE NATHAN

◆ THE HERMIT

MAJOR ARCANA cards signify soul growth and herald lessons and opportunities designed to put us on the right path and help us to evolve. When a Major Arcana appears, we become conscious of something that was previously unknown or face challenges emanating from beyond our personal sphere of influence or control.

PLANETARY INFLUENCE

Sun: Identity. Manner of expression. Direction of energy. Health and vigor. Willpower. Decision making. Beliefs about one's abilities. People in positions of authority or authority issues. Positive thinking. Encounters with men (or masculine, active energy).
Mercury: Reasoning ability. Intellectual prowess. Perceptions. Formulating thoughts. Conveying ideas. Communications of all kinds.

NUMEROLOGICAL ASSOCIATION

The number 9 stands for completion, arrival, integration and realization. When a number 9 surfaces, it marks a transition between what was and what is to come, a parenthesis in time as one pauses to reflect on all that went before and the unknown potential of that which is yet to be.

Why do you think a Major Arcana showed up in your life at this time?

• **What stood out the most in your experience of this card?**

In addition to your recollection, here are some other possibilities you might want to consider:

Were you going through a period of seclusion, introspection or isola- **FOCUS** _____
tion? Was time spent in meditation or in the pursuit of an important
(spiritual?) quest? Was your focus on problem solving, perfecting or
completing? Had you reached a zenith in one area of your life or
work? Was a new plateau awaiting you? Was there a special emphasis on messages, communications and how you were listening, speaking or being heard?

Did you want to change your life, make your time on earth matter, or **DESIRES** _____
get (back) together with someone?

Were you attracting, or attracted to, people younger than yourself? **LOVE** _____
Were you with one person but thinking of another? Did men/women
from your past reappear and then exit your life again? Did someone
who's been estranged return? If so, were you able to work things out
and cement your relationship or were you still strangers? Did you feel
as though you were completing a cycle?

OTHERS

Were you expanding your sphere of influence, making a transition into a new lifestyle or moving back into the mainstream? Did you have a friend who was a teacher, counselor or spiritual adviser? Did someone give you good advice? Were you more comfortable with impersonal relationships than you were with romance or intimate gatherings?

HOME

Did you want to move or sell your home? Did you get a call for work or a message from an admirer? Were you waiting for a delivery or an important letter or document?

TRAVEL

Did you travel afar (or realize that you've come a long way)? Did your studies call for traveling? Did you take a sabbatical or go to a spiritual retreat? Was a flight plan changed or postponed due to an illness in the family?

WORK

Was your work the center of your life? Did it require you to spend long periods of time alone? Was it helping you define yourself spiritually or stretching your observational or intuitive skills? Did you complete an important job or begin a new one? Did your work entail teaching, inspiring or enlightening others? Did people seek you out for your wisdom or light?

BODY/MIND

Were there any upcoming tests or checkups? Did you have a problem with your neck or bronchial tubes? Were you a recluse, "hermit" or celibate? If so, was it by choice?

Did you receive good news, a helpful message or positive acknowl-edgment for your work? Were you at a point in your spiritual un-foldment that allowed you to just be still; to sit in the presence of what represents the Divine to you and *not* need to ask questions or pray for anything?   **SPIRIT**

Did a relative extend an invitation? Did you invite yourself? Did you spend a relaxing or refreshing time with a family member or close friend? If you had a falling out with someone, did you rectify the problem?   **RELATIVES**

Did you augment your income with a part-time job? Did you receive money from the completion of a project? Did you feel successful; that you had money to spend on pleasurable pursuits, helping others or buying the commodities you needed?   **FINANCES**

Did an incident arise that evoked a sense of personal or financial loss? Was it short-lived? Did the situation get resolved within a day or so? If you had been feeling alone, restricted or suppressed, did that come to an end? Was the future beginning to look brighter?   **PROBLEMS**

The impelling force of the number 9 is toward *detachment* and *uni-versality*.   **GUIDANCE**

   How was this energy manifesting in your life? Were you motivated by a desire to serve the common good? Was your appeal to the masses or international trade? Looking back, why do you believe some rela-tionships, jobs or conditions came to an end and others endured?

SUCCESS   Opportunities for a number 9 come through inspirational lines and artistic, creative or motivational people.

Did your success come through inspirational fields, artistic people or working for (or joining forces with) an occult, metaphysical or creative group? Did you attain your goals or find what you sought? Did you succeed in bridging estrangements, beginning a new business or in making the kind of money to which you aspired?

ACTION   What approach did you take to achieve what you wanted? Did your actions advance your inner convictions or spiritual beliefs?

• **In light of your experience, what do you believe The Hermit signified?**

• **What did you learn from it?**

• **If you drew The Hermit in response to a question you asked, in what way did this card answer it?**

• **Now, take another look at your card. Is there anything that stands out about it you didn't notice before?**

- **If you were to make your own Tarot card, what words, pictures or symbols would you put on it?**

SOMETHING TO REFLECT UPON

God knows the things you have need of before you ask Him.

    # THE WHEEL OF FORTUNE

MAJOR ARCANA cards signify soul growth and herald lessons and opportunities designed to put us on the right path and help us to evolve. When a Major Arcana appears, we become conscious of something that was previously unknown or face challenges emanating from beyond our personal sphere of influence or control.

PLANETARY INFLUENCE

Uranus: Unexpected changes. Sudden upheavals. Events that test one's faith or call for new thinking or methods. Awakenings. Invention. Reformation.

Jupiter: New undertakings. Favor. Luck. Improvement. Opportunity. Enlargement. Long-term and future plans. Recognition. Material benefits. Generosity. Feelings of (or beliefs about) success, accomplishment and abundance.

NUMEROLOGICAL ASSOCIATION

The number 1 (1 + 0 = 1) indicates fresh starts, invention, creativity, originality, independence, force and will. During the influence of the number 1, ideas, opportunities and new projects begin to flourish, and although one may know *what* one needs to do, it may take courage or daring to follow through.

The 10 in the Tarot marks the end of one phase and the beginning of another. Although it has the same basic meaning as the number 1, it also signifies a time when one may have to come to terms with something that was previously overlooked, unfinished or avoided.

Why do you think a Major Arcana showed up in your life at this time?

• **What stood out the most in your experience of this card?**

In addition to your recollection, here are some other possibilities you might want to consider:

FOCUS   Were you worried about maintaining your position, profits and losses or the outcome of a new project or venture? Were there unforeseen changes or vicissitudes? Did a new phase commence following the arrival of important news or information?

DESIRES   Did you want to pin something down, resolve a dilemma or end a cycle of misfortune and negativity?

LOVE   Were you undecided about a relationship? Did a disagreeable condition end followed by an important decision or the entry of a new love?

Did bad luck or ill health befall a friend or loved one? Did he/she have   **OTHERS** _____
to go to the hospital? Did you and another (superior, business partner,
associate?) have a falling-out? Was there a conflict of interest?

Did your financial obligations, living expenses or rent increase? Did a   **HOME** _____
service person have to return to complete a job?

Were you considering a *major* trip or move?   **TRAVEL** _____

Did an unexpected event make it necessary to leave your work, look   **WORK** _____
for another job or change your vocation?

Were you up one minute and down the next? Were you drinking too   **BODY/MIND** _____
much caffeine or eating too much sugar or starch? Were suppressed
emotions causing a negative physical reaction? Were you becoming
more aware of, or developing an interest in, your body's nutritional
needs, natural timetable, biorhythms or astrological cycles?

Was pleasure derived through your friends, good books or the for-   **SPIRIT** _____
mation of a new union or partnership? Were you lucky in games of
chance? Did you get a winning (lottery) ticket? Was there a fortuitous
change for the better?

RELATIVES

Was someone a burden to you or a constant source of aggravation? Did you wish you could be free of him/her or of your emotional attachment? If you were worried about a loved one, did you receive information that alleviated your concerns?

FINANCES

Was your salary or income cut? Were you unhappy with your earnings or sales? Did you worry that your profits wouldn't be enough to compensate for your pain, effort or investment? Did something happen to brighten your outlook? Did your amended earnings exceed your expectations?

PROBLEMS

Did you have trouble coping with change, difficulties or unknowns? Were you disheartened by your unsatisfactory love life, work or career? If so, what did you do (or might you have done) to extricate yourself or resolve the problem?

GUIDANCE

The impelling force of the number 1 is toward *creation*.

Were the events in your life compelling you to rediscover your Creator, your creative potential or the future you were creating with your thoughts or deeds? Did you have a vision of something you could attain or aspire to?

SUCCESS

Opportunities for a number 1 come through purposeful intention, leadership and innovative thinking.

Did your determination enable you to work through difficulties, power issues or creative blocks? Did success come through your initiative, inventiveness or leadership skills? Did the changes you went through (physically or psychologically) ultimately move you out of a precarious situation and into a more confident and rewarding position?

How did you conduct yourself? Did standing up to your fears dissolve them? What action was taken to complete your "karma" and change your "fate"?

ACTION

- **In light of your experience, what do you believe The Wheel of Fortune signified?**

- **What did you learn from it?**

- **If you drew The Wheel of Fortune in response to a question you asked, in what way did this card answer it?**

- **Now, take another look at your card. Is there anything that stands out about it you didn't notice before?**

• If you were to make your own Tarot card, what words, pictures or symbols would you put on it?

SOMETHING TO REFLECT UPON

We are never given more than we can bear. If our burden feels heavy, it's because our Creator has great confidence in our ability to handle it. When God closes one door, somewhere He opens another.

JUSTICE

MAJOR ARCANA cards signify soul growth and herald lessons and opportunities designed to put us on the right path and help us to evolve. When a Major Arcana appears, we become conscious of something that was previously unknown or face challenges emanating from beyond our personal sphere of influence or control.

PLANETARY INFLUENCE

Saturn: Structures. Stability. Discipline. Material security. Affairs that demand patience and endurance. Profound learning experiences. Maturing. Feelings of (or beliefs about) failure or powerlessness.

Neptune: Idealism. Confusion. Illusions. Worthiness issues. Dissolving old patterns. Finding new meanings. Perspective. Spiritual, mystical or occult experiences.

NUMEROLOGICAL ASSOCIATION

The number 11 is a master number indicating a higher, more universal application of the number 2 and aspirations that may be loftier than, or superior to, one's current level of understanding or ability.

Why do you think a Major Arcana showed up in your life at this time?

• **What stood out the most in your experience of this card?**

In addition to your recollection, here are some other possibilities you might want to consider:

Were you addressing questions of fairness or evaluating issues like destiny versus choice and free will, mind over matter or cause and effect? Were you involved with the law, legal dealings or a lawsuit? Did justice seem to hang in the balance? Did events have to evolve before they could be understood, weighed or judged? Did you reach an important milestone?

FOCUS _____

Were you looking for emotional fulfillment, an answer to an important financial question or an understanding that would put your world back into perspective?

DESIRES _____

Were you weighing the quality of your relationship(s)? Did you want to find someone who was right for you but felt that you kept meeting Ms./Mr. Wrong? Did you reunite with a man/woman you were previously involved with or married to, renew your vows or marry him/

LOVE _____

her again? Did one cycle end and a new one begin? Did a tense situation become more flexible?

OTHERS

Did others make you feel vulnerable, inhibited or inferior in some way? Did you turn down social opportunities because you felt insecure? If you were having problems, were you the one who needed to change or straighten things out?

HOME

Did you make calls, send letters or receive mail concerning legal, financial or other weighty matters? Did you or a relative want to move into a new home or begin a new life?

TRAVEL

Did you go on a spur-of-the-moment trip? Was the weather cold, windy or unpredictable?

WORK

Were there problems at work? Did something unjust, unfair or upsetting happen? Were you afraid of losing seniority, status, business or time? Did you have to make a "major" decision or do some "major" rethinking? Did you consider starting your own company or opening a large center?

BODY/MIND

Were you more conscious of your physical or nutritional needs, or interested in any rejuvenating products? Were you or a relative having trouble with your teeth, drugs or alcohol? Did you speak with a new physician? Did an earlier prognosis prove to be correct? Did you feel that you were in balance? Were you easily thrown *off* balance?

Were you more intuitive or perceptive? Did you have prophetic dreams? Did being in accord with yourself stimulate productivity? Did you enjoy restoring things? What gave you a sense of peace and harmony? What were you zealous about?

SPIRIT

Was someone in your family worrying about their future? Was a relationship, job or legal problem discussed? Could you trust your family to tell the truth or keep their word? Did you see a relative in a new light?

RELATIVES

Were you feeling a crunch in your pocketbook? Did *another* expense crop up? Did you receive unexpected money or get news that money would be arriving sooner than expected? Was a lawsuit or arbitration settled? Were your finances gradually improving? Were your accounts squared and your bills paid?

FINANCES

Were you frustrated, emotionally unfulfilled or disillusioned by your expectations? Were you isolating, cutting yourself off from others? Was there something you could have done to make your life more meaningful or satisfying? Does the saying "argue for your limitations and sure enough, they're yours"* mean anything to you? What attitudes do you think you needed to revise?

PROBLEMS

The impelling force of the number 11 is toward *illumination*.
    Did you trust your instincts or feel more in tune with inner guidance or spiritual guide(s)? Did you have a revelation about yourself, your beliefs or why you have come to this point in your life? Was time

GUIDANCE

*Richard Bach, *Illusions—The Adventures of a Reluctant Messiah*

the key to understanding? Were the lessons you taught the ones *you* needed to learn?

SUCCESS

Opportunities for a number 11 come through *spiritual* leadership, teaching and uplifting others.

What qualities made you a leader or visionary? How were you using your talents or gifts? Did you consider volunteering your services? Did you entertain the possibility that you may have a *higher* calling? Were you honored for a contribution you made? Did success depend upon your popularity?

ACTION

Did you stand up for yourself or confront your oppressors? Were you able to right wrongs, resolve disputes and come to the correct conclusions? Could you let tomorrow take care of itself?

• **In light of your experience, what do you believe Justice signified?**

• **What did you learn from it?**

• **If you drew Justice in response to a question you asked, in what way did this card answer it?**

- Now, take another look at your card. Is there anything that stands out about it you didn't notice before?

- If you were to make your own Tarot card, what words, pictures or symbols would you put on it?

SOMETHING TO REFLECT UPON

Ask yourself this: "Is what I'm thinking, doing or planning a step up in my spiritual evolvement or a step down?"

If your answer is the latter, what *would* advance your godhood?

> *A mediocre teacher tells. The good teacher explains.*
> *The superior teacher demonstrates. The great teacher inspires.*
> E. C. McKenzie, 14,000 *Quips & Quotes*

◆ THE HANGED MAN

MAJOR ARCANA cards signify soul growth and herald lessons and opportunities designed to put us on the right path and help us to evolve. When a Major Arcana appears, we become conscious of something that was previously unknown or face challenges emanating from beyond our personal sphere of influence or control.

PLANETARY INFLUENCE

Neptune: Idealism. Confusion. Illusions. Worthiness issues. Dissolving old patterns. Finding new meanings. Perspective. Spiritual, mystical or occult experiences.

Jupiter: New undertakings. Favor. Luck. Improvement. Opportunity. Enlargement. Long-term and future plans. Recognition. Material benefits. Generosity. Feelings of (or beliefs about) success, accomplishment and abundance.

NUMEROLOGICAL ASSOCIATION

The number 3 (1 + 2 = 3) indicates expressing one's self, creating, externalizing and relating. With the number 3, group activities or situations involving more than one person are usually emphasized. Although the 3 brings conditions to fruition, there may also be some delay. Growth of an inner, emotional nature is also indicated.

Why do you think a Major Arcana showed up in your life at this time?

• **What stood out the most in your experience of this card?**

In addition to your recollection, here are some other possibilities you might want to consider:

FOCUS
Was there a complete reversal in your activities, plans or way of thinking? Was your world turned upside down? Were you suddenly questioning the value of what you were doing? Did you feel that part or all of your life was not in your control?

DESIRES
Did you wish you could find a way out of your difficulties, release a painful or problematical situation or let go of striving and uncertainty? Was what you wanted or needed beyond material considerations?

LOVE
Were you waiting to see what a lover would do or suspending your decision about him/her? Were you saddened by the fact that

you couldn't have the love you really wanted? If you were involved in a relationship that wasn't working or contemplating one that previously ended, did you feel that your needs were really quite different or that there were formidable communication problems between the two of you? Did it seem like he/she challenged you or your creativity and no matter how you shook them, oil and water just didn't mix?

Were legal, health or other crucial matters "hung up" or left dangling?   **OTHERS**

Was there a sudden flight from home? If so, was it only temporary?   **HOME**

Did a relative or friend travel to see you (or vice versa)? Did you go to a different environment or country? Were you feeling trapped or stranded?   **TRAVEL**

Did your work or the effort you put into it suddenly become meaningless? Were you questioning its caliber or worth? Was something important lost or missing? Did it look as though your future or your financial security was in jeopardy? Were you feeling hamstrung?   **WORK**

Did you have a pinched nerve or "stuffy" head? When you didn't understand something, did it help to sleep on it? Did meditation, prayer   **BODY/MIND** or reading spiritual literature cause a change of heart or perspective? Did you find the wherewithal to handle a rough situation effectively?

SPIRIT

Did something transpire that brought new hope and meaning into your life? Did you have a precognitive dream?

RELATIVES

Did you give your family and friends the dignity of having their own opinions, making their own choices and living their own lives? Did you respect their wishes and put their needs above your own?

FINANCES

Were you tired of waiting for money? Were you bound by financial restrictions? Did problems arise over who should pay or who owed whom what?

PROBLEMS

Were you led astray by aligning yourself with people who only looked like what you wanted, when in fact they had no real substance at all? Did you dislike being at the mercy of others or having to put your plans on hold?

GUIDANCE

The impelling force of the number 3 is toward *self-expression*.

Were you searching for a deeper level of self worth? Was a bigger *Self* beginning to emerge? Did you feel that some of your ideals were being redefined? Were the patterns that weren't working in your life beginning to dissolve? Did a deeper understanding replace them? What was your new perception?

Opportunities for a number 3 come through creative channels, social **SUCCESS**
awareness and interacting with the public.

    Were you inspired by an altruistic cause or something in the arts or
entertainment industry? Did opportunities come through your social
connections? Was your current job, relationship or lifestyle allowing
you to *express* the desires of your heart or pursue the dreams you believed meant the fulfillment of your destiny? If not, how might you
have made better use of your time or talents?

What did you need to sacrifice, suspend or surrender? What did (or   **ACTION**
could) you assume more responsibility for?

- **In light of your experience, what do you believe The Hanged Man signified?**

- **What did you learn from it?**

- **If you drew The Hanged Man in response to a question you asked, in what way did this card answer it?**

- **Now, take another look at your card. Is there anything that stands out about it you didn't notice before?**

• **If you were to make your own Tarot card, what words, pictures or symbols would you put on it?**

SOMETHING TO REFLECT UPON

What if answers come when we stop seeking them? What if the way to attain what we want is to give it? What if, when our life seems like it's completely turned around, it's finally heading in the right direction?

◆   # DEATH

MAJOR ARCANA cards signify soul growth and herald lessons and opportunities designed to put us on the right path and help us to evolve. When a Major Arcana appears, we become conscious of something that was previously unknown or face challenges emanating from beyond our personal sphere of influence or control.

PLANETARY INFLUENCE

Saturn: Structures. Stability. Discipline. Material security. Affairs that demand patience and endurance. Profound learning experiences. Maturing. Feelings of (or beliefs about) failure or powerlessness.

   Pluto: Inner powers and resources. Letting go of what's no longer needed or working anymore. Transformation of consciousness. Integration. Rebirth into a new form or better way of life.

NUMEROLOGICAL ASSOCIATION

The number 4 (1 + 3 = 4) connotes formation, stability and solidification. With the number 4, one's work and dreams are stressed, and although one's eyes may be on a bigger picture, or the promise of future reward, one must concentrate on what *is* and deal with the practical task(s) at hand.

Why do you think a Major Arcana showed up in your life at this time?

• **What stood out the most in your experience of this card?**

In addition to your recollection, here are some other possibilities you might want to consider:

Did you feel that you were going through a *major* change, transition or metamorphosis? Were there "deaths" and "rebirths" in your career, partnerships, love life or psychological makeup?   **FOCUS** _____

Did you want things to radically change or to put something to rest once and for all?   **DESIRES** _____

Did a relationship, or the way you relate to another within a relationship, end? Were you getting the feeling that your attitude or need to be loved was getting in the way of making the right choices or asserting yourself in healthy ways?   **LOVE** _____

OTHERS _____ Did you and another have a discussion about health, death or dying? Was a friend moving away or going out of your life?

HOME _____ Did you want to move or relocate? Did something (or someone) delay your plans or cause them to change? Did you buy or replace an expensive item?

TRAVEL _____ Did you have to travel whether you wanted to or not? Were there any changes or reprieves?

WORK _____ Did your goals, or the focus of your work, completely change? Were you compelled to look for alternatives?

BODY/MIND _____ Did you feel that you needed to eat more organic foods like fruits and vegetables? Were you aware of any tightness or pressure in your body? Did you have a character flaw (explosive temper, obsessive behavior, self-destructive tendency?) that needed to be uprooted and weeded out?

SPIRIT _____ What made you come alive?

RELATIVES _____ Did someone offer words of encouragement? Did your family (and friends) gather 'round? Did you lose, fear you would lose or come close to losing someone you love?

Was your income cut back or severed? Did you come up short in your accounting or estimation? Were you worried about making ends meet? Did a new source of revenue unexpectedly arrive? Was money thought lost, eventually reinstated? Was a financial concern put to rest?

FINANCES

The 13/4 is a karmic number indicating tribulations in relationships, negative or rigid thinking and difficulties in working through limitations or applying oneself appropriately (all or nothing, too much or too little, etc.).

PROBLEMS

Did any of these factors apply to your situation? Were you locked into a mind-set that kept perpetuating itself? Did you lack self-discipline, opt for easy ways out or doggedly cling to people and things even though nothing good could come of it and no improvement could be made by continuing to pursue them?

The impelling force of the number 4 is toward *security*.

GUIDANCE

Was your death experience forcing you to let go of deadening conditions, what you *thought* you needed and illusory forms of security in order to give birth to what you *do* need and more life-affirming situations?

Opportunities for a number 4 come through practical application, work and service.

SUCCESS

What notions, attitudes or behavior had to change for success to be achieved? What did you need to work harder at or release in order for you to evolve and be of greater service? How did the conclusion of one aspect of your life open the door to new opportunities and better conditions?

ACTION   Did you dwell on what you couldn't do or have, or did you act on what you could?

- In light of your experience, what do you believe the Death card signified?

- What did you learn from it?

- If you drew Death in response to a question you asked, in what way did this card answer it?

- Now, take another look at your card. Is there anything that stands out about it you didn't notice before?

- If you were to make your own Tarot card, what words, pictures or symbols would you put on it?

SOMETHING TO REFLECT UPON

You may want to tape this guided meditation and play it back with your eyes closed.

Think about the things you've been struggling with . . . if you're having trouble sorting them out, take a piece of paper and write them down.

Once the issues are clearly defined, pretend that they are lined up in front of you like stick figures, cardboard representations or cue cards.

As you contemplate these things, imagine that a pearl white box is beginning to form from out of the ethers, and when it comes to rest at your feet, take the lid off and one by one, pick up each of your cares and put them in the box. . . . When you have finished, replace the lid and give the box back to the Universe. . . . If there is something you need, ask for it now.

Ask only once, and then *let it go* . . . let go knowing that you turned your problems over to your Higher Power and you don't have to wrestle with them anymore.

Unless a seed falls to the ground, it cannot have life.

TEMPERANCE

MAJOR ARCANA cards signify soul growth and herald lessons and opportunities designed to put us on the right path and help us to evolve. When a Major Arcana appears, we become conscious of something that was previously unknown or face challenges emanating from beyond our personal sphere of influence or control.

PLANETARY INFLUENCE

Mercury: Reasoning ability. Intellectual prowess. Perceptions. Formulating thoughts. Conveying ideas. Communications of all kinds.

Mars: Desires. Knowing what one wants. Methods of attaining goals. Action. Impatience. Conflict (or accidents). Affairs that demand personal evolvement, self-assertion, boldness and courage.

NUMEROLOGICAL ASSOCIATION

The number 5 (1 + 4 = 5) indicates change, fluctuations in fate or fortune, conflict, experiential learning and the expansion of one's thinking. With the number 5, opportunities and challenges go hand in hand and one must look to both the material and spiritual realm if one is to triumph or understand.

Why do you think a Major Arcana showed up in your life at this time?

• **What stood out the most in your experience of this card?**

In addition to your recollection, here are some other possibilities you might want to consider:

FOCUS   Were issues, conditions or relationships you thought you had dealt with or completed resurfacing? Did you feel that your foundations were being rocked or that your beliefs or commitment to something were being challenged? Did the events in your life cause you to ponder metaphysics or the power of thought? Do you think you were learning a lesson about *temperance,* self-discipline or self-control? Were you testing theories or trying to prove something to yourself?

DESIRES   Did you want, need or seek spiritual assistance in solving a problem?

Did men/women you previously knew reenter your life for a final review? Did you have a balanced, committed relationship? Were your feelings for each other consistent? Were your communications easy, honest and clear?

LOVE

Did someone (a secret admirer?) do you a favor or give you a gift? Were old feelings stirred up? Were your boss, peers or friends more kind, loving or demonstrative toward you? Were others living up to their promises or keeping their commitments?

OTHERS

Did your home reflect your internal experience; i.e., if you couldn't see the light, did you need to change a light bulb? If you were exhausting your resources or pushing your endurance to the limits, did an appliance burn out or your computer crash?

HOME

Did you postpone a trip, outing or invitation? Was it because you were too busy? Did someone need or ask you for a ride? Did you believe "a rolling stone gathers momentum"?

TRAVEL

Were you confronting an issue you thought you had overcome, challenging a fear or working through limitations? Did you feel that you simply couldn't go on without relief or gratification? If you were overwhelmed, did it help to concentrate on one project or group of things at a time? Were you or your work in the public eye?

WORK

BODY/MIND

Were you craving change, travel or excitement? Were you nervous, restless or impatient? Did you get frustrated if communications weren't clear or information was incomplete? Did you have to work at staying positive or centered? Were you suffering from a nerve-related affliction? Did a previous health condition resurface? If so, did you need medical attention or were you able to heal yourself? Did you feel as if you were experiencing a clash between the old and the new?

SPIRIT

Did you receive a spiritual answer? Did a flash of insight transform your experience? Were you lucky? Did you feel grateful that someone who had been ill was recovering, or that your finances were improving?

RELATIVES

Were you thrown back to a mind-set you used to have or a problem you thought you had handled? Was a family member (or friend) there for you with the right word or gesture?

FINANCES

Did you receive money for something done in the past? Did you earn (or spend) vacation or holiday pay? Did you make or get phone calls that brought in additional money or purchase something over the phone? Did you win anything? Was a moderate degree of success attained?

PROBLEMS

The 14/5 is a karmic number indicating a lack of commitment (to a person or thing), unaccountability and an unwillingness to learn life's lessons, resulting in repeated lessons, delays and losses.

Were you dealing with any of these issues? Was there something you were avoiding or *still* hadn't learned? Do you think your assessments or expectations of people, conditions or your own abilities tended to be impractical or unrealistic? Did you want to throw in the towel at the slightest provocation or discouragement? Were you unwilling to make the compromises necessary to keep a relationship going or bring your work to a successful conclusion?

The impelling force of the number 5 is toward *freedom*.

GUIDANCE

 Was there a belief, behavior or addiction (mental or physical) that was imprisoning you? Was the desire for change so intense that when it came it brought the very thing you wanted? In the final analysis, did you feel that the Universe was testing your faith or giving you the opportunity to renew it?

Opportunities for a number 5 come through change, progressive thinking and the establishment of something new.

SUCCESS

 Did maintaining (emotional) control over volatile situations turn negative experiences into positive ones? When the right ideas or components came together, did external conditions also change?

Were you willing to confront problems that needed to be addressed and work through limitations? If you needed verification or more understanding, did you ask for it? How were you able to use the transforming aspects of the *temperance* experience to your advantage?

ACTION

- In light of your experience, what do you believe Temperance signified?

- What did you learn from it?

- If you drew Temperance in response to a question you asked, in what way did this card answer it?

- Now, take another look at your card. Is there anything that stands out about it you didn't notice before?

- If you were to make your own Tarot card, what words, pictures or symbols would you put on it?

SOMETHING TO REFLECT UPON

The Rules for Being Human

1. You will receive a body. You may like it or hate it, but it will be yours for the entire period.
2. You will learn lessons. You are enrolled in a full-time informational school called life. Each day in this school you will learn lessons. You may like the lessons or think them irrelevant and stupid.
3. There are no mistakes, only lessons. Growth is a process of trial and error; experimentation. The "failed" experiments are as much a part of the process as the experiment that ultimately "works."

4. A lesson is repeated until learned. It will be presented to you in various forms until you have learned it. Once learned, you will then go on to the next lesson.

5. Learning lessons does not end. There is no part of life that does not contain its lessons. If you are alive, there are lessons to be learned.

6. "There" is no better than "here." When your "there" has become a "here" you will simply obtain another "there" that will again look better than "here."

7. Others are merely mirrors of you. You cannot love or hate something about another person unless it reflects something you love or hate about yourself.

8. What you make of your life is up to you. You have all the tools and resources you need. What you do with them is up to you. The choice is yours.

9. The answers to life's questions lie inside you. All you need to do is look, listen, and trust.

10. You will forget all this.

Cherie Carter-Scott, Ph.D., "The Rules for Being Human," *(Chicken Soup for the Soul,* Canfield and Hansen)

 # THE DEVIL

MAJOR ARCANA cards signify soul growth and herald lessons and opportunities designed to put us on the right path and help us to evolve. When a Major Arcana appears, we become conscious of something that was previously unknown or face challenges emanating from beyond our personal sphere of influence or control.

PLANETARY INFLUENCE

Saturn: Structures. Stability. Discipline. Material security. Affairs that demand patience and endurance. Profound learning experiences. Maturing. Feelings of (or beliefs about) failure or powerlessness.

Jupiter: New undertakings. Favor. Luck. Improvement. Opportunity. Enlargement. Long-term and future plans. Recognition. Material benefits. Generosity. Feelings of (or beliefs about) success, accomplishment and abundance.

NUMEROLOGICAL ASSOCIATION

The number 6 (1 + 5 = 6) indicates the need to make adjustments in one's thoughts, attitudes, behavior or condition. While this may feel burdensome, the number 6 also carries with it the ability to transcend difficulties and oftentimes serendipitously. Responsibilities, family and health may also be emphasized.

Why do you think a Major Arcana showed up in your life at this time?

- **What stood out the most in your experience of this card?**

In addition to your recollection, here are some other possibilities you might want to consider:

FOCUS

Were you in bondage to people, conditions or beliefs that weren't serving you? Did you feel *un*lucky? Were you suffering from spiritual amnesia? Did you feel that there was nothing out there to help you and no hope for improvement? Did problems seem to multiply?

DESIRES

Did you wish you could rise above the negative feelings you were experiencing about money, love, health, (fill in the blank)?

LOVE

Did you feel emotionally chained to a dead-end, or unhealthy, love affair? Were you acting in ways you knew weren't in your best interest? Were you allowing someone to use or take advantage of you? Did you feel that you were unworthy of being loved? Did you want love but accept sex? Were you depressed by the lack of love in your life?

Were you angry with an associate? Did you feel unappreciated or **OTHERS**
overlooked? Did you think that others had the upper hand and you
had little or no say in the matter? Did hearing or seeing people laugh-
ing and enjoying their lives make you feel worse? If so, what do you
suppose that was telling you?

Were you in a state of turmoil? Did you feel that it wasn't a good time **HOME**
to make any major moves or changes; especially if it might incur additional problems, responsibilities or expenses?

Did you go somewhere hoping to escape but your problems went **TRAVEL**
with you? Was a trip put off?

Did you feel that conditions had become so negative, you couldn't **WORK**
continue? Were you a slave to your work? Did you have an upsetting
conversation with someone? Did you feel that success was a never-
ending battle or feel thwarted in your attempts to capitalize on your
potential? Was your opinion of yourself based solely on your ability
to succeed?

Was a depressing condition taking the pleasure out of something you **BODY/MIND**
used to find enjoyable? Was it hard to keep the faith? Did you think
you had to suffer or sell your soul to get ahead in life? Did you experience any sexual inhibitions or aberrations? Was your thinking
askew? Had your vision become myopic?

SPIRIT   Did you find out something to your advantage? Did a delay work in your favor? What did you feel released from or grateful for?

RELATIVES   Did you blame others for your problems or expect them to fix things for you or did you take responsibility?

FINANCES   Did you feel overworked and underpaid? Were you upset about the cost of living, an unexpected bill or money you'd spent? Were you having (or anticipating) major financial difficulties? Was your focus on lack?

PROBLEMS   Did dwelling on your problems or looking for the reason *why* you were having a negative experience only make matters worse? Did you notice that your thoughts were like magnets, attracting like people or conditions into your life? Was your frustration externalized, projected onto others?

GUIDANCE   The impelling force of the number 6 is toward *harmony*.

Were you tuned in to the signs or messages surrounding you or did you feel that you were not in harmony with yourself *or* God? Did the guidance you were receiving seem like a pinprick of light in a cavern of darkness? If so, can you see how you may have gotten off track, i.e., the thoughts, feelings or actions that preceded the discord you were experiencing?

Opportunities for a number 6 come through helping those in need of **SUCCESS**
material or spiritual assistance and expressing the art, beauty or
music of life.

Were *you* the one who was impoverished? If you realized you
needed to change, did you gently reassure yourself? If you were inspired by a great purpose, did it enable you to transcend the limitations you felt bound by or did you let it fall by the wayside? Was there
any way you could have funneled the negative energy you were feeling into some form of creative expression? How did you say yes to
life?

What action did you take to improve your condition? If you were un- **ACTION**
able to help yourself, did you seek out one who could help you? If
you needed a second opinion, did you get one? If not, why not?

• **In light of your experience, what do you believe The Devil signified?**

• **What did you learn from it?**

• **If you drew The Devil in response to a question you asked, in what way did
  this card answer it?**

- Now, take another look at your card. Is there anything that stands out about it you didn't notice before?

- If you were to make your own Tarot card, what words, pictures or symbols would you put on it?

SOMETHING TO REFLECT UPON

There is no point in being pessimistic. It won't work anyway.
ANONYMOUS

◆ # THE TOWER

MAJOR ARCANA cards signify soul growth and herald lessons and opportunities designed to put us on the right path and help us to evolve. When a Major Arcana appears, we become conscious of something that was previously unknown or face challenges emanating from beyond our personal sphere of influence or control.

PLANETARY INFLUENCE
Uranus: Unexpected changes. Sudden upheavals. Events that test one's faith or call for new thinking or methods. Awakenings. Invention. Reformation.
Mars: Desires. Knowing what one wants. Methods of attaining goals. Action. Impatience. Conflict (or accidents). Affairs that demand personal evolvement, self-assertion, boldness and courage.

NUMEROLOGICAL ASSOCIATION

The number 7 (1 + 6 = 7) indicates a period of introspection, analysis or solitude. During the influence of the number 7, one's psychological and spiritual resources are expanded and faith in what can't be seen, but nevertheless exists, is demanded.

Why do you think a Major Arcana showed up in your life at this time?

• **What stood out the most in your experience of this card?**

In addition to your recollection, here are some other possibilities you might want to consider:

Were there unexpected upheavals, losses or reversals? Did you sud-   **FOCUS** _____
denly become aware of something that was completely out of your reality? Were your plans disrupted? Were you fighting for your rights?
What areas of your life were undergoing *major* reconstruction?

Were you praying for an end to difficulties or that you could hold on   **DESIRES** _____
to something that was slipping away?

Was there a breakdown in your relationship or communications?   **LOVE** _____
Did a lie, infidelity or unexpected event cause a separation, parting of
the ways or divorce? Did you think you had a problem establishing
lasting relationships?

OTHERS   Did someone betray, deceive or abandon you? Were your encounters unusual or strange? Did you feel that no one heard or understood you? Did you have trouble fitting in?

HOME   Was there a total change in the status quo? Were you having problems with household appliances? Did you lose a home you wanted to buy?

TRAVEL   Were there any perils, near misses or mishaps in your travels? Did you feel the need to exercise more caution than usual? Did your plans unexpectedly change?

WORK   Was there something that just wasn't working; something you were reluctant to change or give up? Were you worried about your business (or the lack thereof)? Did you contemplate a different career? Was it in music, speaking or writing?

BODY/MIND   Were there any accidents, illnesses or catastrophes? Were you pessimistic, uncertain or filled with doubt or fear? Was money received for an accident, injury or something that caused you pain or suffering? Were your medical bills high?

SPIRIT   Did you feel lucky in business or finance or that your good fortune slipped away as fast as it came? What helped you to regain a sense of rightness?

Were there problems at home? Was anyone in your family concerned about his or her future or an impending decision? Were there any disciplinary problems?

RELATIVES

Were you worried about your finances? Was funding canceled? Did a source of income abruptly end? Did you incur any unwanted expenses? Were there discussions about a court action, the collection of money or a contractual issue? How did you fare?

FINANCES

The 16/7 is a karmic number indicating shattered dreams; impermanence in status, fortune or love; tests of faith; and a tendency to want to flee rather than deal with emotional issues and the expression of one's feelings.

    Did any of these factors apply to your situation? If so, in what way?

PROBLEMS

The impelling force of the number 7 is toward *wisdom*.

    Was there a rude awakening, sudden flash of inspiration or an important breakthrough? What thoughts or fears were ruling your life? How were your beliefs helping or imprisoning you? What negative patterns or unrealistic fantasies did you need to cast out? What wisdom did you glean from the ordeals you had to suffer? How did the overthrow of an existing condition build a stronger personal or spiritual foundation?

GUIDANCE

Opportunities for a number 7 come through what is *brought* to one, inner poise and the spiritual, unseen realm, rather than what is actively pursued.

SUCCESS

What was brought to you that you *didn't* seek, or *couldn't* do, for yourself? Was what was right, essential or meaningful, preserved, recovered or replaced by something better? Did you suddenly come into an abundance of love or money? What unseen *force* was urging you on to greater victory or reward?

ACTION   Were you able to remain calm in the face of challenge or setbacks? What new plans or decisions were you making?

• In light of your experience, what do you believe The Tower signified?

• What did you learn from it?

• If you drew The Tower in response to a question you asked, in what way did this card answer it?

• Now, take another look at your card. Is there anything that stands out about it you didn't notice before?

• **If you were to make your own Tarot card, what words, pictures or symbols would you put on it?**

SOMETHING TO REFLECT UPON

You may want to tape this guided meditation and play it back with your eyes closed.

Close your eyes and think about the issue that's troubling you. As you bring this thought forward, notice the *feelings* that accompany it and the way you react to people or your environment when you're experiencing those feelings. . . . Do you push away the very thing you need the most? Do you contract, shut out God and everyone else?

Close your eyes once more and recall a time when you were in a relationship or situation that didn't work out. . . . What were your thoughts, actions or feelings shortly before it came to an end or failed?

Now think back and recollect an event that *did* work out, something that you thought wouldn't . . . what were your thoughts, actions or feelings then?

There is but one cause of human failure and that is man's lack of faith in his true Self.

WILLIAM JAMES

 # THE STAR

MAJOR ARCANA cards signify soul growth and herald lessons and opportunities designed to put us on the right path and help us to evolve. When a Major Arcana appears, we become conscious of something that was previously unknown or face challenges emanating from beyond our personal sphere of influence or control.

PLANETARY INFLUENCE

Sun: Identity. Manner of expression. Direction of energy. Health and vigor. Willpower. Decision making. Beliefs about one's abilities. People in positions of authority or authority issues. Positive thinking. Encounters with men (or masculine, active energy).

Jupiter: New undertakings. Favor. Luck. Improvement. Opportunity. Enlargement. Long-term and future plans. Recognition. Material benefits. Generosity. Feelings of (or beliefs about) success, accomplishment and abundance.

NUMEROLOGICAL ASSOCIATION

The number 8 (1 + 7 = 8) connotes the potential for success, accomplishment or recognition and the capacity to achieve one's goals; but unless one seeks the Power Within, these may not be easily attained. Although a positive change of mind or status almost always accompanies the number 8, moral integrity, fortitude and emotional equilibrium will also be required.

Why do you think a Major Arcana showed up in your life at this time?

• **What stood out the most in your experience of this card?**

In addition to your recollection, here are some other possibilities you might want to consider:

FOCUS   Did you want to know what the future held? Were you thinking about what *could* be? Were you following your own star?

DESIRES   Were you wishing for clarity or financial betterment? Did you hope your future would be better than your past?

Was your heart yearning for something you couldn't quite put your **LOVE**
finger on or have? Did you feel destined to be with or meet someone
special? Did something occur to encourage that wish? Was there a
man/woman you felt emotionally or karmically tied to? Did you feel
that you held the greater power in a relationship and the fate of it depended on you?

Did you meet, or connect with, any important people? Were papers **OTHERS**
or the exchange of ideas significant? Did others like and respect you?
Did you feel like a shining star? If you were in need of assistance,
backing or insight, did you receive it?

Were you reassessing your future as the result of a call or caller? Did **HOME**
a wish become a requirement? Did you lease, sell or have a debate
about a home?

Did you contemplate, or go on, a long-distance trip? Did someone **TRAVEL**
travel to see you or tell you that he/she would soon be traveling?

Did your job or your status change? Were bright opportunities avail- **WORK**
able to you? Did you discover a new talent or a new way to make
money?

Were there any physical or emotional matters that had to be at- **BODY/MIND**
tended to? Did you gain insight into something and take steps to correct it? Were there any medical tests or prescription changes? Were

you becoming a more positive person? Did you feel that it was important to not give negative thoughts any power?

SPIRIT

Did you have a foretelling dream? Did something lead you to believe that you would prosper in the future? Did you have a knack for making timely or profitable discoveries or win money in a lottery, sweepstakes or game? What made you happier than you thought was possible?

RELATIVES

Was someone in your family worrying about another or dealing with reservations, confirmations or legal documents?

FINANCES

Were you manifesting the kind of money to which you aspired? Did you receive news, calls or letters related to finance or profit?

PROBLEMS

Were you hurt by someone's words or deeds? Did unavoidable circumstances impede your progress? Did you have trouble keeping your emotions on an even keel? Were there any health flare-ups? Did you feel that you were regressing?

GUIDANCE

The impelling force of the number 8 is toward *authority*.

Were you searching for, or listening to, a Higher Authority? Were *you* becoming an authority on something you learned, mastered or acquired special skills in? What insights or special guidance were you receiving?

Opportunities for a number 8 come through assisting those in need **SUCCESS** of direction, worthwhile goals and large, progressive organizations.

Did you feel that you could be a guiding light? Were you motivated by a sense of purpose? Did you strive toward your goal with a deep sincerity and firm resolve? Were large corporations involved? How did (or could) you use the gifts you currently possess? What did you feel *destined* to do or become?

Did you feel that your plan was aligned with the Divine plan? How **ACTION** did following your star lead you in the right direction or take you where you wanted to go?

- **In light of your experience, what do you believe The Star signified?**

- **What did you learn from it?**

- **If you drew The Star in response to a question you asked, in what way did this card answer it?**

- **Now, take another look at your card. Is there anything that stands out about it you didn't notice before?**

- If you were to make your own Tarot card, what words, pictures or symbols would you put on it?

SOMETHING TO REFLECT UPON

If you knew with absolute certainty that you were destined to fulfill your deepest desire, what would that desire be?

> *Ask and you shall receive. Seek and you will find. Knock and the door will be opened unto you.*
>
> THE GOSPEL ACCORDING TO ST. MATTHEW

◆   # THE MOON

MAJOR ARCANA cards signify soul growth and herald lessons and opportunities designed to put us on the right path and help us to evolve. When a Major Arcana appears, we become conscious of something that was previously unknown or face challenges emanating from beyond our personal sphere of influence or control.

PLANETARY INFLUENCE

Moon: Feelings about oneself. Responses to life. Instability. Changeability. Cycles and rhythms. Intuition. Psychic sensitivity. Tendency toward negative thinking. Encounters with women (or feminine, passive energy).

Neptune: Idealism. Confusion. Illusions. Worthiness issues. Dissolving old patterns. Finding new meanings. Perspective. Spiritual, mystical or occult experiences.

NUMEROLOGICAL ASSOCIATION

The number 9 (1 + 8 = 9) stands for completion, arrival, integration and realization. When a number 9 surfaces, it marks a transition between what was and what is to come, a parenthesis in time as one pauses to reflect on all that went before and the unknown potential of that which is yet to be.

Why do you think a Major Arcana showed up in your life at this time?

• **What stood out the most in your experience of this card?**

In addition to your recollection, here are some other possibilities you might want to consider:

Were you unfulfilled in, or disillusioned by, the very thing that mattered most? Did you lose your way or faith in your goals? Was it hard not to succumb to the pull of your emotions? Were you in the process of completing a cycle or entering a new phase?   **FOCUS** _____

Did you want your dreams to come true but fear they wouldn't?   **DESIRES** _____

Were you disappointed in love or by a relationship you thought would work but didn't? Did an infatuation come to an end? Do you think you were deluding yourself or you didn't *want* to see the truth? Were there *major* problems or differences that made trying to make a relationship work pointless?   **LOVE** _____

OTHERS
Were you upset by someone's actions, words or conduct? Did you have conflicting emotions or trouble sorting out your feelings? Were you deceived, lied to or in danger of being taken in by a con artist, cult or fanatic?

HOME
Did a phone call or caller bother you? Did a get-together turn out to be a disappointment? Was there an upsetting occurrence you had absolutely no control over?

TRAVEL
Was there something about travel that was disturbing you? Were there unforeseen problems or hazards? If you traveled, did you wish you hadn't gone? Did your journeys involve the spirit realm, dream work or the astral plane?

WORK
Were you having misgivings about what you initially thought would be a good idea or an enjoyable and profitable enterprise? Did your ideas meet with opposition? Did a company reject your proposal or return your merchandise?

BODY/MIND
Did you struggle with bouts of depression, self-doubt or feelings of dread or foreboding? Were you sleeping or eating more (or less)? Did you experience any strange psychic or physical disturbances (premonitions, lumps, bumps, cysts, etc.)? Was your thinking confused or disjointed? Were you shedding silent tears? Where did your passions take you?

Did you enjoy the arts, music or dance? What made you a happier, **SPIRIT**
healthier or more well-rounded person? What did you *think* you
needed to feel that way?

Did you have trouble connecting with your family or conveying your **RELATIVES**
feelings? Were there too many emotional or distracting elements involved?

Were you keeping a watchful eye on your property and investments? **FINANCES**
Did you feel short-changed, cheated or ripped off?

Were you crushed by a huge disappointment? Did you know that the **PROBLEMS**
only way out of the pain you were feeling was to find a way through it?

The impelling force of the number 9 is toward *detachment* and *uni-* **GUIDANCE**
versality.
    Were you being forced to let go of relationships, business associ-
ates or diversions that were wasting your time or going nowhere? If
you were accustomed to relying on external sources of guidance and
other people to do things for you, did you find that it wasn't working
anymore? Was something urging you to become a fuller, more *Self-*
directed person? How did a personal loss bring the realization of a
greater gain? What confirmations were you receiving?

SUCCESS

Opportunities for a number 9 come through inspirational lines and artistic, creative or motivational people.

Were the people you cared about supporting what you were doing or hoped to do or become? Who or what inspired you or stirred your soul? What did you *want* to do? What might that tell you about your path or desire?

ACTION

Were you able to cling to your Inner Light? What made you feel grounded? What did you need to discard or integrate in order to evolve?

• In light of your experience, what do you believe The Moon signified?

• What did you learn from it?

• If you drew The Moon in response to a question you asked, in what way did this card answer it?

• Now, take another look at your card. Is there anything that stands out about it you didn't notice before?

- **If you were to make your own Tarot card, what words, pictures or symbols would you put on it?**

SOMETHING TO REFLECT UPON

What are five positive things that *could* or did come out of your situation?

1. _____

2. _____

3. _____

4. _____

5. _____

   Believing something is possible is nine-tenths of the battle . . . and sometimes it takes going through a lot of what we don't want to arrive at that conviction.

 # THE SUN

MAJOR ARCANA cards signify soul growth and herald lessons and opportunities designed to put us on the right path and help us to evolve. When a Major Arcana appears, we become conscious of something that was previously unknown or face challenges emanating from beyond our personal sphere of influence or control.

PLANETARY INFLUENCE

Mars: Desires. Knowing what one wants. Methods of attaining goals. Action. Impatience. Conflict (or accidents). Affairs that demand personal evolvement, self-assertion, boldness and courage.

Sun: Identity. Manner of expression. Direction of energy. Health and vigor. Willpower. Decision making. Beliefs about one's abilities. People in positions of authority or authority issues. Positive thinking. Encounters with men (or masculine, active energy).

NUMEROLOGICAL ASSOCIATION

The number 1 (1 + 9 = 1) indicates fresh starts, invention, creativity, originality, independence, force and will. During the influence of the number 1, ideas, opportunities and new projects begin to flourish, and although one may know *what* one needs to do, it may take courage or daring to follow through.

Why do you think a Major Arcana showed up in your life at this time?

- **What stood out the most in your experience of this card?**

In addition to your recollection, here are some other possibilities you might want to consider:

FOCUS   Was there an emphasis on self-expression, creative endeavors, love or spiritual pursuits? Were you looking for happiness or your life's purpose? Did humanity, society, politics or glamour come into play?

DESIRES   Did you want a partner or a lasting marriage? Were you seeking professional recognition or Cosmic consciousness?

Were you a good judge of character? Did you jump right into rela- **LOVE**
tionships? Looking back on your love affairs, if you knew then what
you know now, would you have gotten involved? Did you retain
your individuality or did you become what you thought your
lover/mate wanted you to be? Were you afraid to reveal your true
self? Was the one you really wanted missing from your life? If so, did
others vie to take his/her place?

Did your work, or something you wanted to accomplish, involve the **OTHERS**
public or public opinion? Were you offered a job as a speaker or lecturer? Did you work for a charitable cause? Did someone offer you a
glamorous opportunity or propose a joint venture or partnership?
Was mixing business with pleasure a good idea?

Were you experiencing problems with legal forms, important papers, **HOME**
bills or documents? Were you uncertain as to how to proceed? Did
you want to get away but something kept pulling you back? Were
you house-sitting, taking care of someone's home or speaking with
someone about their house?

Did your work or health take you away from home? If you traveled, **TRAVEL**
were you pleased that you went? Did you make a call on someone
with a package, gift or your suitcase in hand?

Was business slow? Did you feel like not working? Conversely, did **WORK**
you become so preoccupied with your work, or trying to make your
business a success, you lost all sense of balance? Did any new ideas

begin to formulate? Did you change direction or do something other (or better) than what you started out to do?

BODY/MIND   Did you feel energized or enervated? Was there something that was careening out of control (temper, emotions, binges, drugs)? Were you becoming more aware of your self-talk? Did you want to change your appearance or create a new self-image? Did you need a healing of heart or spirit? Did you donate something to a health organization?

SPIRIT   Did selfless giving or counting your blessings lift your spirits? Did friends and social activities offer simple pleasures? Did someone do you a (huge) favor?

RELATIVES   Did you feel that your family was mentally or emotionally available? Were you paying attention to *them?* Did you help someone out of a jam? Did you drop in on a relative or go on a special outing together?

FINANCES   Were you worried about money? If a source of income had run out or was cut off, was it reinstated? Did you receive good news concerning your finances? Did a financial or contractual issue get settled amicably? Was an appeal won?

PROBLEMS   The 19/1 is a karmic number indicating power issues and tests of courage, endurance and independence.

Did you vacillate between extremes: bold and independent or shy and needy; controlling or a pushover; totally optimistic or hopelessly depressed? Did you pretend to be what you were not? If someone criticized you or your work, did it destroy your confidence or make you think less of it? Did challenges unleash feelings of powerlessness or cause you to lose faith in yourself or others? Did feelings of insecurity prevent you from promoting yourself, utilizing your skills or profiting through your talents? Was an engagement broken? Did the future look uncertain?

The impelling force of the number 1 is toward *creation*.   **GUIDANCE**

How were you expressing your creative energy? What did you most enjoy doing? When you pursued your hobbies and interests, did you discover a talent you didn't think you had, or a world you never knew existed? What childlike quality did you need to let emerge?

Opportunities for a number 1 come through purposeful intention,   **SUCCESS**
leadership and innovative thinking.

Were you on purpose and determined? What areas were you the most successful in? What skills had you perfected? Did succeeding in the things you *liked* to do build confidence and help you define your purpose? Did you use your gifts to lead, enrich or inspire others? Were you beginning to realize that you couldn't wait for life to happen, *you* had to make life happen?

What limitations or obstacles did you have to push through or rise   **ACTION**
above? If something was beyond your present ability, were you learning to work within the confines of what *was* available to you? Did it help to turn your attention elsewhere temporarily or to constrain your ambition to twenty-four hours at a time?

- In light of your experience, what do you believe The Sun signified?

- What did you learn from it?

- If you drew The Sun in response to a question you asked, in what way did this card answer it?

- Now, take another look at your card. Is there anything that stands out about it you didn't notice before?

- If you were to make your own Tarot card, what words, pictures or symbols would you put on it?

SOMETHING TO REFLECT UPON

When we photograph an image and send it out to be developed, we don't think of the actual process, only the final picture. Similarly, when we envision what we want in life (a lasting relationship, a successful career, financial security, enlightenment, etc.) we tend to overlook the process it's going to take to get us there. Like film, we must also develop. We will have to go through the growing pains of becoming; and when our road seems bleak or murky we need to remind ourselves that what appears to be "negative" is really a developing "positive," and eventually that which is deepest within us will shine forth.

JUDGEMENT

MAJOR ARCANA cards signify soul growth and herald lessons and opportunities designed to put us on the right path and help us to evolve. When a Major Arcana appears, we become conscious of something that was previously unknown or face challenges emanating from beyond our personal sphere of influence or control.

PLANETARY INFLUENCE

Mars: Desires. Knowing what one wants. Methods of attaining goals. Action. Impatience. Conflict (or accidents). Affairs that demand personal evolvement, self-assertion, boldness and courage.

Pluto: Inner powers and resources. Letting go of what's no longer needed or working anymore. Transformation of consciousness. Integration. Rebirth into a new form or better way of life.

NUMEROLOGICAL ASSOCIATION

The number 2 (2 + 0 = 2) connotes assimilation, balancing polarities and dealing with unknowns. When the number 2 is present, partial success can be realized but one may also find oneself having to repeat previous lessons or experiences in order to eliminate flaws or continue to progress. Reunions, reconciliations and an element of surprise could also be indicated.

Why do you think a Major Arcana showed up in your life at this time?

• **What stood out the most in your experience of this card?**

In addition to your recollection, here are some other possibilities you might want to consider:

FOCUS —————— Were you trying to put bits and pieces of information into a cohesive whole? Were you getting the feeling that the future was still unfolding and you needed to withhold judgement until you gained a clearer understanding? Were you growing into new levels of awareness or "adeptmanship"?

DESIRES —————— Did you want to know if you should invest time or money in a relationship or enterprise, or to have more positive, joyful or loving experiences in your life?

LOVE —————— Did someone's actions make you think twice about seeing him/her again? Were you sensing that there was more to the person than he/she wanted you to believe? Did something occur that caused you to feel differently about having a relationship with him/her?

OTHERS —————— Did you hear a voice from out of the past? Were your friends and loved ones nurturing and supportive? Did your relationship with one in particular need to improve or end?

HOME —————— Did a lover call or an unexpected visitor arrive? Was an important decision made as a result? Were you handling, moving or having trouble with sound equipment?

TRAVEL —————— Did an expedition, trip or deviation from your normal routine prove to be a beneficial experience? Did a connection you made in the past play a prominent role in the present?

Did the resolution of a conflict (internal or external) mark the end of suffering and bring new hope, purpose or meaning to your work? **WORK**

Were you experiencing dizzy spells? Did you wish you were more together than you were? Did you need to recharge your emotional or spiritual batteries or take charge of your physical fitness? **BODY/MIND**

Was your quest for clarity, purpose or *Self*-evolvement beginning to supersede all transitory considerations? Were there any correlations between your dreams and your waking life? Was the truth about someone (or something) finally revealed? **SPIRIT**

Did you receive good news from a relative? Was there a surprising reunion? Were you making plans for a future event? **RELATIVES**

Were you troubled by an unexpected confrontation over money or legal rights? Was there a judgement in your favor? Were you seeing returns on your investments? Was money coming in through a job referral, partnership or previous business transaction? **FINANCES**

Did you have difficulty committing or letting go? Were you getting the feeling that you were being too judgmental or carrying around a lot of karmic baggage? If so, did you ask for spiritual assistance in dissolving the mental blocks or emotional patterns that kept you from embracing the blessings life has to offer? Did you consider using any visualization techniques like picturing yourself in the environ- **PROBLEMS** ment of the future, living the life you'd like to lead or having the thing(s) you wanted?

GUIDANCE

The impelling force of the number 2 is toward *association*.

Were you getting the impression that you needed to find a force greater than you were capable of mustering to align yourself with? Were you willing to persevere without immediate results until you were able to make the right connections?

SUCCESS

Opportunities for a number 2 come through friends, groups and communities.

Did a new friend, position or relationship provide opportunities that weren't available to you before? Were the people you were involved with showing you the lessons you needed to learn or how much you've grown? Did you get a positive response?

ACTION

If you were unsure about something, did you find that it was better to hold off rather than advance prematurely? Did a change of consciousness follow a period of intense personal growth?

• **In light of your experience, what do you believe Judgement signified?**

- **What did you learn from it?**

- **If you drew Judgement in response to a question you asked, in what way did this card answer it?**

- **Now, take another look at your card. Is there anything that stands out about it you didn't notice before?**

- **If you were to make your own Tarot card, what words, pictures or symbols would you put on it?**

SOMETHING TO REFLECT UPON

If you were reborn as the person you wanted to be or into the lifestyle you wanted to live, what would you do differently and why?

Can you do some or all of that now?

Significant problems cannot be solved at the same level of thinking we were at when we created them.

ALBERT EINSTEIN

THE WORLD

MAJOR ARCANA cards signify soul growth and herald lessons and opportunities designed to put us on the right path and help us to evolve. When a Major Arcana appears, we become conscious of something that was previously unknown or face challenges emanating from beyond our personal sphere of influence or control.

PLANETARY INFLUENCE

Saturn: Structures. Stability. Discipline. Material security. Affairs that demand patience and endurance. Profound learning experiences. Maturing. Feelings of (or beliefs about) failure or powerlessness.

Mars: Desires. Knowing what one wants. Methods of attaining goals. Action. Impatience. Conflict (or accidents). Affairs that demand personal evolvement, self-assertion, boldness and courage.

NUMEROLOGICAL ASSOCIATION

The number 3 (2 + 1 = 3) indicates expressing one's self, creating, externalizing and relating. With the number 3, group activities or situations involving more than one person are usually emphasized. Although the 3 brings conditions to fruition, there may also be some delay. Growth of an inner, emotional nature is also indicated.

Why do you think a Major Arcana showed up in your life at this time?

- **What stood out the most in your experience of this card?**

In addition to your recollection, here are some other possibilities you might want to consider:

FOCUS   Was your personal awareness expanding? Did world events, ecology or planetary conditions affect you more profoundly? Were your encounters with others, public gatherings or organizations more consequential? What obligations, responsibilities or patterns were you completing? Was something finally coming together? What significant changes did you notice?

Did you want to be successful, liberated from restraints or to live a life that left its mark?

DESIRES

Did obstacles or adverse conditions prevent you from meeting new men/women or uniting with the one you wanted to be with? Were you worried that you'd never have the relationship you wanted? Did it seem that no matter how you tried, nothing worked? Were you a better friend or lover than a marriage partner? Did the world have to take a turn before a new day could emerge bringing with it the possibility of beginning again on a new foundation?

LOVE

Were you inspired by somebody you wanted to emulate? Did someone's irrational, wasteful or cruel behavior upset you? Was there something you could do about it? How did the world respond to you?

OTHERS

Were you feeling pressured, stressed or conflicted? Was an appointment broken? Were you chastised for something that you had no control over? Was someone thinking about building or moving into a new home? Did you think it was time to move? Did you mail or receive an important letter, box or package?

HOME

Did you want to leave home, the country or the world behind? Did you travel? If so, was it to attend a symposium, exhibition or outdoor

TRAVEL

event? Did your attitude shift as a result? Was the weather change-able; rainy, sunny, cloudy, balmy, humid?

WORK

Were you in a position you didn't want to be in (unemployed, work-ing too hard, disliking your job)? Did your status change? Did a dif-ferent procedure or new information make your work easier? Were you given the chance to advance or expand?

BODY/MIND

Did you run the gamut between heights of bliss to depths of despair? Were you recovering from an illness, infection, accident or injury? Were you being forced to slow down or take it easy? Was your nose, bladder or skin bothering you? Did you switch doctors or pay to see a doctor who wasn't covered by your medical plan? Did you think you were too materialistic or, conversely, not worldly enough?

SPIRIT

Did you have a dream about the issues you were experiencing? What thoughts, actions or activities inspired you, pleased you or gave you a sense of peace or purpose? Did you know what would make you happy?

RELATIVES

Did a relative or separation in the family cause unhappiness? Were in-laws (or pets) a burden you didn't want to contend with? How did you handle it? Did you need to be more tolerant, understanding or forgiving?

Did you acquire money from more than one source? Were you capable of doing so if you applied yourself? Did you know what you needed to do in order to make a profit? Did you get a refund?

FINANCES

Were you preoccupied with the past or frustrated by your inability to break free from a negative or restricting influence? Did you want to change conditions (physically, spiritually, worldly, politically, etc.) but felt powerless to do so? Did you feel like Atlas, that the weight of the heavens rested on *your* shoulders? Did opportunities come disguised as problems or obstacles?

PROBLEMS

The impelling force of the number 3 is toward *self-expression*.

Did you feel compelled to express yourself in a different way? Were you beginning to understand that what you *do* doesn't determine who you are, but that who you *are* determines what you do? What were you discovering about yourself? What unique talents/gifts do you possess?

GUIDANCE

Opportunities for a number 3 come through creative channels, social awareness and interacting with the public.

How did (or could) you become more visible in the world? What part of you was connecting successfully: your mind (wit, originality, creativity, intellect); body (a healing touch, physical appearance, athletics, etc.); spirit (desire to serve, a sense of inner connectedness)? What worked the best for you: personal, one-on-one interactions or an impersonal approach geared toward the world at large? What achievement *felt* the most rewarding?

SUCCESS

ACTION _____ What action did you take to support your goals? What did you need to transcend?

_____

• In light of your experience, what do you believe The World signified?

• What did you learn from it?

• If you drew The World in response to a question you asked, in what way did this card answer it?

• Now, take another look at your card. Is there anything that stands out about it you didn't notice before?

• If you were to make your own Tarot card, what words, pictures or symbols would you put on it?

SOMETHING TO REFLECT UPON

To whom much is given, much shall be required.

THE FOOL

MAJOR ARCANA cards signify soul growth and herald lessons and opportunities designed to put us on the right path and help us to evolve. When a Major Arcana appears, we become conscious of something that was previously unknown or face challenges emanating from beyond our personal sphere of influence or control.

PLANETARY INFLUENCE

Pluto: Inner powers and resources. Letting go of what's no longer needed or working anymore. Transformation of consciousness. Integration. Rebirth into a new form or better way of life.

Jupiter: New undertakings. Favor. Luck. Improvement. Opportunity. Enlargement. Long-term and future plans. Recognition. Material benefits. Generosity. Feelings of (or beliefs about) success, accomplishment and abundance.

NUMEROLOGICAL ASSOCIATION

The number 0 represents the God force and it is an ancient symbol for the number 22. Since the number 4 (2 + 2 = 4) points to manifestation, I see The Fool as the spirit of God in man. The number 22 is a master number indicating a higher, more universal application of the number 4, and aspirations that may be loftier than, or superior to, one's current level of understanding or ability.

Why do you think a Major Arcana showed up in your life at this time?

• **What stood out the most in your experience of this card?**

In addition to your recollection, here are some other possibilities you might want to consider:

FOCUS

Were you experiencing an energy shift? Was the small self being overshadowed by a greater Self? Were you watching the Cosmic play of the Universe as it unfolded in your life or having a mini-enlightenment experience? Were you looking forward to a brighter tomorrow? Did you have choices to make? Were you about to take a leap of faith?

DESIRES

Did you want to do what came naturally, what you felt led or inspired to do? Were you searching for happiness or a better understanding of the workings of God or the way in which He speaks to you?

LOVE

Did someone tell you that he/she was falling in love with you? Were the men/women in your life positive acknowledgments of your spiritual growth or advancing your godhood? If not, did you move on? Were you seeing someone who was more evolved than you? If you didn't have a relationship, did you feel certain that you would and that he/she would be a perfect complement? Were you the "chooser" instead of the "choosee"?

OTHERS

Were you unconcerned with the opinions of others? If someone tried to make you feel like a fool, did you realize that it was more of a statement about them than about you?

HOME

Did you feel a special affinity for nature and all of its creatures? Did an unexpected visitor or guest arrive? Were you considering or putting off a move?

Was there a question about travel plans or car insurance? If you planned to travel for business reasons, did you conduct the meeting over the phone instead? Did you go on a "walk about"? Were you on a journey for the Self? Were you traveling your own path? **TRAVEL**

Were you afforded the opportunity to teach or work with the public on a greater scale? Did you enact a daring business plan or embark on a new (creative) endeavor? If you were thinking about terminating a job or taking a leave of absence, did you? Did you work part of the time, rest, then take on more? **WORK**

Did you feel impervious to life's vicissitudes? Were you optimistic and carefree? Were old wounds beginning to heal? Did you speak with someone in the healing arts? If you had a question concerning your health, did you wait for clarity before proceeding with something that might be unnecessary? Did you look at the same things in different ways? **BODY/MIND**

Were you happy with your life? Did events turn out the way you hoped they would? Were desires fulfilled before the need arose? Were questions answered before you asked? Were you becoming more aware of the *way* God answers your prayers? Did you feel the power of Grace in your heart and affairs? Did revelations spring from within? **SPIRIT**

Was a relative job hunting? Did someone need attending to? Was there a decision that had to be made? Did you take time off to spend with your loved ones? Were you and your family close? Did you confide in them, laugh with them, cherish them? **RELATIVES**

FINANCES

Did you make a decision concerning your career and finances? Was forgotten interest from a savings account or CD suddenly available? Did you open a new account or put your money into something with a higher yield? If you were expecting a check, did it arrive? Did you have a wealthy partner, lover or friend? Did you profit through a phone call or caller(s)?

PROBLEMS

Were you having mixed emotions about someone? Were you worried that something a lot of time was invested in might not succeed? Did you fear that you had gotten in over your head, took on more than you could handle, or the work it would entail might push you over the edge? Did you run into problems when you listened to others instead of your*Self*?

GUIDANCE

The impelling force of the number 22 is toward *power on all planes*.

Were you feeling the pangs of a different calling? Do you think that a "Divine discontent" was urging you forward toward a better way of life? Did you have the conviction that no matter what life hands you, you had the power to deal with it? What insights or special guidance were you receiving? How was your consciousness expanding? What did you need to stop questioning?

SUCCESS

Opportunities for a number 22 come through self-mastery, extraordinary achievements and working with the masses.

Were your aspirations different from the general populace or the ordinary workaday world? Were you able to bring your higher ideas or spiritual vision down into the tangible world of form? Did success come through terminating the things in life that were keeping you from expressing your highest potential? What did you excel in?

Were you attached to the way you *thought* things should be or did   **ACTION**
you let go, let God and just let them be?

• **In light of your experience, what do you believe The Fool signified?**

• **What did you learn from it?**

• **If you drew The Fool in response to a question you asked, in what way did this card answer it?**

• **Now, take another look at your card. Is there anything that stands out about it you didn't notice before?**

• **If you were to make your own Tarot card, what words, pictures or symbols would you put on it?**

SOMETHING TO REFLECT UPON

For one entire day, practice the presence of God. When you go to work, imagine that you are doing your job in God's presence. When you speak with others, imagine that you are addressing the God within them. When you sit down to eat with your family, imagine that you are gathered together in the presence of God. . . . In everything you do, think or say, imagine that God is present.

Meditate on yourself. Honor yourself. Worship yourself. Understand yourself. God dwells within you as you.

SWAMI MUKTANANDA

THE
WANDS

YOUR QUERY SHEET

You can use this query sheet in addition to your weekly notes for questions you may have during the course of your workbook experience and in times to come.

Date:	Card:	Your Questions and Answers:
		Q:
		A:
		Q:
		A:
		Q:
		A:
		Q:
		A:
		Q:
		A:
		Q:
		A:
		Q:
		A:
		Q:
		A:
		Q:
		A:
		Q:
		A:
		Q:
		A:
		Q:
		A:
		Q:
		A:
		Q:
		A:
		Q:
		A:
		Q:
		A:
		Q:
		A:

THE ACE OF WANDS

Wands relate to ideas, growth, creativity and expansion.

Aces represent new beginnings; they also signify a season. The Ace of Wands represents the autumn months—September, October, November.

What season is it now? _____ What season does it *feel* like? _____

Numerologically, Aces correspond with the number 1 indicating fresh starts, invention, creativity, originality, independence, force and will. During the influence of the number 1, ideas, opportunities and new projects begin to flourish, and although one may know *what* one needs to do, it may take courage or daring to follow through.

Constructive: Confidence. Determination. Assuming responsibility. Strengthening one's abilities and sense of self. Singular effort.

Undermining: Willfulness. Unreasonable force. Fear of taking the initiative, promoting one's self or standing on one's own. Discouragement.

• **What stood out the most in your experience of this card?**

In addition to your recollection, here are some other possibilities you might want to consider:

Was your focus on potential: that which could develop or become actual? Was there an increase in activity or productivity? Were you driven by the desire to create? Were there several options to consider? Did you feel that life had become more abundant?   **FOCUS** _____

Were you hoping to start something new or get an answer, response or go-ahead?   **DESIRES** _____

Did you feel that the opposite sex found you more attractive? Did someone catch your eye? If so, what were the qualities that attracted   **LOVE** _____ you? Were there any invitations or proposals? Was marriage or living together discussed? Did you have a happy union even if there were problems in the past?

OTHERS

Did you and another have a discussion about your work, money or returns? Was it productive? Were you debating the idea of going with a different partner? Did you speak with someone you hadn't seen in awhile?

HOME

Were you working at home or contemplating a career that you could do at home? Were there discussions about buying a new home, moving out of the state or living in a different country?

TRAVEL

Did you take a "must go" or impulsive trip? What was the nature of your travels? Were you considering a trip or move to the East?

WORK

Were you good at intuiting information, improvising or coming up with original ideas? Was your work creative, artistic, musical or inspirational? Did you start your own company or begin a new enterprise?

BODY/MIND

Did your thinking or attitude change? Did you feel more positive, energetic or inspired? Were you more productive during one time of the day than at another? Did you begin a new treatment or (exercise) regime?

Were you happiest when you were creating something? Did you enjoy being busy?

SPIRIT

What role, if any, did your family play in your life?

RELATIVES

Did your efforts pay off? Were you rewarded by cash and sales? Did you feel good about spending your money?

FINANCES

Were you worried that your product or project wouldn't be in demand? Did you lack the determination to carry on or see it through to its completion?

PROBLEMS

Were you inspired by a new idea or winning concept? Did the way to proceed suddenly come to you?

GUIDANCE

Did you succeed in one particular field or undertaking or did you have equal success in several?

SUCCESS

How was your energy being put to use? Were you active or passive, a leader or a follower? Did you wait for others to come around or did you make the first move? If your first attempts were incomplete or unsuccessful, what were your alternatives? Did you follow up on them?

ACTION

- In light of your experience, what do you believe the Ace of Wands signified?

- What did you learn from it?

- If you drew the Ace of Wands in response to a question you asked, in what way did this card answer it?

- Now, take another look at your card. Is there anything that stands out about it you didn't notice before?

- If you were to make your own Tarot card, what words, pictures or symbols would you put on it?

SOMETHING TO REFLECT UPON

Whatever you can do, or dream you can, begin it. Boldness has genius, power, and magic in it.

GOETHE

THE TWO OF WANDS

Wands relate to ideas, growth, creativity and expansion.

Numerologically, the number 2 connotes assimilation, balancing polarities and dealing with unknowns. When the number 2 is present, partial success can be realized but one may also find oneself having to repeat previous lessons or experiences in order to eliminate flaws or continue to progress. Reunions, reconciliations and an element of surprise could also be indicated.

Constructive: Patience. Tolerance. Cooperation. Nurturing, developing or refining what one has before commencing something new. Combined efforts. Personal interaction.

Undermining: Impatience. One-sidedness. Isolation. Lack of commitment or steady purpose.

- **What stood out the most in your experience of this card?**

In addition to your recollection, here are some other possibilities you might want to consider:

Was most of your energy directed toward your work and/or improving your performance, image or status? Were you expanding your ability to express yourself, command your thoughts or open your heart to others? What new worlds, opportunities or possibilities were you exploring?

FOCUS

Were you hoping something good would happen or waiting for something to materialize or become clear?

DESIRES

Did you have (or wish you had) a relationship that made you feel loved and secure? If single, did a new (or married) man/woman enter

LOVE

your life? If you broke up with someone, did he/she want or win you back? Was living together (or a different offer) proposed? Did you find that longevity in a relationship wasn't due to a lack of problems but through the ability to resolve them amicably?

OTHERS

Were you well liked, respected and appreciated? Did you have (or meet) a benefactor? Did a chance encounter bring an unexpected blessing or gain? Did someone call on the pretext of business but what he/she *really* wanted was something else? Did you have like-minded friends?

HOME

Did you receive an important letter, fax or package and/or get good news about a home or a product you use at home? Did a lover call or visit? Did you purchase something you've been wanting or waiting for?

TRAVEL

Did you travel? Was your means of transportation different? Were there a few stops and starts along the way? Did you take a boat trip or go to a resort-like environment?

WORK

Were you in a position of power or a leader in your field? Was your business expanding? Did your work demand accuracy, attention to detail or patience? Were you considering a business proposal or perusing an important document? Did you make new business connections? Was a new partnership in the works?

Were you eating foods that gave you more energy or stimulated your mental faculties (fish, fruits, nuts, etc.)? Did you increase your vitamin intake? Were you more conscientious or feeling more secure, mature or capable? Did you want to change your (or someone else's) wardrobe, appearance, behavior or way of thinking? **BODY/MIND**

Were you invited to a party, dinner or social event? Did your focus shift from work to pleasure or romance? Did you hear something that pleased you or boosted your faith in a cherished wish? **SPIRIT**

Did you enjoy the time you spent with your family? Were your relatives understanding and your children playful and happy? If you didn't have children, were your creations your offspring? If you and another weren't getting along, did you patch things up? Did you introduce a new beau; ask a relative to act in your behalf; or receive positive, encouraging or surprising news? **RELATIVES**

Was a financial proposal discussed and agreed upon? Were your profits increasing? Did you get a promotion or a large check? **FINANCES**

Were you disturbed about a late payment or a delay in finalizing a deal? Was there a loss of income or a cancellation of funding? Did you worry about a feeling you had, an action you took or money that was spent? Did you have a poverty consciousness? Did something cause your perspective to change for the better? **PROBLEMS**

GUIDANCE   Were facts that were previously vague becoming clear to you? Was a thought you had, or a message you received, later confirmed? If, in the past, you distrusted your intuitive impressions or your inner connection, were you feeling more confident now?

SUCCESS   Were you determined to succeed? Was your work well received? Were you praised for its quality, thoroughness or sales? Did you have the opportunity to make more money or advance your position?

ACTION   Did you proceed in a prudent, gradual manner, doing only that which you were sure about or *wanted* to do? If you didn't feel right about something, did you convey your thoughts or put it on hold until you *were* sure about it? How were you using your resources or putting what you've learned into practice?

- In light of your experience, what do you believe the Two of Wands signified?

- What did you learn from it?

- If you drew the Two of Wands in response to a question you asked, in what way did this card answer it?

- Now, take another look at your card. Is there anything that stands out about it you didn't notice before?

- If you were to make your own Tarot card, what words, pictures or symbols would you put on it?

SOMETHING TO REFLECT UPON

Have you ever noticed how some inner promptings feel uplifting or exciting while others feel heavy or burdensome?

Try this experiment:

The next time you wonder if it's your intuition, as opposed to your intellect, that's urging you to do something, notice the accompanying feelings. Once you've acted on the thought, note the results of your action. Were your feelings right?

 # THE THREE OF WANDS

Wands relate to ideas, growth, creativity and expansion.

Numerologically, the number 3 indicates expressing one's self, creating, externalizing and relating. With the number 3, group activities or situations involving more than one person are usually emphasized. Although the 3 brings conditions to fruition, there may also be some delay. Growth of an inner, emotional nature is also indicated.

Constructive: Synthesizing. Conceptualizing. Becoming more selective or giving something your all. Embracing the lighter side of life. Keeping a positive, optimistic frame of mind. Allowing events to unfold.

Undermining: Ennui. Scattering energies. Overreacting or overindulging. Refusing to accept life on life's terms.

• **What stood out the most in your experience of this card?**

In addition to your recollection, here are some other possibilities you might want to consider:

FOCUS

Was your mind on promising unions, large (or small) companies, contracts or documents? Were you waiting for your ship to come in? Did you feel that bright prospects and golden opportunities lay ahead? Were the events in your life expanding your horizons or causing you to plumb your emotional or spiritual depths?

DESIRES

Did you want to quash a nagging apprehension?

LOVE

Was your love life improving? Did someone declare his/her love for you or apologize for his/her actions toward you? Were there several people vying for your affection? Did you have to make a difficult decision? If you worried that you and another weren't going to get together, did everything work out?

OTHERS

Were you unflappable in your dealings with others or did people sway your thinking or determine your happiness? If you had reservations about a friend, business associate or an authorization, was your anxiety dispelled? Was a friendship renewed or a new partnership established?

Did you leave home in search of something you hoped might be enjoyable? Was your house a peaceful haven? Were you experiencing better relations with your friends and neighbors?   **HOME**

Did you travel for work or pleasure, lease or return a car or drive somebody somewhere?   **TRAVEL**

Did someone offer practical assistance or help you achieve a goal? Did you work for more than one firm or under an "umbrella" company? Was your business flourishing? What type of work were you doing?   **WORK**

Did you trust yourself and your decisions? If you were concerned about a possible medical problem, did you get a clean bill of health?   **BODY/MIND**

Did you sense things *before* they occurred? Did touching another convey feelings that words could not?   **SPIRIT**

Were you or a family member expressing concern over a contract, business associate or company policy? If you needed support, was your family there for you? Were you concerned about a loved one's well-being?   **RELATIVES**

FINANCES   Did business take an upward swing? Did friends send you referrals or assist you monetarily? Did you conclude a financial transaction that brought in extra money or an additional income? Were there any bonuses?

PROBLEMS   Were you discouraged about something you didn't understand or that didn't appear to be working out? Were you beginning to lose faith? If so, did you turn to people who sustained you or put your energy into channels that supported you in positive ways?

GUIDANCE   Did you feel connected to your inner Self? What guidance were you receiving? Did acting on your inner promptings help to build more confidence?

SUCCESS   Did your talents find expression? Were you able to turn a thought or dream into a reality? Was there a major breakthrough in your business affairs, personal life or way of thinking?

ACTION   Did you trust that your ideas could be realized and expect the best?

• **In light of your experience, what do you believe the Three of Wands signified?**

• **What did you learn from it?**

• **If you drew the Three of Wands in response to a question you asked, in what way did this card answer it?**

• **Now, take another look at your card. Is there anything that stands out about it you didn't notice before?**

• **If you were to make your own Tarot card, what words, pictures or symbols would you put on it?**

SOMETHING TO REFLECT UPON

You may want to tape this guided meditation and play it back with your eyes closed.

Close your eyes and imagine that you are standing shoulder deep in a whirlpool of your thoughts and emotions . . . feel the density of this mass as it swirls around you . . . as you continue to observe it, notice that the level is beginning to recede . . . slowly at first and then faster as it moves down your chest, your stomach, your hips and your knees . . . as it reaches your feet, you breath easier and you realize that you are standing atop a mountain and the flood of your thoughts and feelings is flowing down into the ocean below. . . . As you look out over the horizon, you become aware of a little boat calmly sailing in from sea . . . and as you watch it come closer . . . and closer . . . you realize how effortlessly it glides toward its destiny . . . and now, as it fully appears beneath the setting sun, trust that *your* ship will come in fully laden with the fruits of your labor, rewards for work well done.

Obstacles are those frightful things we see when we take our eyes off our goal.
WHILE THE ORIGIN OF THIS QUOTE IS UNKNOWN,
HANNA MORE SEEMS TO BE FAVORED AS THE AUTHOR.

THE FOUR OF WANDS

Wands relate to ideas, growth, creativity and expansion.

Numerologically, the number 4 connotes formation, stability and solidification. With the number 4, one's work and dreams are stressed, and although one's eyes may be on a bigger picture, or the promise of future reward, one must concentrate on what is and deal with the practical task(s) at hand.

Constructive: Deliberation. Constructive application. Down-to-earth practicality. Functionality and workability. Building solid, concrete foundations.

Undermining: Impractical dreaming. Pie-in-the-sky risk taking. Too much attention focused on the material aspects of life and not enough on the spirit.

- **What stood out the most in your experience of this card?**

In addition to your recollection, here are some other possibilities you might want to consider:

FOCUS

Was there a greater emphasis on travel and interpersonal interactions? Were you growing (mentally, emotionally or spiritually) through your work and/or relationships?

Do you think you were learning a lesson about sharing, compromise or handling conflict constructively? What were you trying to build, construct or expand?

DESIRES

Did you think things should be better than they were? Did you want to quit or give up?

LOVE

Were you disappointed in your plans to unite with someone? Did you wonder if the person you were involved with was as he/she seemed, wanted to build a relationship or was being totally honest with you?

Were you beginning to realize that although much could be achieved by improving yourself, some people are easier to love or get along with than others?

Did you feel coerced into doing something you didn't want to do or make a commitment you weren't ready for? Did a business partner, friend or associate upset you? Did you refuse to be put in a precarious position?

OTHERS

Did you get a letter or call from an old friend or loved one? Did you have mounds of (paper) work or chores to do? Were there any unpleasant problems, confrontations or tête-à-têtes?

HOME

Did you have numerous errands to run? Did you travel all over town looking for something? Did you see someone you wanted to meet or talk to? Were your travels profitable or beneficial? Did you go out to dinner with your family or friends?

TRAVEL

Did you have trouble applying yourself toward your work? Were you beset by obstacles or distractions? Do you think you were lacking the right focus or direction? Did you turn down a job? Did you write something in order to sell your idea, introduce a new product or get a consent?

WORK

Was your body stiff or sore? Were you irritated, frazzled or disorganized? Was sex with your partner unfulfilling? Did you *know* you needed nurturing but not know how to ask for it or give it to your-

BODY/MIND

self? Were you feeling self-conscious or trying to live up to an impossible standard? Did you believe that you deserved to be happy?

SPIRIT

Was a small gift given or received? Did you enjoy social outings, books, window shopping or dabbling with creative projects? Was an emotional or spiritual need fulfilled? Did you experience a healing of ills? If so, what caused it?

RELATIVES

Were you concerned about someone's approval or peeved by something a relative said or did? Was your anger contained or did you explode? Was blood thicker than water? Did peace prevail?

FINANCES

Did you receive a large check? Were you paid by the hour or did your earnings come through commissions, royalties or residuals? Did you make more than you thought you would? Were you discussing a financial matter or better ways to invest your money?

PROBLEMS

Were you dispirited by the magnitude of the work you had to do or disappointed in your inability to connect with others in a satisfactory way? Did it occur to you that you might not be upset for the reason you thought or that your burdens were self-imposed?

GUIDANCE

Were you getting the impression that you didn't *have* to do or comprehend everything now, that some things were meant to come together later? Did you have a spiritual revelation or experience an event that enabled you to better understand the workings of God? Did you trust the Universe?

Did you or your circumstances change? Was a stumbling block over-come? Did your best success come through printed material, teaching or public exchanges?   **SUCCESS**

Did you act in your own best interest and produce the best you were capable of? Instead of quitting, did you persevere?   **ACTION**

- **In light of your experience, what do you believe the Four of Wands signified?**

- **What did you learn from it?**

- **If you drew the Four of Wands in response to a question you asked, in what way did this card answer it?**

- Now, take another look at your card. Is there anything that stands out about it you didn't notice before?

- If you were to make your own Tarot card, what words, pictures or symbols would you put on it?

SOMETHING TO REFLECT UPON

Adversity, pain, anger, fear and frustration all contain a message and an opportunity for growth. Ask your Higher Self, guardian angel or Higher Power, "What am I to learn from this?"

        # THE FIVE OF WANDS

Wands relate to ideas, growth, creativity and expansion.

Numerologically, the number 5 indicates change, fluctuations in fate or fortune, conflict, experiential learning and the expansion of one's thinking. With the number 5, opportunities and challenges go hand in hand, and one must look to both the material and spiritual realm if one is to triumph or understand.

Constructive: Discrimination. Resourcefulness. Revision. Re-creation. Self-reliance. Inner conviction.

Undermining: Little faith in one's self or abilities. Panic. Distress. Rebellion.

- **What stood out the most in your experience of this card?**

In addition to your recollection, here are some other possibilities you might want to consider:

Were you analyzing win/lose factors with regard to decision making, **FOCUS** outcomes or relationships with others? Was business or romance accentuated? What was changing in your life?

Did you want to do the right thing, handle communications effec- **DESIRES** tively or succeed in a challenging undertaking?

Was your love life on hold? If you were undecided about your feel- **LOVE** ings for someone, did you make up your mind? If you cast aside a lover, did you let him/her back into your heart (or bed)?

Were you praised for your efforts, perceptions or personal growth? **OTHERS** Did an acquaintance from the past return or a friendship blossom?

Did a phone call disturb you? Were you wrestling with a predicament **HOME** there didn't seem to be an answer to? Were you worried about your assets, theft, vandals or fire? Was there a problem with an insurance policy?

Did you travel for business, health or social reasons? Was your car, or **TRAVEL** a decision involving travel, a focal point?

WORK   Did you need to be more courageous or determined? Did the completion of a project bring an unexpected gain?

BODY/MIND   Was your health, diet or sex life improving? Was it imperative to maintain a positive attitude?

SPIRIT   Did you enjoy sensual pleasures, physical forms of recreation, striking bargains, or acing out your competitors?

RELATIVES   Were you concerned about the treatment of a family member or the safety of a pet? Were problems in the process of being resolved?

FINANCES   Were you weighing your profits against your losses? Did they balance out? If you were involved in a financial dispute or worried about money, were you ultimately victorious? Did you make out like a bandit? Was there an increase in sales, mail orders or commissions?

PROBLEMS   Did problems arise from unexpressed desires or unfulfilled emotional needs? Were you feeling compromised? Were you forced to take a serious look at the way you handled situations, the choices you were making or what you wanted out of life? Were your real battles inner ones?

GUIDANCE   Did the thought cross your mind that you weren't wasting your time pursuing your goal, you were wasting your time *worrying* about it?

Did success come through a revision of attitude or summoning the **SUCCESS**
courage it took to make effective changes or get the job done? Did
your business expand or your love life improve?

Did you realize that if you were feeling angry, fearful or defeated it **ACTION**
was because you weren't being honest with yourself (or others) or
you were looking at conditions from a "lose" instead of a "win"
point of view? Did you make decisions that put *you* in the driver's
seat?

• **In light of your experience, what do you believe the Five of Wands signified?**

• **What did you learn from it?**

• **If you drew the Five of Wands in response to a question you asked, in what way did this card answer it?**

• **Now, take another look at your card. Is there anything that stands out about it you didn't notice before?**

- **If you were to make your own Tarot card, what words, pictures or symbols would you put on it?**

SOMETHING TO REFLECT UPON

Ask yourself: "What limiting thought might I be harboring?" Then, "Why do I believe it?" What if it weren't true? How would you act or be?

> *Don't be afraid to take a big step if one is indicated. You can't cross a chasm in two small jumps.*
>
> DAVID LLOYD GEORGE

 # THE SIX OF WANDS

Wands relate to ideas, growth, creativity and expansion.

Numerologically, the number 6 indicates the need to make adjustments in one's thoughts, attitudes, behavior or condition. While this may feel burdensome, the number 6 also carries with it the ability to transcend difficulties and oftentimes serendipitously. Responsibilities, family and health may also be emphasized.

Constructive: Thoroughness. Resoluteness. Serving, giving or adapting to the needs of others. Love. Compassion.

Undermining: Indifference. Irresponsibility (toward self and others). Fixed opinions, beliefs or attitudes. Imbalance.

- **What stood out the most in your experience of this card?**

In addition to your recollection, here are some other possibilities you might want to consider:

Did the way you were expressing yourself verbally or creatively take **FOCUS** _____ on more significance? Were you learning about your strengths and limitations or going through psychological changes? Were people the catalyst for growth? Was there an unexpected shift in a new direction?

Were you determined to overcome challenges imposed upon you by **DESIRES** _____ time or circumstance? Did you want things to be different than they were? Were your desires changing?

Did a new element cause you to rethink your relationship or make any **LOVE** _____ changes? Was someone impetuous, amorous or younger than you trying to win your heart? If so, what were your thoughts about him/her?

Were people friendly, cooperative and supportive? Were you becom- **OTHERS** _____ ing more aware of the way you interacted with others? Did the response of another to something that you said or did surprise you? Did you make new professional friends? Did someone in a prominent position offer to promote you or send business your way?

Were things breaking, sticking, coming unglued or falling apart? Did **HOME** _____ you (or were you planning to) visit the home of a friend or relative? Did someone (or something) you were waiting for arrive? Did a suitor call on you?

TRAVEL   Did you go on a pleasure trip or an outing with a friend? Was there something you hoped you could put off or get out of? Were you irritated by the way some people parked or drove? Did you fly to another state or country or speak with someone who was intending to travel?

WORK   Did you take a break from your work or usual routine? Did you take up a creative hobby, attend a seminar or teach a class? Did the arts, music or communication industry influence or attract you?

BODY/MIND   Were you catching up on your rest or nursing someone (yourself?) back to good health? If you weren't at your best (emotionally or psychologically), were you able to pull yourself out of it? Were your sexual passions growing? Were your needs satisfied?

SPIRIT   Did you receive good news about a literary endeavor, sale of a book or an article you wrote? Did good luck come through professional people or people-related activities? Did you receive a gift you were pleased about?

RELATIVES   Was a relative having a problem that ended up costing you? Did you pay a relative for his/her help? Was someone in your family having problems at work? Did a relative need more of your time or consideration? If you made a mistake, were you quick to admit you were wrong?

Was your income moderate or less than you hoped for? Was there **FINANCES**
tension related to financial matters or business partnerships? Was the
difficulty overcome? Did you have to spend money to make money?

Were things just not gelling the way you wanted them to or thought **PROBLEMS**
they would? Did resistance or resentment only make matters worse?

Did new information become available to you? Were you beginning **GUIDANCE**
to see that your "teacher" was everywhere?

Did compassion, ingenuity or gentle persistence succeed where force **SUCCESS**
failed? Was something done or accomplished that made you feel tri-
umphant?

Was a decision made that ended an internal conflict? Did acceptance **ACTION**
and dealing with "what is" take the pressure off?

• **In light of your experience, what do you believe the Six of Wands signified?**

- **What did you learn from it?**

- **If you drew the Six of Wands in response to a question you asked, in what way did this card answer it?**

- **Now, take another look at your card. Is there anything that stands out about it you didn't notice before?**

- **If you were to make your own Tarot card, what words, pictures or symbols would you put on it?**

SOMETHING TO REFLECT UPON

Sometimes that which we fear most is the very thing that we must do.

The mind, like a parachute, works best when it's open.
JAMES DEWAR

THE SEVEN OF WANDS

Wands relate to ideas, growth, creativity and expansion.

Numerologically, the number 7 indicates a period of introspection, analysis or solitude. During the influence of the number 7, one's psychological and spiritual resources are expanded and faith in what can't be seen, but nevertheless exists, is demanded.

Constructive: Evaluation, research or investigation. Experimenting and being willing to look at things differently. Waiting for what you want to come to you. Trusting your intuition and Higher Self.

Undermining: Pessimism. Separatism. Perfectionism. Living in one's head.

• **What stood out the most in your experience of this card?**

In addition to your recollection, here are some other possibilities you might want to consider:

Was your focus on travel, love, schedules and personal commitments? Was your workload becoming stressful? Were important connections put to the test? Did you experience a tug-of-war of some kind? Were you defending or opposing anything? If so, what was it? **FOCUS**

Did you want a clear direction, a yes or no answer or a (marriage?) commitment on the part of another? **DESIRES**

Were you spending time in the arms of the lover of your dreams? Did you feel that you've never been so completely happy? Did the two of you share a sexual intimacy you never experienced before? Were the moments you shared together never enough? Did you want to spend **LOVE** your life with him/her? If you were single, did you meet someone who swept you off your feet (or wanted to)?

OTHERS

Were your dealings primarily with teachers, writers, publishers or other professionals? Did a business associate, client or company confirm an appointment or extend an invitation? Did someone give you something that meant a sacrifice for him/her but ended up benefiting you both?

HOME

Were you trying to manage your work, appointments, love life and social affairs all at the same time? Were you successful at it? If business called you away from home, were you able to conduct it over the phone instead? Did you give someone (your lover?) keys to your house? Did you finally handle something you've been putting off?

TRAVEL

Were you planning a trip with a sweetheart or a vacation with a loved one? Did you send information over the Internet? Was anything in transit?

WORK

Did your work go well, smoothly, quickly and effortlessly? Did you complete all projects to your satisfaction? Did your job call for special skills or something out of the ordinary? Was love (or your desire to be in a loving relationship) becoming more important than your work?

BODY/MIND

Were you trying to accomplish too many things at once? Was it a strain trying to keep up with it all? Did you make any health or dietary decisions or eat something that made you ill? Was there a sexual breakthrough?

Did someone let you know that he/she had a crush on you or loved you? Was a union proposed? Were there any special moments or peak experiences?

SPIRIT

Did a relative call with an answer you requested or news about his/her home or finances? Was someone trying to reach a relative through you? Did you invite an in-law to your home?

RELATIVES

Did someone give you a discount or a financial break? Was a difficulty surmounted? Were your negotiations successful? Was a deal finalized, contract signed or a check made good? Did you receive money through a grant, advance or settlement? Was it as much as, or more than, you hoped for?

FINANCES

Did you want to complete something or be with the one you love but time, circumstances or others prevented it? Were you disappointed when people broke their commitments, didn't follow through or dropped the ball? Were you easily swayed or distracted?

PROBLEMS

Were you beginning to realize that if you wanted conditions to change, *you* needed to change? What messages, thoughts or impressions were you receiving?

GUIDANCE

Were some of your greatest accomplishments born out of isolation or frustration? Did you feel that you were on a roll that nothing could thwart? What was your greatest achievement?

SUCCESS

ACTION   Were you committed to your goals? Did you refuse to let anything
veer you off your course? Were you being true to yourself?

- **In light of your experience, what do you believe the Seven of Wands signified?**

- **What did you learn from it?**

- **If you drew the Seven of Wands in response to a question you asked, in what way did this card answer it?**

- **Now, take another look at your card. Is there anything that stands out about it you didn't notice before?**

- **If you were to make your own Tarot card, what words, pictures or symbols would you put on it?**

SOMETHING TO REFLECT UPON

How would you feel or act if you *had* an answer, or you knew for certain that you'd reach your goal or have *exactly* what you wanted?

Use what talent you possess; the woods would be very silent if no birds sang except for those that sang the best.

HENRY VAN DYKE

THE EIGHT OF WANDS

Wands relate to ideas, growth, creativity and expansion.

Numerologically, the number 8 connotes the potential for success, accomplishment or recognition and the capacity to achieve one's goals; but unless one seeks the Power Within, these may not be easily attained. Although a positive change of mind or status almost always accompanies the number 8, moral integrity, fortitude and emotional equilibrium will also be required.

Constructive: Attending to business, finance and material matters. Asserting one's self or one's authority. Enacting daring plans. Becoming proficient.

Undermining: Strain. Overemotionalism. Oppression. Careless disregard for the spiritual or material realities of life.

• **What stood out the most in your experience of this card?**

In addition to your recollection, here are some other possibilities you might want to consider:

Was there an emphasis on productivity, enterprise, travel or meetings? Were you always on the move? Did you feel that you were advancing toward your goal(s)? Was romance in the air? Were constructive changes taking place? **FOCUS**

Did you wish something would speed up or get resolved? **DESIRES**

Was there someone special in your life? If not, was it a positive time for romance? If you didn't begin a new relationship, could you have? Did a persuasive suitor call and want to romance you? If you were in a relationship, was it going the way you wanted it to? Did you feel passion- **LOVE** ately about him/her? Did the two of you think alike or express affection in similar ways? Was marriage discussed, planned or announced?

OTHERS

Did someone cause you to make changes in your thinking or plans? Was it a positive development? Were you considering a new partner, agent or promoter? Did you receive an unexpected (romantic) proposal or invitation? Was a friendship renewed or turning into love?

HOME

Did activities keep you on the go or away from home? Did you want to move or live by the sea? Did you have the opportunity to purchase your home or property if you wanted to? Did important news or papers arrive? Were you experiencing a time of happiness and domestic harmony?

TRAVEL

Did you travel in search of one thing, but found something better? If there were problems related to travel or travel arrangements, were they settled in a fortunate way? Did a trip lead to a new way of life or an enlightening discovery? Did you think about selling your car?

WORK

Were you enterprising and tireless? Did you correspond with, or send letters to, companies or clients? If you had fallen behind or were off the mark, were you getting caught up or back on target? Did you find a new outlet for your talents or have a new priority or objective? Did you feel differently about your work or your future based on an insight you recently had or an understanding you came to?

BODY/MIND

Were you feeling lighter, healthier or more capable? If you felt pressured in the past, were you still feeling that way or were conditions improving? Did something about your sex life, or what you thought about it, change?

What did you do for pleasure and entertainment? Did you feel fortu-   **SPIRIT**
nate, lucky or blessed? Did a twist of fate help you find something
you were looking for, or didn't realize you needed?

Did you receive good news from someone in your family? Were you   **RELATIVES**
planning a rendezvous? Did you acknowledge your children in positive, loving ways?

Did you spend money more freely? If you were looking for a product   **FINANCES**
you wanted, did you find it? Was your cash flow increasing? Was
your business booming, improving or beginning to yield a profit? Did
any moneymaking opportunities come your way?

Were you unhappy with your business affairs or love life? Were there   **PROBLEMS**
any frustrating delays, unexpected complications or legal problems?
Were you wasteful? Did you need to take a closer look at your spending habits or the value you place on money or your material possessions?

Were you getting the impression that the reason you were previously   **GUIDANCE**
held back was so that the world could catch up? If you couldn't attain something your mind was set on having, did you realize you
probably didn't need it?

SUCCESS _____ Did you feel that success may be getting what you want, but happiness was wanting what you had? If some of the events in your life were still undecided, did you think that it really didn't matter, because you were going to succeed anyway?

ACTION _____ Were you finding your own truth or forging your own path? Did you need to be more accountable or assertive? Were you willing to do some investigating, travel or make yourself more available to others?

• **In light of your experience, what do you believe the Eight of Wands signified?**

• **What did you learn from it?**

• **If you drew the Eight of Wands in response to a question you asked, in what way did this card answer it?**

• **Now, take another look at your card. Is there anything that stands out about it you didn't notice before?**

- If you were to make your own Tarot card, what words, pictures or symbols would you put on it?

SOMETHING TO REFLECT UPON

We have what we seek. It is there all the time, and if we give it time, it will make itself known to us.

THOMAS MERTON

 # THE NINE OF WANDS

Wands relate to ideas, growth, creativity and expansion.

Numerologically, the number 9 stands for completion, arrival, integration and realization. When a number 9 surfaces, it marks a transition between what was and what is to come, a parenthesis in time as one pauses to reflect on all that went before and the unknown potential of that which is yet to be.

Constructive: Broadness of viewpoint, perspective and understanding. Having faith in one's source of supply. Discard. Detachment. Impersonal interaction.

Undermining: Self-centeredness. Dissipation. Suffering.

- What stood out the most in your experience of this card?

In addition to your recollection, here are some other possibilities you might want to consider:

FOCUS Were you pondering the progress you've made or how far you had yet to go? Was there an emphasis on character development, discipline or stamina? Were you waiting for something to develop or your efforts to bear fruit? Did you feel that you were progressing but greater application would be required?

DESIRES Did you want to finalize a deal, go out with others or improve your health?

LOVE Were you torn between two people or trying to reconcile two sides of one? Was your lover hard to pin down? Did you worry that he/she wasn't telling you the whole truth or was seeing someone else? Did you want more personal freedom if a commitment wasn't made? Did dallying or impulsiveness force a showdown?

OTHERS Were you waiting for someone to call or for an answer to something you said, mailed or recently completed? Did you refuse to be pressured into doing or accepting something you didn't want? Did an enemy become a friend? Did you receive or offer someone sound advice?

HOME Did your plans or the thrust of your activities change? Did your personal or domestic life also change? Did a doctor, friend or suitor call? If the latter is true, did he/she arrive and stay?

Did you travel? If so, was it for business or social reasons? Did you enjoy yourself? Did anything interesting occur? Were weather conditions favorable? **TRAVEL**

Did you feel that your work entailed a gradual progression of accumulated information and that, bit by bit, you'd gather enough experience or understanding to set you on the road to success? Were you learning to work within reasonable limits so that you could avoid burnout? Did you think you would make a good teacher? Were you contemplating a metaphysical profession? **WORK**

Did you feel sick, tired or run down? Did you have or catch a cold? Was anyone else ill? Did something need to be changed, diagnosed or rechecked? Were you considering a new (or stronger) medication or thinking about consulting a different doctor? Were sexual restrictions or your inhibitions fading away? Were you learning to think, act or respond in different ways? **BODY/MIND**

Did happiness or good fortune come through social activities, work done in the past or the arrival of someone (or something) you needed? Did you enjoy giving to another or being in the arms of one who is extremely engaging and quite different than the other men/women you've known? **SPIRIT**

Was someone in your family having money, job or relationship problems? Did it affect you in any way? **RELATIVES**

FINANCES

Were your transactions lucrative? Were you making money at your craft? Did you have enough to cover your expenses? Did an opportunity arise that enabled you to make more?

PROBLEMS

Were you troubled by an incident that reminded you of a problem you had in the past? Did you force a resolve rather than deal with the suspense or sit on the fence of indecision? If you ignored your intuition, acted in haste or issued an ultimatum, did you regret it? Were you ready to face the consequences of your actions?

GUIDANCE

Were you cognizant of your inner cues? Were you able to draw upon your spiritual resources or wisdom gleaned from previous experiences? Were your beliefs strong enough to sustain you?

SUCCESS

Did success depend upon your intention or continued effort? If at first you didn't succeed, did you try again?

ACTION

Did you have to promote, defend or restrain yourself? Did you wait until you gathered strength, more was revealed or the moment to act became apparent? In personal relationships, were you building walls or bridges?

- In light of your experience, what do you believe the Nine of Wands signified?

- What did you learn from it?

- If you drew the Nine of Wands in response to a question you asked, in what way did this card answer it?

- Now, take another look at your card. Is there anything that stands out about it you didn't notice before?

- If you were to make your own Tarot card, what words, pictures or symbols would you put on it?

SOMETHING TO REFLECT UPON

For the next day or so, practice detaching yourself from outcomes and the way you think people and things *ought* to be. Take note of any expectations or preconceptions you may have and if/how they influence your state of mind, reactions or decisions.

Men do not fail; they give up trying.
ELIHU ROOT

THE TEN OF WANDS

Wands relate to ideas, growth, creativity and expansion.

The 10 in the Tarot marks the end of one phase and the beginning of another. Although it has the same basic meaning as the number 1, it also signifies a time when one may have to come to terms with something that was previously overlooked, unfinished or avoided.

• **What stood out the most in your experience of this card?**

In addition to your recollection, here are some other possibilities you might want to consider:

FOCUS   Was there an emphasis on work, labor or responsibilities? Was a relationship (or forming a new partnership) important? Were you considering a career change or residential move? Were you tying up loose ends?

DESIRES   Did you feel overburdened by responsibilities and wish you could escape? Was there something you wanted to complete or be done with?

LOVE   Were you working on a relationship? Did you feel the effort you were putting into trying to make it work was worth it or that it was an impossible situation and you were just wasting your time? Did you know where you stood with him/her or were you totally in the dark?

Did others cause you to make difficult adjustments? Did you and another have a tiff? Was there a problem you didn't know how to deal with or correct?   **OTHERS**

Did you, or someone you know, move, lease a home or acquire property? Did a letter arrive containing money? Did you entertain a house guest? Were there any unforeseen developments?   **HOME**

Did making money require travel or distant business transactions? If you traveled, was your trip enjoyable? Was the weather warm? Did you purchase any useful commodities? Was someone (delayed in) returning home?   **TRAVEL**

Was your job becoming monotonous? Was paperwork a chore? Did throwing yourself into your work keep you from thinking about the things that were missing from your life? Were you planning to market an idea that required a license, copyright or legal representation? Did you change your routine or do something along different lines? **WORK**

Was something you once loved becoming a burden? Did you feel that you were constantly busy, working all hours of the day and night with barely enough time to eat or be with your friends and family? Did your mind keep working even when you wanted to stop? Were you emotionally overwrought?   **BODY/MIND**

Were you grateful for all that you have or were given? Did pleasure come through helping others or completing projects, tasks or ven-   **SPIRIT** tures successfully? Were you lucky in ferreting out facts that were previously hidden?

RELATIVES

Did a family member call on you to help them move or do something that required work or labor on your part? Did you appreciate your loved ones?

FINANCES

Were you worried about money or was your financial situation gradually improving? Did you find that you were able to do, buy or have more? Were large sums of money changing hands? Were there any setbacks or losses?

PROBLEMS

Did you trust other people's opinions over your own? Did you think you made a mistake by pursuing the wrong people, projects or goals? Did you fear that after all was said and done, your efforts might still come to naught?

GUIDANCE

Did your experience help you find a higher path, purpose or direction? As your faith increased did your need to control or manipulate decrease?

SUCCESS

Did you get caught up, find workable alternatives or recover any losses? Did you discover something you were *really* glad you had? Did something from the past assist you in the present? Was a new way of life (personally, financially or professionally) finally in sight?

Were you determined to have what you wanted? Did you refuse to **ACTION**
settle for mediocrity? Did follow-through or doing more preparation
or research help you in any way? If not, what did?

• **In light of your experience, what do you believe the Ten of Wands signified?**

• **What did you learn from it?**

• **If you drew the Ten of Wands in response to a question you asked, in what way did this card answer it?**

• **Now, take another look at your card. Is there anything that stands out about it you didn't notice before?**

• **If you were to make your own Tarot card, what words, pictures or symbols would you put on it?**

SOMETHING TO REFLECT UPON

Lao-tzu said, "A journey of a thousand miles must begin with a single step." How often have we looked at our road ahead and thought to ourselves, "This is just too hard; I will never make it." Yet once we take that first step, our focus shifts; and instead of contemplating the distance, we get wrapped up in the moment, and in no time at all, we find that we have arrived.

◆   # THE PAGE OF WANDS

Astrological Sign: Sagittarius

Sagittarius rules the ninth house and activities related to higher learning (education, expanding one's horizons, discovering oneself); vision (dreams, ideals, wisdom gained, sharing what one learns); long journeys (physical or mental).

Time frame: November 22–December 21

Type: Adventurous. Autonomous. Philosophical. Broad-minded. Jocular. Charismatic. Straightforward.

Thrust: Inner growth. The search for meaning. Liberation. New dimensions. The future.

Cornerstone: To enrich and inspire.

Life lesson: Prudence

Wands relate to ideas, growth, creativity and expansion.

Pages are commonly referred to as messengers, children or youths, but they can also represent one's maturing self, lovers or problems.

The Page of Wands connotes a person who is enthusiastic, impetuous and passionate, one who wants more from life and will seek high and low to get it. Although this Page has acquired some metaphysical knowledge, he/she may just be learning how to apply it. Traditionally, Wands represent a person with blond, red or light-colored hair and blue or green eyes.

Did you feel that you resembled this card type? Have you recently come in contact with someone who does?

- **What stood out the most in your experience of this card?**

In addition to your recollection, here are some other possibilities you might want to consider:

Did you feel that you were on a quest for truth or understanding? Were you taking a personal inventory? Did you have a dream you hoped to manifest or vision you wanted to share with the world? Were you learning to apply spiritual principles to your everyday life and material affairs?   **FOCUS** _____

Did you want to break free of something that was bringing you down or stifling you? Did you long for something indefinable or never experienced before? Was there something you wished would work or change?   **DESIRES** _____

Were you involved with an ardent lover? If so, was it a satisfying, enriching union or was it an infatuation and tend to be more sexual, flighty or superficial? Did you need to stand back and take stock of a relationship or guard against love affairs that were more imaginary than real? Were you, or the person you were involved with, moving toward commitment or backing away?   **LOVE** _____

OTHERS   Did you engage in any philosophical or religious discussions? Were you a guide, counselor or an inspiration to others? Did you think you could be? Did you tend to side with the underdog? Did a friend extend an invitation? If you felt distant, withdrawn or indifferent, was it because you inwardly longed for more substance, meaning or depth?

HOME   Did a visitor or love interest call on you? Were there any uncomfortable changes? If so, what caused them?

TRAVEL   Did you think about traveling to distant places? Did you take any lengthy journeys or travel to see a friend, lover or relative? Did your work call for travel? What kind of trips did you take?

WORK   Vocations suited for a Sagittarian type are publishing, sports, philosophy or religion, advertising, entrepreneur, law, explorer, forest ranger, teacher, import-export dealer, politics.

Do any of these professions sound like something you're doing or would like to do? Did you speak to, or associate with, someone who worked in one of these trades?

Did people like your work and acknowledge your skills? Did you find a new approach? Were there any job opportunities or referrals? Were you working on a long-range project? Was it related to one of the vocations associated with a Sagittarian type? Did you and another discuss a business venture? Were you good at fixing things? Was your career lucrative?

Health issues associated with a Sagittarian type are hips, thighs, mus- **BODY/MIND**
cles, liver, hepatitis, weight gain, colds, bronchitis, arthritis, growths,
tumors, boils and abscesses.

   Have you experienced problems related to any of these areas recently? Has anyone close to you?

   Did you feel stimulated, enthusiastic and energetic or were you irritable, moody and edgy? Were you more interested in sports or
physical fitness or did you tend to be lazy and lackadaisical? Were
you always hungry? Did you have an infection? If so, what kind? Did
you need prompt medical attention or was it something you could
put off?

Were you invited to a special event or showered with praise, love **SPIRIT**
or affection? Did someone help you see the light or attain a new
perspective? Did you do or accomplish something that you were
proud of?

Were you abrupt, uninvolved or impatient with your family? Did lit- **RELATIVES**
tle ones need to be watched more carefully? Was there a previous
commitment you wished you could get out of?

Were you worried about your monetary status (or someone else's)? **FINANCES**
Did you receive news pertaining to financial gain or profit? Were
there any disputes or delays? Were you in a position to increase your
earning power? Overall, was your financial outlook improving?

PROBLEMS   The negative characteristics of a Sagittarian type are excessiveness, indiscrimination, tactlessness, explosiveness, overindulgence, exaggeration.

Did you see these traits in yourself or notice them in another? What troubles or disappointments were you experiencing?

GUIDANCE   Did you have an experience or vivid dream that told you something about yourself, answered a question or accurately predicted a future event? If you were encountering difficulties, was it because warning lights were being ignored? Was something telling you to pay attention, back off or take it easy? Did you find that life treated you better when *you* treated *yourself* better?

SUCCESS   Were you successful at the things you applied yourself toward or did you lose interest and never get them done? Did success come through new avenues or by making do or sticking with the old?

ACTION   Did you tend to think about things more than you acted on them? What activity, hobby or interest did you pursue?

• **In light of your experience, what do you believe the Page of Wands signified?**

- **What did you learn from it?**

- **If you drew the Page of Wands in response to a question you asked, in what way did this card answer it?**

- **Now, take another look at your card. Is there anything that stands out about it you didn't notice before?**

- **If you were to make your own Tarot card, what words, pictures or symbols would you put on it?**

SOMETHING TO REFLECT UPON

If not having, being or doing what you want is making you unhappy, want, be or do something else.

THE KNIGHT OF WANDS

Knights symbolize comings or goings, beginnings or endings and direction of thoughts or energy. When a Knight appears, long-term conditions will change.

There is no astrological or numerological correlation to the Knights.

Wands relate to ideas, growth, creativity and expansion.

• **What stood out the most in your experience of this card?**

In addition to your recollection, here are some other possibilities you might want to consider:

FOCUS Were documents, partnerships or residential issues emphasized? Were you at a crossroad? Was there an important decision pending? Did you feel pressured or stressed? Did someone or something enter your life that changed things for the better?

DESIRES Did you want to reverse a negative trend or settle a matter once and for all?

LOVE Was a heartfelt desire met? Were you seeing a man/woman who awakened your romantic heart or inspired thoughts of marriage? Was he/she someone you met before (or felt as if you had)? Did the depth of your emotions astonish you? Were your feelings for each other mutual? Did a passionate liaison ensue? Were you pursued by many admirers?

Were you in a social mood? Was the atmosphere conducive to social-   **OTHERS**
izing or meeting new people?

Did spiritual material come in the mail? If so, what did it mean to   **HOME**
you? Were you thinking about moving in with someone or having
them come to live with you? Did you do any spring cleaning? Did a
suitor arrive or invite you to his/her home?

Did you take any short trips or jaunts? Did you travel with a sweet-   **TRAVEL**
heart? If so, did it prove to be a turning point in your relationship?
Was a friend or family member planning to travel? Did someone
want to borrow your car?

Did you have to deal with unpleasant people or circumstances? Did   **WORK**
something make you feel that you wasted your time or effort? Were
you scrutinizing, rewriting or revamping documents? If so, did you
find something to your benefit? In time, did tensions vanish? Did you
move in a new, better or happier direction?

Were you feeling self-conscious or clumsy? Were there any awkward   **BODY/MIND**
moments? Did you have problems with doctors or dentists? Were
you teeming with energy or did you feel tired or listless? Were you
more sexually active or were you dispassionate or disinterested?

SPIRIT

Did you have a prophetic dream? Were your psychic impressions accurate? Was something provided *before* the desire was expressed? Did you feel fortunate in matters of the heart? Was there a positive change in your environment, lifestyle or attitude? If so, what created it?

RELATIVES

Did your plans go as anticipated? Did everyone get along? Were there any uncomfortable or embarrassing situations?

FINANCES

Were you concerned about your finances or an impending decision? Was a payment late? Were you negotiating a contract or bickering about money, percentages or commissions? Did you reach an agreement? Did money come in through a new undertaking or a different source?

PROBLEMS

Did you feel that you were out of sync or that nothing made sense? Were you worried that something wouldn't work out or get finished on time? Did you have a compulsive need to right wrongs or fix things? Did you run into difficulties trying to assess situations or effect solutions in advance?

GUIDANCE

Were you getting the impression that if you trusted God and the right outworking of your affairs, you would know what to do when the time came? Did you believe that there was a Divine Order to things? What feelings, messages or guidance were you receiving?

Were you able to navigate the straits in difficult business or financial   **SUCCESS**
matters? Did success come after difficulty? What gave you the greatest sense of satisfaction, fulfillment or accomplishment?

Was one part of your mind saying one thing and the other, another?   **ACTION**
If so, which part did you listen to?

- **In light of your experience, what do you believe the Knight of Wands
  signified?**

- **What did you learn from it?**

- **If you drew the Knight of Wands in response to a question you asked, in what
  way did this card answer it?**

- **Now, take another look at your card. Is there anything that stands out about
  it you didn't notice before?**

- **If you were to make your own Tarot card, what words, pictures or symbols
  would you put on it?**

SOMETHING TO REFLECT UPON

Spend the day observing your thoughts. . . . Notice what you think about and the energy that accompanies it. If you can, carry a pencil and note pad with you, and at the beginning of each hour, write down exactly what you're thinking. If you say to yourself, "I'm not thinking anything," that's a thought too.

◆   THE QUEEN OF WANDS

Astrological Sign: Leo

Leo rules the fifth house and activities related to pleasurable pursuits (creative expression, hobbies, entertainment, social activities, etc.); speculative ventures (gambling, new enterprises, personal risks); romance; and children.

Time frame: July 23–August 22

Type: Affectionate. Openhearted. Magnanimous. Proud. Forthright. Inventive. Dramatic.

Thrust: Self-expression. Inspiration. Interaction. Recognition. Enjoyment. Happiness.

Cornerstone: To be adored

Life lesson: Modesty

Wands relate to ideas, growth, creativity and expansion.

The Queen of Wands connotes one who is talented, intelligent and alluring, a charming individual who is well liked, sought after and admired. She/he is adept at managing both a career and a relationship, and although ambitious, is equally devoted to love, family and home. Traditionally, Wands represent a person with blond, red or light-colored hair and blue or green eyes.

Did you feel that you resembled this card type? Have you recently come in contact with someone who does?

• **What stood out the most in your experience of this card?**

In addition to your recollection, here are some other possibilities you might want to consider:

Were your activities similar to those described in the fifth house? **FOCUS**
Were you pursuing new avenues or taking more creative, expressive or personal risks? Did love, fulfillment or family play an important role in your life?

Did you wish you had an answer to a business, personal or spiritual **DESIRES**
question?

Did you meet someone you were wondering if you should or will **LOVE**
have a relationship with? Was he/she a foreigner or someone from a different country, culture or background? Did you have a passionate affair or marriage? If so, was it also a spiritual bonding or a spiritually awakening experience? Did you think your union was or would be a lasting one? If you couldn't have the real thing, would you rather have nothing? What were your relationship priorities?

Were you open and accessible to others or was it difficult for you to **OTHERS**
let go and let a friendship develop or a love affair happen? Was there a misunderstanding between you and another? Did a friend or social activity bring the opportunity for romance? If you were looking for a counselor or adviser, did you find one? Were your questions answered?

HOME

Did you spend much of your time at home? Did your career allow you to work from home? Did you entertain a guest or lover? What interests were you pursuing? What did you *want* to be doing?

TRAVEL

Did you put off a trip or move? Did you go somewhere entertaining? Did your career take you to distant locations?

WORK

Vocations suited for a Leo type are anything in the performing arts or luxury trades (actor, playwright, make-up artist, stylist, wardrobe or fashion designer, etc.), artist, illustrator, stockbroker, kindergarten teacher, professional sports.

Do any of these professions sound like something you're doing or would like to do? Did you speak to, or associate with, someone who worked in one of these trades?

Did you feel that your work or talents inspired others or helped people recognize their own gifts? Did you wonder if your way of seeing things might raise a few eyebrows? If, in the past, you were having problems that interfered with your productivity or limited your effectiveness, did you bounce back even stronger? Did you receive any good news?

BODY/MIND

Health issues associated with a Leo type are the heart, back and spine: heart attacks, angina, spinal meningitis, rheumatism, mononucleosis, sunstroke or heat sensitivity, perspiration, poor recuperative powers.

Have you experienced problems related to any of these areas recently? Has anyone close to you?

Did you feel more cheerful or confident about yourself and your abilities? Did you smile when the chips were down, knowing they'd come up again? Was sex important, sensual or fulfilling? Was the chemistry right? Were you more health or fitness conscious than you usually are?

Did a stroke of good luck cause your spirits to soar or were your spirits soaring anyway? If you've been off the spiritual path, was your interest renewed? What ideas inspired you?   **SPIRIT**

Did you want to have children? Did children play an important role in your life? Did you favor pets instead? Were you concerned with birth control? Were family get-togethers significant? Did a choice in affections have to be made? Was it concerning a lover?   **RELATIVES**

Did you feel that you were basically secure and/or that more profits could be expected in the future? Were there any (impromptu) expenditures that you regretted? Did you make money in an unexpected way? What was your income derived from?   **FINANCES**

The negative characteristics of a Leo type are bossiness, conceit, self-absorption, pretentiousness, impetuousness, foolhardiness.   **PROBLEMS**
    Did you see these traits in yourself or notice them in another? What troubles or disappointments were you experiencing?

GUIDANCE _____ Did you believe that if you were patient, everything would fall into place? Did the thought occur to you that if you were in doubt or didn't know what to do, it was probably to prevent you from going forward too soon? If you forced results, did you run into difficulties or have to backtrack?

SUCCESS _____ Were you able to attract what you needed or wanted? Was what was missing provided? Did you think the true mark of success was doing what you enjoyed?

ACTION _____ Did you ask for guidance and then follow up on leads, hunches or inner promptings?

_____

• In light of your experience, what do you believe the Queen of Wands signified?

• What did you learn from it?

• If you drew the Queen of Wands in response to a question you asked, in what way did this card answer it?

- Now, take another look at your card. Is there anything that stands out about it you didn't notice before?

- If you were to make your own Tarot card, what words, pictures or symbols would you put on it?

SOMETHING TO REFLECT UPON

Decisions usually make themselves when the time comes.

In time, one's teacher arrives. The message may come through a person you've met only once, a brief relationship or someone you've known all your life. It might be felt as you read a passage in a book, a poster on a wall or an article in a magazine. It could make its presence known through a hunch, song, dream or sudden insight you had as you were walking or driving down the street. . . . However it comes, rest assured, it is *always* at the right moment.

 # THE KING OF WANDS

Astrological Sign: Aries

Aries rules the first house and activities related to beginnings, one's physical self (appearance, disposition, persona, etc.) and one's outlook on the world.

Time frame: March 21–April 19

Type: Ambitious. Idealistic. Optimistic. Enthusiastic. Pioneering. Ardent. Daring.

Thrust: Self-growth, awareness and reliance. Starting. Discovering. Developing. The untried and the new.

Cornerstone: To initiate

Life lesson: Patience

Wands relate to ideas, growth, creativity and expansion.

The King of Wands represents someone who is independent, high-spirited and influential, a professional person who stands out from the crowd and likes to assume positions of authority. He/she is also described as a family man/woman, spiritual mentor or inspiring friend. Traditionally, Wands represent a person with blond, red or light-colored hair and blue or green eyes.

Did you feel that you resembled this card type? Have you recently come in contact with someone who does?

• **What stood out the most in your experience of this card?**

In addition to your recollection, here are some other possibilities you might want to consider:

FOCUS   Were you more assertive or independent? Was your mind on business, finance, planning or constructing? Was the way others perceived you (or how you felt you looked) important to you? Did you feel ambitious? Were you more aware of the way you responded to events, expressed yourself or internalized your experiences?

DESIRES   Did you want to connect with someone or be successful in a (new) business venture?

LOVE   How did you feel around the opposite sex? Were you confident and self-assured or were you afraid of letting people get to know you or revealing too much of yourself? Did you meet (or were you involved with) someone who uplifted you or made you feel secure? Did a new relationship begin? Were there any proposals?

Were your social involvements linked to business or were they of a personal or spiritual nature? Was an important contact made? Did you feel that you could delegate responsibilities or that you had to handle everything on your own? Were you more interested in inspiring people than in holding their hands?

OTHERS

Was there more emphasis on things or property matters? Did something make you feel cramped or uncomfortable? Did you have discussions about your house or moving into a new home? Did someone call on you or invite you to his/her home? What kind of activities, projects or hobbies were you involved in?

HOME

Did you receive or extend a travel invitation? Did something change related to, or as a result of, your travels? Did a new arrangement make you happy?

TRAVEL

Vocations suited for an Aries type are explorer, firefighter, department head or manager, surgeon, hairdresser, professional motivator, leader, comedian, race car driver, director, coach, developer, inventor, writer (self-help material, short stories or columnist).

WORK

   Do any of these professions sound like something you're doing or would like to do? Did you speak to, or associate with, someone who worked in one of these trades?

   Were you better at initiating projects and telling others what to do than taking orders or following through? Were you thinking of ways to promote yourself or to get your ideas across? If your work involved papers, did your thoughts dissipate before you could write them down? Did your business or phone sales increase? Were there any important new beginnings? Did you enjoy discovering new things?

BODY/MIND

Health issues associated with an Aries type are head, face or brain injuries; eyes; headaches; stomach or kidney problems; inflammatory afflictions; acne; dizziness; fevers; accidents; strokes; paralysis or numbness.

Have you experienced problems related to any of these areas recently? Has anyone close to you?

Were you more aware of your physical requirements? Did you feel that you really *should* take better care of yourself or shape up? Were you watching your health or diet?

Did you suffer from migraines or backaches? Did you begin any new treatments or exercise regimes? How did you cope with conflict? Did problems cause you to become irritable or shut down emotionally? Were you hard on yourself when things went wrong or you didn't have the know-how to change?

SPIRIT

Did you enjoy being productive, coming up with creative ideas or beginning new projects? Did you find something that was sought after, such as a metaphysical teaching, (spiritual) teacher or a new love? Did you get good news concerning test results, making the grade or graduating? What gave you the most satisfaction: inner rewards or outward manifestations?

Was your family more important to you now than at other times? If **RELATIVES**
you felt distant or alienated in the past, did you experience a change
of heart? Were you tolerant or were you a tyrant?

Were you thinking about creating money or ways to make more **FINANCES**
money? Did you contemplate rich rewards for something you accomplished? Did you see large returns for your investments? Did
your earnings come through new or repeat business contacts?
Where/what did money come from? How did you approach financial
matters? Did the signing of a contract change your life?

The negative characteristics of an Aries type are impulsiveness, self- **PROBLEMS**
ishness, bossiness, willfulness, abruptness, arrogance, being unfocused or leaving things unfinished.
   Did you see these traits in yourself or notice them in another?
What troubles or disappointments were you experiencing?

Did you feel supported by the Universe or did you feel that you had **GUIDANCE**
to go it alone?

Did you think you could do just about anything you set your mind **SUCCESS**
to? Were you able to get your concept across to others? Were you
successful in your ventures? Was there something you still had to
wait for or let unfold? In what area did you experience the most
growth? What did you feel the most empowered by?

ACTION   What action did you need to take to get what you wanted or achieve success? Was your decision, determination or opinion a deciding factor?

- In light of your experience, what do you believe the King of Wands signified?

- What did you learn from it?

- If you drew the King of Wands in response to a question you asked, in what way did this card answer it?

- Now, take another look at your card. Is there anything that stands out about it you didn't notice before?

- If you were to make your own Tarot card, what words, pictures or symbols would you put on it?

SOMETHING TO REFLECT UPON

You may want to tape this guided meditation and play it back with your eyes closed.

Imagine that it is night and you are walking through the darkness toward a mountain illuminated only by the moon and stars. . . . Near the top, you notice a golden glow emanating from what appears to be a temple. As you draw nearer, the doors open, beckoning you to come in. At first the room looks empty, but then, as if by magic, a pedestal with a book upon it begins to materialize. . . . As you watch you notice that it opens as if inviting you to read a special page. . . . So you walk up to the book and you read your message and it says, "You are *always* being guided although you are not always aware of it. You need not worry when you think you're on your own. . . . God *is* there. . . . It's just that He's teaching you how to *feel* His love, not just understand it."

THE
CUPS

YOUR QUERY SHEET

You can use this query sheet in addition to your weekly notes for questions you may have during the course of your workbook experience and in times to come.

Date:	Card:	Your Questions and Answers:
		Q:
		A:
		Q:
		A:
		Q:
		A:
		Q:
		A:
		Q:
		A:
		Q:
		A:
		Q:
		A:
		Q:
		A:
		Q:
		A:
		Q:
		A:
		Q:
		A:
		Q:
		A:
		Q:
		A:
		Q:
		A:
		Q:
		A:
		Q:
		A:

THE ACE OF CUPS

Cups represent emotions, pleasure seeking, intuition and spiritual awareness.

Aces represent new beginnings; they also signify a season. The Ace of Cups represents the summer—June, July, August.

What season is it now? _____ What season does it *feel* like? _____

Numerologically, Aces correspond with the number 1, indicating fresh starts, invention, creativity, originality, independence, force and will. During the influence of the number 1, ideas, opportunities and new projects begin to flourish, and although one may know *what* one needs to do, it may take courage or daring to follow through.

Constructive: Confidence. Determination. Assuming responsibility. Strengthening one's abilities and sense of self. Singular effort.

Undermining: Willfulness. Unreasonable force. Fear of taking the initiative, promoting one's self or standing on one's own. Discouragement.

• **What stood out the most in your experience of this card?**

In addition to your recollection, here are some other possibilities you might want to consider:

Was there a fresh start in love or creative activities? Did you begin or revise a project that involved color or the formulation of ideas? Was there an emphasis on romance, giving, favors or pleasurable endeavors?   **FOCUS**

Were you looking for clarity or for the truth in a situation where your heart said one thing and your mind another? Did you hope an idea would become a reality?   **DESIRES**

LOVE

Did someone surprise you or actively pursue you? Did a call from (or to) an admirer lead to a refreshing change or new beginning? Were you attracted to a person you hadn't considered before? Did you find the one your heart had been yearning for? Did you marry or set a wedding date?

OTHERS

Did you require the services of a professional in matters concerning papers, licenses, copyrights or patents? Were you feeling pressured to perform or to give more than you felt capable of? Did you make a new friend? Was it hard to keep a platonic relationship going or a friendship platonic?

HOME

Did you purchase something you've wanted or longed for (a house, computer, new furniture or something to create with)? Did you have a happy home life? Did a friend or admirer call on you? If you needed assistance with your household chores, projects, child care or yard work, did you find someone to help you?

TRAVEL

Were your travels fortunate or rewarding? Did you find something you were searching for? Was it in a way or place you hadn't thought of? Were you discussing travel plans? Did you walk instead of drive? Were you considering a trip or move to the West?

WORK

Was activity renewed? Were you inspired all over again? Were you full of creative ideas? Did you have a natural talent for blending color or mixing creative mediums? Did your work receive praise or admiration? Did your ideas meet with success?

Were you in good health? Did you feel happy, content or inspired? **BODY/MIND**
Were you more centered or spiritually connected? If you didn't start
out that way, did you end up that way?

Did you hear a pleasing disclosure or receive an unexpected blessing? **SPIRIT**
What excited you or filled your heart with joy?

Did a relative call? Were you making plans to visit a relative in the **RELATIVES**
near future? Did you get along well with your in-laws? Were you
starting a family of your own?

Did you receive money for your artistic or creative endeavors or **FINANCES**
funding through a pension plan or scholarship? Were you able to
support yourself doing what you wanted to do? Did you begin a new
project to supplement your income or defray some of your expenses?

Were you discouraged by love, unhappy with the state of your affairs **PROBLEMS**
or fed up with malfunctioning products or expensive repair bills?
Was someone mistreating you or giving you unwanted or thoughtless
advice? Did your moods or reactions demand analysis? Were you be-
rating yourself for not feeling or acting differently?

Was something (or someone) telling you to stay focused on what you **GUIDANCE**
want to happen? Did it occur to you that what you want, God wants
for you? Did something that was previously difficult or obscured become easier or crystal clear?

SUCCESS   Did success come through your creative, inspired or innovative ideas? Were you able to turn an art, hobby or concept into a successful product, business or conglomerate? Was a heartfelt desire realized?

ACTION   How were you using your creative potential: desiring, visualizing, making a treasure map,* thinking positively? Did you act on new ideas, try new avenues or say yes? What was the result?

• **In light of your experience, what do you believe the Ace of Cups signified?**

• **What did you learn from it?**

• **If you drew the Ace of Cups in response to a question you asked, in what way did this card answer it?**

• **Now, take another look at your card. Is there anything that stands out about it you didn't notice before?**

*A montage of pictures and words that symbolize the attainment of your hopes and wishes.

• **If you were to make your own Tarot card, what words, pictures or symbols would you put on it?**

SOMETHING TO REFLECT UPON

Close your eyes and imagine that you are sitting by a lily pond. As you become aware of the sounds of nature and the way the water droplets glisten on the lily pads, imagine that a white dove appears before you bearing a tiny white scroll in its beak. You reach out your hand, accept the offering and read the message. . . . What does it say?

THE TWO OF CUPS

Cups represent emotions, pleasure seeking, intuition and spiritual awareness.

Numerologically, the number 2 connotes assimilation, balancing polarities and dealing with unknowns. When the number 2 is present, partial success can be realized, but one may also find oneself having to repeat previous lessons or experiences in order to eliminate flaws or continue to progress. Reunions, reconciliations and an element of surprise could also be indicated.

Constructive: Patience. Tolerance. Cooperation. Nurturing, developing or refining what one has before commencing something new. Combined efforts. Personal interaction.

Undermining: Impatience. One-sidedness. Isolation. Lack of commitment or steady purpose.

• **What stood out the most in your experience of this card?**

In addition to your recollection, here are some other possibilities you might want to consider:

FOCUS

Did relationships, physical unions and choices of the heart become more meaningful? Were you learning to accept, work with or adapt to others, or was the cooperation you sought mostly within yourself? Was love or pleasure the strongest emotion you felt? Were there any warm reunions or happy surprises?

DESIRES

Did you want to be in accord with life and love or quell the doubts you had concerning your path, career or the relationship you hoped to have?

LOVE

Were you longing for a loving relationship, spiritual companion or life mate? Were your affections torn between two people, one old and one new? Did you feel capable of attracting or sustaining the love you aspired to? Were you, or the person you were involved with, suffering from low self-esteem? Did you have a sudden clarity about what you wanted in a relationship you never considered before?

OTHERS

Were the people you came in contact with cooperative and accommodating? Did someone invite you to a special event or propose a glamorous offer? Did you and another share a mutual affinity or have a glorious time together? Were you deeply touched by a friend or lover? Did you feel as though you had met a soul mate or kindred spirit?

Did an admirer call and want to spend time with you? If something **HOME**
was lost or in need of repair, was it finally found or fixed? Were you
redecorating or working on any creative projects?

Was something in or on your car not working right? Did you travel in **TRAVEL**
search of a job or for something related to your business, or was it
mostly for pleasure? Were your travels pleasant, fruitful or productive?

Did you wish you could be more effective in your work, or in getting **WORK**
your message across? Did you want to reach a larger audience? Were
you looking for a different employer or more support in your working environment? Did you feel that your success depended on someone or something in addition to, or other than, yourself?

Were you concerned about your health or the health of another? **BODY/MIND**
Were you and your lover sexually compatible? Was there a physical
or emotional problem you were hard-pressed to overcome? Did you
discuss or act upon a personal injury case?

Did someone send you a love letter or give you a card or gift? Did you **SPIRIT**
enjoy giving as much as or more than receiving?

Did you feel comforted, secure or lighthearted in the company of **RELATIVES**
your loved ones? Were you in harmony with your brother(s) or sis-
ter(s)? If, in the past, communications were strained or you had a
falling out, were tensions resolved? Did you feel that your efforts
were appreciated?

FINANCES

Were you making a living doing what you loved to do? Did money come through a partnership? Was a financial issue settled in a positive way? Could you afford to buy what you wanted?

PROBLEMS

Did you expect too much from yourself or others? Were you afraid to enjoy the good times for fear that they might be taken away? Did you feel personally responsible for everything?

GUIDANCE

Were you beginning to see that it was humanly impossible to take every contingency into account? Did you trust your intuition and have faith that you would be Divinely led? Did you have an inspired idea? How were you helped, healed, directed or guided?

SUCCESS

Were problems, arguments or inner conflicts resolved? What attainment meant the most to you?

ACTION

Did you communicate your needs? If you had to wait for what you wanted, were you at peace with it? Did you celebrate your accomplishments?

• **In light of your experience, what do you believe the Two of Cups signified?**

• **What did you learn from it?**

• **If you drew the Two of Cups in response to a question you asked, in what way did this card answer it?**

• **Now, take another look at your card. Is there anything that stands out about it you didn't notice before?**

• **If you were to make your own Tarot card, what words, pictures or symbols would you put on it?**

SOMETHING TO REFLECT UPON

Dare to look within your heart.
Dare to expose your deeply felt wishes and most cherished dreams.
Dare to believe that what you are compelled to seek is your Oversoul's plan for you.
Dare to defy your fear.
Dare to let go . . . to trust . . . to wait and see.

THE THREE OF CUPS

Cups represent emotions, pleasure seeking, intuition and spiritual awareness.

Numerologically, the number 3 indicates expressing one's self, creating, externalizing and relating. With the number 3, group activities or situations involving more than one person are usually emphasized. Although the 3 brings conditions to fruition, there may also be some delay. Growth of an inner, emotional nature is also indicated.

Constructive: Synthesizing. Conceptualizing. Becoming more selective or giving something your all. Embracing the lighter side of life. Keeping a positive, optimistic frame of mind. Allowing events to unfold.

Undermining: Ennui. Scattering energies. Overreacting or overindulging. Refusing to accept life on life's terms.

• **What stood out the most in your experience of this card?**

In addition to your recollection, here are some other possibilities you might want to consider:

FOCUS
          Was your focus on self-improvement, creative projects, nourishment or love? Were you enjoying your existence or did you feel rushed, anxious or pushed by circumstances, with never enough time to do the things you wanted in life? Were you faced with dichotomies (quality or quantity, security or seduction, ideal versus real, etc.)?

DESIRES
          Did you want to heal, revise or change your attitude about something? What were your goals?

LOVE
          Was a lover or admirer trying to reach you? Was a personal dilemma resolved sooner than you thought it would be? Did a new beginning

(or new romance) make problems a thing of the past? Was marriage considered or discussed? What were your feelings with regard to relationships in general?

Did you interact with more people than usual? Were you surrounded by friends or making new ones? Were the contacts you made for social reasons or were they motivated out of necessity?

OTHERS _____

Was your environment peaceful? Did any visitors, guests or packages arrive?

HOME _____

Did you take a vacation or spend time away from home? Was a family get-together planned or confirmed? Did you travel (or postpone a trip) to a healer, doctor or vet?

TRAVEL _____

Was your mind on your work? Were you contemplating a new line of work (something less taxing) or thinking about what you were going to do with your time/life once your work was completed? Did your job involve conceptualizing, correlating information or hand-to-eye coordination? Were there any self-expressive or artistic projects in the works? Did you do anything to make your current job easier or more enjoyable?

WORK _____

BODY/MIND

Were you coping well or were you overreactive, overindulgent or overemotional? Were you troubled by a weight problem or abusing pills or alcohol? If so, was the source of the problem caused by external events or did your real issues stem from within? What emotional (or sexual) decisions were you making?

SPIRIT

Did something give you cause to celebrate? Did people, animals or nature influence your disposition in a positive way? Were you lucky with money, clothes or merchandise? Did you receive or buy yourself something you liked? Did you allow yourself to be happy?

RELATIVES

Did you feel supported? Was your family accommodating? Were there any emotionally charged incidents involving your family or pets?

FINANCES

Did you receive payments, checks or money orders? Were you able to sustain yourself on your earnings? Did you spend money foolishly? Were you relieved about a financial matter? Were there any unexpected expenditures or advantages? Were some or all of your expenses paid by another?

PROBLEMS

Were you disappointed by someone's callous, lukewarm or disinterested response? Did somebody's actions, words or deeds infuriate you? Were you involved in a love triangle? Did you have to tell someone that you weren't interested in him/her romantically, or that you no longer required his/her professional services?

Did you have a spiritually awakening experience? Was there a helping hand in your affairs? If so, was it an actual person or an unseen force? What do you believe your inner guidance was urging you to do?

GUIDANCE

Did your friends, family or social connections advance your goals? Did anything happen that proved to be a turning point or caused you to experience a renewed sense of satisfaction about who you were, what you've accomplished or what you were capable of attaining?

SUCCESS

Did you need to get clear about what your priorities were, what you were striving for or what you valued most? Were you willing to give your ideas a try even if it meant risking failure? Was there anything you could have done but didn't? Looking back, is there anything you would have done differently?

ACTION

- **In light of your experience, what do you believe the Three of Cups signified?**

- **What did you learn from it?**

- **If you drew the Three of Cups in response to a question you asked, in what way did this card answer it?**

• Now, take another look at your card. Is there anything that stands out about it you didn't notice before?

• If you were to make your own Tarot card, what words, pictures or symbols would you put on it?

SOMETHING TO REFLECT UPON

You may want to tape this guided meditation and play it back with your eyes closed.

Take a few deep breaths and contemplate what it is that you want. . . . Begin to observe the thoughts, fears or comments that make your goal seem far away or your excitement grow dim . . . now imagine a tiny white light starting to form just below your breastbone . . . as you continue to observe it, notice that it's growing brighter, filling your body and mind with its pervading glow . . . and as it begins to radiate outward, notice that there is nothing but the light . . . nothing to fear, nothing but the warm feeling within . . . and now, imagine that this is the light of your Inner Spirit and that It is *encouraging* you to be happy, to believe in yourself, to fulfill all of your deepest desires . . . knowing this, how do you feel about your situation now?

THE FOUR OF CUPS

Cups represent emotions, pleasure seeking, intuition and spiritual awareness.

Numerologically, the number 4 connotes formation, stability and solidification. With the number 4, one's work and dreams are stressed, and although one's eyes may be on a bigger picture, or the promise of future reward, one must concentrate on what *is* and deal with the practical task(s) at hand.

Constructive: Deliberation. Constructive application. Down-to-earth practicality. Functionality and workability. Building solid, concrete foundations.

Undermining: Impractical dreaming. Pie-in-the-sky risk taking. Too much attention focused on the material aspects of life and not enough on the spirit.

• **What stood out the most in your experience of this card?**

In addition to your recollection, here are some other possibilities you might want to consider:

Were you reaching for something that wasn't immediately apparent or attainable? Was your focus on the material aspects of life? Were you reassessing your worldly gains or what you've become in your efforts to attain them?   **FOCUS**

Did you have an obsessive desire for something or want a new job or source of income?   **DESIRES**

Was there an unresolved togetherness in matters of the heart? Were you contemplating a union that may never be or wondering if you would ever be satisfied with what you have?   **LOVE**

Did you speak with, discuss or need to get a mediator, agent or legal representative? How did you respond to others? What did people teach you? What did you have to offer them?   **OTHERS**

HOME —————— Were you busying yourself with the practical duties of life? Was there a problem in the neighborhood or a housing, management or property matter you needed to attend to? Did a neighbor or roommate say or do something that bothered you?

TRAVEL —————— Were you preparing for a trip? Did someone from a distance call you or assist you in some way?

WORK —————— Did your business or workload increase? Did a prospective employer, client or partner respond to your inquiry or offer you a job?

BODY/MIND —————— Were you emotionally or sexually unfulfilled? Did something happen to remind you of your own mortality? Were you feeling a sense of chagrin? What did you do to take charge of your happiness?

SPIRIT —————— Did you have a poignant talk with a friend or connect with someone who fulfilled a deep desire? What gifts were given to you?

RELATIVES —————— Was a relative planning to travel? Were you taught, or teaching your children, healthy values? Did your parents approve of your lover/mate, or his/her family respond favorably to you?

FINANCES —————— Did you have some accounting to do? Were you resourceful when it came to money and acquiring sustenance or means?

Did you feel like a lost soul fighting a lost cause? Were you experi-   **PROBLEMS**
encing a spiritual emptiness no earthly thing could fill? Did you fear
that you would never *have* what you want, never *be* what you want,
but you couldn't stop *wanting?*

Did you wish your guidance was clearer? Were you finding that the   **GUIDANCE**
answers you sought could not be *given,* they had to be *learned?*

Was there a positive change in your business, finances or emotional   **SUCCESS**
state? Did a solution, benediction or an avenue of fulfillment come
out of the blue?

Did it help to take your mind off your love life, your work or "the   **ACTION**
problem" and turn your attention elsewhere for the time being? Did
you have to give up before you got what you wanted?

• **In light of your experience, what do you believe the Four of Cups signified?**

• **What did you learn from it?**

- If you drew the Four of Cups in response to a question you asked, in what way did this card answer it?

- Now, take another look at your card. Is there anything that stands out about it you didn't notice before?

- If you were to make your own Tarot card, what words, pictures or symbols would you put on it?

SOMETHING TO REFLECT UPON

Do you have an idol or cherished spiritual mentor? If not, take a moment and think about someone you respect and admire, someone you would like to be or emulate. . . .

When you think of that person, being, teacher or guru, close your eyes and visualize him/her standing before you, lovingly telling you what your heart wants/needs to hear. . . .

Now, imagine that what you heard was *really* the truth and your fear was the lie.

 # THE FIVE OF CUPS

Cups represent emotions, pleasure seeking, intuition and spiritual awareness.

Numerologically, the number 5 indicates change, fluctuations in fate or fortune, conflict, experiential learning and the expansion of one's thinking. With the number 5, opportunities and challenges go hand in hand and one must look to both the material and spiritual realm if one is to triumph or understand.

Constructive: Discrimination. Resourcefulness. Revision. Re-creation. Self-reliance. Inner conviction.

Undermining: Little faith in one's self or abilities. Panic. Distress. Rebellion.

- **What stood out the most in your experience of this card?**

In addition to your recollection, here are some other possibilities you might want to consider:

Were you worn down by challenges, reversals or delays? Were restrictions keenly felt? Were you so intent on what was wrong, you couldn't see what was right? Did your attachment to a person, place or thing change? **FOCUS** _____

Did you wish you had a satisfying relationship or long for something fun, interesting or fulfilling to happen? **DESIRES** _____

Did you wonder what it would be like to have a love that didn't fade once the romance was over, or when (if) you'd be in love again? Were you tired of having to contend with a relationship you didn't want? If you were married, was it a happy union? If not, what would have made you feel more loved? **LOVE** _____

Did someone's behavior annoy you? Did you outgrow (or end) a friendship? Were business meetings put off or answers postponed? Did you feel like you were getting the runaround? How did you react to these events? **OTHERS** _____

HOME   Were you waiting for news or a package to arrive? Did it come? Did an unexpected guest appear? If so, what were your feelings about him/her?

TRAVEL   Did you travel for emotional or sentimental reasons? If you had to travel, did you want to go? If you were returning from a trip, was your house in order and your possessions intact when you arrived?

WORK   Did you believe that you had to keep on plodding or your work wouldn't get done? Was something (or someone) telling you to stop?

BODY/MIND   Were you feeling fatigued or burned-out? If so, did you rest when you were tired, eat when you were hungry and back off when you felt overwhelmed, or did you neglect your needs and push yourself even harder? Were you constipated or suffering from hemorrhoids? Was a poor diet making you irritable?

SPIRIT   What did you feel lucky about or grateful for?

RELATIVES   Were you depending on a relative's assistance or support? Did he/she come through for you? Were there any unavoidable obligations or sad partings?

Were you worried about your finances? Did you have cause to be? **FINANCES**
Were you in a financial bind? Did you need to be more assertive or
thrifty?

Was your body tired and your spirit undernourished? Were you feel- **PROBLEMS**
ing neglected or victimized? If you knew something wasn't right for
you did you have the courage to let it go? Did you make yourself a
promise and then break it? If so, what were the consequences?

Did it occur to you that you didn't *have* to feel the way you did, that **GUIDANCE**
your desires *could* be realized and there were other options and ways
to look at things?

Did you successfully overcome a problem? Was it because you asked **SUCCESS**
for what you needed or revised something you started earlier?

Do you think you took positive, self-affirming action? If not, what **ACTION**
stopped you? What could you have done to get your needs met?

• **In light of your experience, what do you believe the Five of Cups signified?**

- **What did you learn from it?**

- **If you drew the Five of Cups in response to a question you asked, in what way did this card answer it?**

- **Now, take another look at your card. Is there anything that stands out about it you didn't notice before?**

- **If you were to make your own Tarot card, what words, pictures or symbols would you put on it?**

SOMETHING TO REFLECT UPON

We don't have to be victims. We don't have to fixate on our problems. We can stop right now, throw off our cloak of despair and turn our attention to the resources we *do* have. If we don't have what we want, we can bridge that empty gap by asking ourselves what we believe *having* what we want will give us and then looking at other things we can do to give ourselves the same feeling. We can stop waiting for life to give us what we want; we can give it to ourselves. It may take practice, but we have an eternity to learn.

Though we travel the world over to find the beautiful, we must carry it with us or we find it not.

RALPH WALDO EMERSON

THE SIX OF CUPS

Cups represent emotions, pleasure seeking, intuition and spiritual awareness.

Numerologically, the number 6 indicates the need to make adjustments in one's thoughts, attitudes, behavior or condition. While this may feel burdensome, the number 6 also carries with it the ability to transcend difficulties and oftentimes serendipitously. Responsibilities, family and health may also be emphasized.

Constructive: Thoroughness. Resoluteness. Serving, giving or adapting to the needs of others. Love. Compassion.

Undermining: Indifference. Irresponsibility (toward self and others). Fixed opinions, beliefs or attitudes. Imbalance.

• **What stood out the most in your experience of this card?**

In addition to your recollection, here are some other possibilities you might want to consider:

Were you feeling nostalgic about a time that has long since passed, a childhood sweetheart or a person you thought you were over? Did your circumstances or needs change? Were you moving into a different realm of experience or potential?   **FOCUS** _____

Did you want to phase out one thing or path in favor of another? Were you anticipating a future event?   **DESIRES** _____

Did you meet, or were you involved with, someone extraordinary or well-known? Did others look up to him/her? If you and your   **LOVE** _____ lover/mate broke up but you couldn't stop caring for him/her, did a new experience bring about a change of heart?

OTHERS — Were you in a position where you could meet noted or famous people? Did you want to be in the limelight? Did you receive any accolades?

HOME — Did you attend a social function? Was there a gathering of family and friends? Was an old friend or lover among them? Did something re- mind you of your childhood or make you feel like a child? Did you want to "go back home again"?

TRAVEL — Were you busy making travel arrangements or traveling back and forth?

WORK — Did you get a job offer or a new assignment? Were you marching to the beat of a different drummer? What career were you pursuing?

BODY/MIND — Did it seem like your body was out of sync (tired during the day and wide awake at night, etc.)? Did you have an earache? If you were tired but had work to do, or obligations to meet, did you manage to get through it?

SPIRIT — Was a need met or a wish granted? Did you realize that you were liv- ing the event/dream you thought about or prayed for?

Were you devoted to your loved ones? Did you long for a large family? Did you wish you could be a child again? Did a relative you hadn't seen in awhile call or visit?   **RELATIVES**

Were you financially well off? Did you make more money than you thought you would? If your resources were modest, was luck with you in attaining money or in having a family that fed or clothed you?   **FINANCES**

Did you let delays, criticism or appearances contrary to your desire discourage you?   **PROBLEMS**

Did it occur to you that God was so close to you, you mistook His/Her voice for your own? Or that your desire was a Divine one and you were being led to that end?   **GUIDANCE**

Did something work out better or faster than you anticipated?   **SUCCESS**

What adjustments did you make?   **ACTION**

- In light of your experience, what do you believe the Six of Cups signified?

- What did you learn from it?

- If you drew the Six of Cups in response to a question you asked, in what way did this card answer it?

- Now, take another look at your card. Is there anything that stands out about it you didn't notice before?

- If you were to make your own Tarot card, what words, pictures or symbols would you put on it?

SOMETHING TO REFLECT UPON

What are some of the "miracles" that have happened in your life?

_____

_____

_____

_____

    Contemplating the times when we felt blessed before will put us back in that receiving flow again.

THE SEVEN OF CUPS

Cups represent emotions, pleasure seeking, intuition and spiritual awareness.

Numerologically, the number 7 indicates a period of introspection, analysis or solitude. During the influence of the number 7, one's psychological and spiritual resources are expanded and faith in what can't be seen, but nevertheless exists, is demanded.

Constructive: Evaluation, research or investigation. Experimenting and being willing to look at things differently. Waiting for what you want to come to you. Trusting your intuition and Higher Self.

Undermining: Pessimism. Separatism. Perfectionism. Living in one's head.

• **What stood out the most in your experience of this card?**

In addition to your recollection, here are some other possibilities you might want to consider:

Did you feel uncentered or confused? Did it seem like you were traveling from one challenge or relationship to another? Did your life feel meaningless or uneventful? Were there too many choices to make? Did you think you *had* choices? Were you having a difficult time coping with events? Were you searching for the truth?   **FOCUS** _____

Did you wish you had a better handle on your emotional reactions or that you could find the reason for your experience(s)?   **DESIRES** _____

Were you lonesome? Did you wonder how many relationships would come and go before you found him/her again? Did you vacillate in matters of the heart? If you were involved with someone, was he/she difficult to fathom? Did you have to make concessions? Were there   **LOVE** _____ so many other things on your mind, a relationship was the furthest thing from it?

OTHERS   Did someone or something cause you to change your thinking or plans? Did you come to the aid of a friend? Did a friend help you? Were there any significant business discussions, transactions or calls?

HOME   Did you want or need to be outdoors? Did you receive troubling news or worry about your mail? Did anything (or anyone) come into your home that caused a disruption? Did a compromise or difficult decision have to be made?

TRAVEL   Were you debating an issue involving travel? Did you have to travel because of a relative or friend? Did weather conditions change? Were there any problems or unnerving incidents?

WORK   What kind of work were you doing? Was it more mental than physical or was the reverse true? Were you achieving what you wanted, or did your life feel so empty there was nothing to fill it but work and even that was unrewarding?

BODY/MIND   Were your feelings jumbled or your thoughts running together? Were you getting ahead of yourself? Did anything traumatic happen? Were your feet or legs bothering you? Did you consult a physician? If so, what was his/her suggestion? Did rest help?

Did you have a mystical or cosmic-contact experience? What made **SPIRIT**
you feel uplifted, grateful or content?

Were you worried about a relative (or friend)? Did a little one want **RELATIVES**
or need more of your attention? Were you challenged by your family
life? Did you consider counseling?

Were there any unexpected losses or gains? Did you make a mistake **FINANCES**
or find an error? Did you receive a small amount of money? Was a
debt absolved or a loan repaid?

Were you feeling powerless or inadequate? Did you think that what **PROBLEMS**
you wanted was impossible to find or light-years away from attaining? Did you lose money or something of value?

Were you faced with a situation that was beyond your understand- **GUIDANCE**
ing? Did you feel disconnected from your inner Self or the Source of
all life? Did you realize the only thing worth seeking was a better connection with that Source? Did someone (or something) change your
feelings or make your way easier?

Did you feel capable of succeeding? Were you beginning to recognize **SUCCESS**
the source of your success or failure?

ACTION   Did you realize that you needed to develop a more positive approach to life and/or to look for the good (or the Divine) in people, things and conditions? Were you able to accept your situation and work on creating something better?

- In light of your experience, what do you believe the Seven of Cups signified?

- What did you learn from it?

- If you drew the Seven of Cups in response to a question you asked, in what way did this card answer it?

- Now, take another look at your card. Is there anything that stands out about it you didn't notice before?

- If you were to make your own Tarot card, what words, pictures or symbols would you put on it?

SOMETHING TO REFLECT UPON

You may want to tape this guided meditation and play it back with your eyes closed.

Take a few deep breaths and then allow your eyelids to slowly close. . . . As you breathe in and out, become aware of the darkness behind your eyes and what it feels like to be inside of your body . . . notice the rise and fall of your chest, your shoulders and the weight of your body sitting on the chair . . . feel the density of the darkness inside of you. . . . And now, take another deep breath, and as you breathe out, begin to imagine that your body is expanding . . . each time you breathe in and out, feel it becoming a little bigger . . . and as your body expands, imagine that your cells and molecules are beginning to separate . . . as these particles drift apart, notice that you are beginning to feel lighter. . . . As you continue to breathe in and out and the particles of energy and matter drift farther and farther apart, imagine that you can see the space between them and parts of the room through them . . . feel your breath coming in and then seeping out through the spaces . . . as you continue to breathe in and out, imagine that you are becoming one with the room . . . that there are no longer any boundaries between you and your surroundings . . . all the particles are flowing around as if they were one big sea of energy . . . and now, imagine that the room is expanding and the atoms that make up the walls are coming unglued . . . see the trees, the sky and the ground beginning to appear between the spaces in the wall . . . notice that everything is moving and flowing . . . nothing is distinct anymore . . . every particle of everything you are aware of is flowing in and through everything else like dancing particles of light. . . . And now, imagine that this entire substance, the walls, the trees, the ground, the sky, is all God . . . and just as the drops in the ocean are a part of the ocean, you are a part of God, and He is part of you and everything you see. . . . As you inhale, say to yourself, "God in". . . . And as you exhale, say, "God out . . . God in, God out . . . God in, God out. . . ." Repeat this a few more times and then bring your attention back to your body. . . . As you become aware of your cells and atoms coming together again, keep repeating, "God in, God out" until you feel completely centered within yourself. . . . And when you are ready, take another deep breath and open your eyes. . . .

From the spiritual point of view, the only important thing is to realize Divine Life and to help others realize it by manifesting it in everyday happenings. All other happenings, incidents, and attainments in themselves can have no lasting importance.

MEHER BABA

THE EIGHT OF CUPS

Cups represent emotions, pleasure seeking, intuition and spiritual awareness.

Numerologically, the number 8 connotes the potential for success, accomplishment or recognition and the capacity to achieve one's goals; but unless one seeks the Power Within, these may not be easily attained. Although a positive change of mind or status almost always accompanies the number 8, moral integrity, fortitude and emotional equilibrium will also be required.

Constructive: Attending to business, finance and material matters. Asserting one's self or one's authority. Enacting daring plans. Becoming proficient.

Undermining: Strain. Overemotionalism. Oppression. Careless disregard for the spiritual or material realities of life.

• **What stood out the most in your experience of this card?**

In addition to your recollection, here are some other possibilities you might want to consider:

FOCUS   Did you recently complete a tiring ordeal? Were you seeking a different kind of fulfillment? Were you on a self-discovery or spiritual quest? Did you feel that you were learning a lesson about empowerment? Were your feelings, attitudes or emotional values changing?

DESIRES   Did you want to do something entirely different from what you were previously doing? What were you in search of or hoping for?

LOVE   Was your love life unfulfilling? Were you tired of meeting people you had nothing in common with? If you were interested in someone, did you, in the end, become cold, distant and eventually withdraw? Did you make any decisions concerning your relationships or one person in particular?

Did an answer you were seeking come through the voice or experience of another? Did you need someone's consent or agreement in order to achieve your aim? Did you speak with a friend (or relative) who was under the weather or feeling blue?   **OTHERS**

Did an awaited call, document or letter finally come? Were any improvements made?   **HOME**

Did you and another go on a trip together or make arrangements that involved travel?   **TRAVEL**

Was it more important to perform one task well than several poorly? Was your business expanding? Did people seek your expertise? Had you gone as far as you could (or wanted to) go with something? Were you on the verge of making an important discovery or career change?   **WORK**

Did you have an infection? Were you having problems with your vision? Did you need to address the ways in which you were trying to nurture yourself and find alternatives that made you feel more supported by life?   **BODY/MIND**

SPIRIT

What did you do for pleasure? Did someone give you a gift of silver or gold? Did you come into a sudden windfall? What were you happy about or thankful for?

RELATIVES

Did you do a favor for a relative? Did someone in your family receive a gift of money?

FINANCES

Were you anxious about your finances? Did you worry that a deficit might take a long time to recoup? Did it seem like the moment your head was above water, another expense would come up? Was lack a good motivator? Did you embark on any new projects or money-making ventures?

PROBLEMS

Were you uncomfortable when you thought about the future in terms of your love life, finances or career? Had something taken longer to accomplish than you thought it would?

GUIDANCE

Did dwelling on the past or worrying about your future keep you from connecting with the *feeling* part of you that was guiding you in the present? Were you beginning to realize that anything you try too hard to have, control or hold robs you of your power? If you felt that you were being led to move in a different direction than your logical mind thought you should go, were you comfortable with it?

Was there a considerable improvement in your finances? Did long-awaited money arrive? Was a settlement received or a lawsuit won? Did you succeed in finding direction, companionship or inner resolve?   **SUCCESS**

Did you need to challenge some of your less desirable responses? Who or what did you need to walk away from or move toward?   **ACTION**

- **In light of your experience, what do you believe the Eight of Cups signified?**

- **What did you learn from it?**

- **If you drew the Eight of Cups in response to a question you asked, in what way did this card answer it?**

- **Now, take another look at your card. Is there anything that stands out about it you didn't notice before?**

- **If you were to make your own Tarot card, what words, pictures or symbols would you put on it?**

SOMETHING TO REFLECT UPON

What your heart knows today your mind will understand tomorrow.

 # THE NINE OF CUPS

Cups represent emotions, pleasure seeking, intuition and spiritual awareness.

Numerologically, the number 9 stands for completion, arrival, integration and realization. When a number 9 surfaces, it marks a transition between what was and what is to come, a parenthesis in time as one pauses to reflect on all that went before and the unknown potential of that which is yet to be.

Constructive: Broadness of viewpoint, perspective and understanding. Having faith in one's source of supply. Discard. Detachment. Impersonal interaction.

Undermining: Self-centeredness. Dissipation. Suffering.

- **What stood out the most in your experience of this card?**

In addition to your recollection, here are some other possibilities you might want to consider:

FOCUS   Were your primary concerns external (food, making a good living, a roof over your head, etc.), or were they internal? Were you absorbed in the things that money could buy or did your interest lean toward love, emotional gratification, spiritual pursuits or self-improvement?

Did you want to correct or eliminate something that wasn't working   **DESIRES**
in your life or keep the faith in the ultimate outworkings of good despite appearances to the contrary?

Were you happy with your love life or did you want it (or the next   **LOVE**
person you got involved with) to be better? If you were dissatisfied,
was it because you worried about what *might* happen or whether or
not someone wanted you, instead of noticing what *was* happening
and asking yourself if that was what *you* wanted?

Did you feel that you were spending too much time alone or that you   **OTHERS**
needed to cultivate more spiritual, uplifting or inspirational friends?
Did a friend or business associate call with exciting news?

Were you happy at home? Did you like the way it looked and felt?   **HOME**

Were you undecided about a trip? Were there any unexpected diver-   **TRAVEL**
sions? Did you travel for pleasure? If you planned to do one thing,
did something better come up? What were the weather conditions?

Did you worry that something you said or did was wrong, or that it   **WORK**
might have dire consequences? If your situation looked impossible,
was success just around the corner?

BODY/MIND   Were you taking good care of yourself and your emotional requirements or were you neglecting your needs and indulging your hedonistic
impulses? Did you have trouble sleeping or were you sleeping more?

SPIRIT   Were you satisfied with your life and the *things* the world had to
offer? Were you grateful for the material comforts you had? Did you
send a card to, or prepare a gift for, someone who was away?

RELATIVES   Did you have a hard time understanding a loved one, or trouble with
an in-law who said one thing but meant another? Were you con-
cerned about the care or treatment of a family member? Was someone having problems with papers, land or finalizing a deal?

FINANCES   How were you handling your finances? Were you thrifty, budgeting
and cutting down on frivolous expenditures, or were you extrava-
gant, lavish or wasteful? Did money that was promised or anticipated finally arrive? Were there any other financial gains?

PROBLEMS   Were you an emotional wreck? Were you becoming aware of a pattern
that kept repeating itself? Did you feel as if you were constantly being
shown the same lesson? Were you angry with yourself because you *still*
didn't get it and wish you could get off that particular turn of the spiral?

GUIDANCE   Did you connect with someone who stirred your soul, someone you
recognized as the embodiment of the Divine? Did you feel, hear or
see something that made you realize there were no mistakes in the
Universe, that *all* things worked for *good*?

Were you able to achieve something others only dreamed of? Was a
wish finally fulfilled? Did it take another form than what you thought
it would, started with or envisioned? Did what *seemed* like a failure
help you to succeed? What gave you the most satisfaction or feeling
of accomplishment?

SUCCESS

Were you practicing new behaviors? Was there something you needed
to withhold judgment on? Instead of trying to stop the flow of your
thoughts, did you follow the ones that took you where you wanted
to go?

ACTION

• **In light of your experience, what do you believe the Nine of Cups signified?**

• **What did you learn from it?**

• **If you drew the Nine of Cups in response to a question you asked, in what
way did this card answer it?**

• **Now, take another look at your card. Is there anything that stands out about
it you didn't notice before?**

• **If you were to make your own Tarot card, what words, pictures or symbols
would you put on it?**

SOMETHING TO REFLECT UPON

To paraphrase a poem by Portia Nelson:*

> *I walk down the street.*
> *There is a hole.*
> *I don't see it.*
> *I fall in.*
> *It isn't my fault.*
> *It takes a very long time to get out.*
>
> *I walk down the same street.*
> *There is still a deep hole.*
> *I pretend not to see it.*
> *I fall in.*
> *I pretend it's still not my fault.*
> *It takes a long time to get out.*
>
> *I walk down the same street.*
> *There is still the same deep hole.*
> *I see it.*
> *I fall in anyway.*
> *It's a habit.*
> *I get out quicker this time.*
>
> *I walk down the same street.*
> *There is a deep hole.*
> *I see it.*
> *I walk around it.*
> *I don't fall in.*
>
> *I walk down a different street.*

* "Autobiography in Five Short Chapters," Beyond Words Publishing, Inc.

THE TEN OF CUPS

Cups represent emotions, pleasure seeking, intuition and spiritual awareness.

The 10 in the Tarot marks the end of one phase and the beginning of another. Although it has the same basic meaning as the number 1, it also signifies a time when one may have to come to terms with something that was previously overlooked, unfinished or avoided.

- **What stood out the most in your experience of this card?**

In addition to your recollection, here are some other possibilities you might want to consider:

Were you experiencing a time of peace and harmony? Did you feel happy, content and carefree? Were you unfettered by duties or responsibilities? Were problems a thing of the past? Was there a celebration in the offing? Were there any impromptu trips or purchases? Did you quickly sense the advent of change? **FOCUS**

Were your desires minimal? Did you simply want to enjoy life, be loved and stay connected with your Inner Self? **DESIRES**

Did you encounter an old flame or somebody who carries a torch for you? Did you feel a special empathy toward someone or fall in love? Did you marry or feel that your love was so deep and abiding, nothing could keep you apart? Was your relationship unusual in some way or different in the way it inspired you to think or feel? Did being around him/her help you appreciate your own inner beauty and/or reflect the relationship you had with God? **LOVE**

OTHERS   Were you flexible and easy to get along with? Did you enjoy the company of others? Were the people you came in contact with friendly and cooperative? Did you feel supported and nurtured? Were you acknowledged for your professional contributions, talents or emotional growth?

HOME   Did your environment change? Did you wish it would? Did a friend or neighbor invite you over or help you out of a jam? Did someone need or want your assistance?

TRAVEL   Were your inner-city travels enjoyable? Were you packing for a trip? Did you fly to another state?

WORK   Was it hard to buckle down to business? Did you long to get away from the workaday world? Did your work entail any special correspondence or application, letter writing, phone calls, something out of the ordinary? Was there anything you glossed over, had to repeat or needed to rework?

BODY/MIND   Were you feeling confident about yourself and where you were headed in life? Did you feel relaxed and unhurried? If you were previously ill, were you recovering? Were your eating, sleeping or sexual habits changing? Did you feel that giving your mind time to rest and unwind was just as important as using it?

Did you do something that brought enjoyment, helped you unwind **SPIRIT**
or fulfilled you emotionally, like entertain friends, make someone a
gift or take up a creative hobby? Did you think that people who
chased rainbows were the ones most likely to find them?

Did you spend more time with your family? If you didn't have chil- **RELATIVES**
dren, were you thinking you'd like to? Was there a relative you were
particularly fond of? Did you make a conference call? Were there any
long-distance communications? Was someone going on an ocean
voyage or overseas trip?

Were you holding your own financially? Was your income steady? **FINANCES**
Did you have money to spend on yourself and others? Did your financial prospects look as though they were improving?

Were you treating yourself better? Were you more accepting, flexible **PROBLEMS**
or adaptable?

Did you trust yourself or have the feeling that you needed to trust **GUIDANCE**
yourself more?

Were you rich in spirit? Was most of your satisfaction derived from **SUCCESS**
travel, love or pleasurable pursuits?

ACTION _____ Did you let inspiration rather than desperation or perspiration be your guide?

_____

• In light of your experience, what do you believe the Ten of Cups signified?

• What did you learn from it?

• If you drew the Ten of Cups in response to a question you asked, in what way did this card answer it?

• Now, take another look at your card. Is there anything that stands out about it you didn't notice before?

• If you were to make your own Tarot card, what words, pictures or symbols would you put on it?

SOMETHING TO REFLECT UPON

And the Master said unto the silence, "in the path of our highest happiness shall we find the learning for which we have chosen this lifetime" . . .
                    RICHARD BACH, *Illusions: The Adventures of a Reluctant Messiah*

THE PAGE OF CUPS

Astrological Sign: Pisces

Pisces rules the twelfth house and activities related to institutions (hospitals, health care, prisons, religious, etc.); the psychic realm; self-undoing (blind spots that cause needless suffering, frustration or limitation); and karma (unresolved past-life issues or obligations to self and others).

Time frame: February 19–March 20

Type: Impressionable. Imaginative. Telepathic. Idealistic. Child-like. Other-worldly. Tenderhearted.

Thrust: Soul growth. The Higher Self. Intuiting information. Understanding.

Cornerstone: To heal, relieve and inspire

Life lesson: Faith

Cups represent emotions, pleasure seeking, intuition and spiritual awareness.

Pages are commonly referred to as messengers, children or youths, but they can also represent one's maturing self, lovers or problems.

The Page of Cups connotes a *"heart*istic," compassionate person whose interests lean toward the arts, humanities and the ethereal realm. He/she tends to be reflective in nature and emotional in his/her response to life. The Page of Cups is also described as a dreamer and/or someone who may be going through a personal, physical or spiritual transformation. Traditionally, Cups represent a person with light brown hair and hazel eyes.

Did you feel that you resembled this card type? Have you recently come in contact with someone who does?

• **What stood out the most in your experience of this card?**

In addition to your recollection, here are some other possibilities you might want to consider:

FOCUS ———— Were you examining, researching or seeking a resolution to something? Were you involved with service-type people, health care or institutions? What karma do you think you were working through?

DESIRES ———— Were you hoping for an improvement or anxious for the future to take shape?

LOVE ———— Were you driven by the desire for romance or companionship? Did you feel terribly alone without it? Did you meet a new love at a bookstore, work or church? Did he/she seem to be pulled in two different directions (like extending an invitation and then drawing back)? Did you have to do a little coaxing? Did you go somewhere (a cafe?) to talk? Did you want the relationship to progress faster than it was or he/she wanted it to?

OTHERS ———— Did your social activities increase? Was your phone or doorbell always ringing? Did you receive several invitations? Were you more talkative than usual? Did you get an important phone call? Was it from a Pisces? Were you in a position that enabled you to express yourself or meet like-minded people you could relate to? Did you have any strange or uncomfortable encounters? Did you offer your services to those in need of assistance?

HOME ———— Did your routine change? Were you, or someone close to you, moving or forced to move?

Were you making travel plans? Did a trip bring a new discovery? Did you spend more money than you intended to?

TRAVEL

Vocations suited for a Piscean type are anything that deals with illusion, love or behind-the-scenes work; television or motion pictures (actors or crew); clairvoyant; poet; dancer; songwriter; photographer; bartender; clown, mime or magician; institution worker; podiatrist; fisherman; working with animals.

WORK

Do any of these professions sound like something you're doing or would like to do? Did you speak to, or associate with, someone who worked in one of these trades?

Was it difficult to concentrate? Was something disturbing you? Were you having trouble bringing matters to a head? Do you think you were shirking your duties or responsibilities? Were you getting the feeling that you needed to make room for love?

Health issues associated with a Piscean type are the feet and toes; lymph, sweat and pineal glands; liver; mucous membranes; sinuses; pinched nerves; toxic conditions; overdoses; poisoning; contagious diseases.

BODY/MIND

Have you experienced problems related to any of these areas recently? Has anyone close to you?

Did you intuitively pick up on what others were thinking or feeling? Do you think you were too impressionable, sensitive or suggestible? Were your emotional responses appropriate? Did you have problems with your feet, knees or legs? Were you sexually immature or shy about sex?

SPIRIT

Did you move into a happier or more relaxed atmosphere? Was it because you were in love? Did you go to a party?

RELATIVES

Did a relative or pet give you a scare? Were you annoyed with someone (a family member, ex-spouse or close friend)? Did somebody want you to be his/her constant panacea? Were other relatives or in-laws immensely enjoyable?

FINANCES

Could you afford to buy what you wanted or needed? Did you receive monetary compensation for your services? Did anyone owe you money?

PROBLEMS

The negative characteristics of a Piscean type are hypersensitivity, susceptibility, gullibility, escapism, delusion, lack of conviction or commitment.

Did you see these traits in yourself or notice them in another? What troubles or disappointments were you experiencing?

GUIDANCE

What were your inner promptings urging you to do? Were you able to trust your intuitive hunches or interpret the messages you were receiving?

SUCCESS

Was an ongoing problem finally solved? Did you meet or speak with someone who helped you realize your goals or innermost wishes? Did you succeed in work that was done behind the scenes or in self-help or self-discovery areas? Were you getting positive feedback?

Were you acting in ways that nurtured your inner child? What action   **ACTION**
did you take to improve yourself or your situation? If you needed
help or advice, did you ask for assistance?

- **In light of your experience, what do you believe the Page of Cups signified?**

- **What did you learn from it?**

- **If you drew the Page of Cups in response to a question you asked, in what way did this card answer it?**

- **Now, take another look at your card. Is there anything that stands out about it you didn't notice before?**

- **If you were to make your own Tarot card, what words, pictures or symbols would you put on it?**

SOMETHING TO REFLECT UPON

Do not push yourself farther than you are prepared to go. It's very important to respect your reservations and your natural rhythm for growth.

THE KNIGHT OF CUPS

Knights symbolize comings or goings, beginnings or endings and direction of thoughts or energy. When a Knight appears, long-term conditions will change.

There is no astrological or numerological correlation to the Knights.

Cups represent emotions, pleasure seeking, intuition and spiritual awareness.

• **What stood out the most in your experience of this card?**

In addition to your recollection, here are some other possibilities you might want to consider:

FOCUS　　　　　Did the thrust of your activities change? Was travel, movement or advancement emphasized? Were you, your family or your friends branching out into new worlds? Were your thoughts turned toward love and leisurely pursuits? Did you feel that conditions were in a state of flux?

DESIRES　　　　Did you hope that if you maintained a positive attitude and kept your mind on what you wished to accomplish, you'd get what you wanted?

LOVE　　　　　Were you in a romantic or flirtatious mood? If you were feeling lonely, did anything happen to change the way you felt? Were there any surprising proposals, flirtations or romantic interludes? Did you believe that you and the person you were involved with could have a future together, or that he/she had nothing of real substance to offer and/or was incapable of making any long-term commitments?

Were you more sociable or outgoing? Did others make you think of **OTHERS**
love and romance? Did your friends (or family) try to "fix you up" or
extend social invitations? Did you accept them? Were the opinions of
others important?

Did you spend time in the home of a relative? Was it a lengthy stay? **HOME**
Did being in a different locale make you feel renewed? If you didn't
leave home, did you create a vacation-like environment?

Did you travel a great deal or go on any pleasure trips? Were you (or **TRAVEL**
your thoughts) in constant motion? Were you thinking about moving
to another city?

Did you enjoy your work? Was the atmosphere positive or convivial? **WORK**
Were there discussions concerning advertising or promotion? Were
you satisfied with your accomplishments? Did you take time off? If
so, did you feel that it was well deserved? Did you think that getting
where you wanted to go ought to be just as rewarding as having arrived?

Was your health improving? Did you feel that things were looking **BODY/MIND**
up? If you had a problem in the past, was it under control? Did you
exercise, bike or engage in some other form of physical activity? Did
you tend to be accident prone? Did you *refuse* to be negative or entertain a negative thought?

SPIRIT

Did you feel like having fun? Were you cheerful and optimistic? Did you laugh a lot? What did you most enjoy doing?

RELATIVES

Was your family on the move? Were they traveling or returning home? Did you work on a project together? Was the atmosphere lighthearted?

FINANCES

Were there any financial decisions to make? Was your income improving? Did your pecuniary requests or inquiries receive a swift, affirmative response? Did you feel that you had adequate means to support yourself and your family?

PROBLEMS

Did you feel that you made a mistake in your affections? Did it seem like the right choice at the time? If something was bothering you or you caught yourself doubting your ability to succeed, how did you deal with it? Did you refuse to let it gain a stronghold?

GUIDANCE

Were you humming happy songs? Did you notice the words or sentiment they were expressing? Were there any synchronistic events confirming what you thought or felt? Were you able to tap into a sustaining Source that soothed your soul or guided you in a time of need?

SUCCESS

Did success come through "following your bliss"; i.e., doing the things that you enjoyed? Did a new project succeed beyond your expectations? Did it surpass even your previous success(es)?

If you decided on a course of action, were you determined to follow   **ACTION**
through? If something didn't feel right, did you trust that inner urging and put it aside or look for an alternative? If you went against
your hunches, what were the results?

- In light of your experience, what do you believe the Knight of Cups
  signified?

- What did you learn from it?

- If you drew the Knight of Cups in response to a question you asked, in what
  way did this card answer it?

- Now, take another look at your card. Is there anything that stands out about
  it you didn't notice before?

- If you were to make your own Tarot card, what words, pictures or symbols
  would you put on it?

SOMETHING TO REFLECT UPON

For one entire day, pretend your intuitive thoughts, feelings or promptings are 100 percent accurate and *act* on them. Notice what happens when you follow your inner guidance and what comes up to stop you. If you're not sure what you're thinking or feeling, *guess.* . . .

When we consciously live life, we find our answers everywhere.

 # THE QUEEN OF CUPS

Astrological Sign: Scorpio

Scorpio rules the eighth house and activities related to death and regeneration (actual or symbolic); personal sacrifices; occult activities (mysticism, the psychic realm, life after death, etc.); legacies, joint resources and other people's money.

Time frame: October 23–November 21

Type: Intense. Complex. Psychic. Secretive. Shrewd. Magnetic. Mysterious.

Thrust: One's spiritual reality and inner connectedness. Total involvement.
    Uncovering that which is hidden. New levels of awareness.

Cornerstone: To improve, conquer or transform

Life lesson: Forgiveness

Cups represent emotions, pleasure seeking, intuition and spiritual awareness.

The Queen of Cups is a paradox. On the one hand, she/he is intense, powerful and visionary and on the other, a romantic dreamer, artist or poet. This is a person who is highly perceptive, intuitive and strong, but can also be too trusting, gullible and easily drained. There is a deeply felt spiritual or religious core to this individual, and she/he is often involved in a tug-of-war between the desire for inner rewards and the drive for worldly success and material gain. Traditionally, Cups represent a person with light brown hair and hazel eyes.

Did you feel that you resembled this card type? Have you recently come in contact with someone who does?

• **What stood out the most in your experience of this card?**

In addition to your recollection, here are some other possibilities you might want to consider:

Was there something you felt driven to convey or attain? Was a property matter, inheritance or collective effort a priority or concern? Were you going through a metamorphosis or becoming more aware of the need to transform your feelings, passions or sexual energy?   **FOCUS**

Were you seeking the cooperation, support or approval of others? Was there a special wish or prayer you hoped would be answered?   **DESIRES**

Did you want to have an intimate, passionate relationship? Did you meet someone you were attracted to? If so, was he/she a professional person or someone you met close to home? If you were already involved, did you feel that the two of you were on the same wavelength? Was it hard not to let your passion get the best of you? Did you talk about a union or marriage?   **LOVE**

Did people respond favorably to what you wanted to do or sell? Were there any problems with agents, buyers or publishers? Were your friends a pleasure to be around? Did opportunities and invitations come your way? Did someone inspire, help, motivate or enlighten you? If there was a discussion about a merger, did you initiate it?   **OTHERS**

HOME

Were you having problems at home? Were you unhappy about something in or around your home (noise, inconsiderate neighbors, pests, a guest who overstayed his/her welcome, etc.)? If you were trying to sell your house, did the escrow fall through?

TRAVEL

Did something cause you to rethink or postpone your plans? Did you want/need a ride?

WORK

Vocations suited for a Scorpio type are anything that's engrossing or requires concentrated effort, (sex) therapist, counselor, occultist, evangelist, psychic (healer), psychic investigator, detective, spy, espionage agent, surgeon, acupuncturist, hypnotist, dramatic stage or screen actor.

Do any of these professions sound like something you're doing or would like to do? Did you speak to, or associate with, someone who worked in one of these trades?

Did you want your work to have value for, or inspire, others? Were you looking for career direction? Were you pursuing a spiritual or metaphysical line of work? Did your job entail some form of psychic or clairvoyant skill? Did others understand your ideas or readily accept what you had to offer? Were you having problems with paperwork or getting the business response you wanted? Did you branch out into a new or different area?

BODY/MIND

Health issues associated with a Scorpio type are sexual organs, rectum, bladder, ovarian cysts, gynecological problems, prostatitis, hernias, constipation, nose, adenoids, fistulas, gland troubles, sexually transmitted diseases.

Have you experienced problems related to any of these areas recently? Has anyone close to you?

Were your emotions strained or exceptionally intense? Were you more sexually oriented or active? Were your olfactory senses more pronounced? Did you practice hatha, siddha or tantra yoga, or any other spiritual discipline designed to raise the Kundalini and attain enlightenment? Were you losing weight? Did you think about becoming a vegetarian?

SPIRIT

Were you lucky in attracting money, gifts, advantages or leverage? Were you sought after personally or professionally? Were you clairvoyant or able to predict the future?

RELATIVES

Was your family life discordant? Were you having problems with a child or pet? Did you need to keep your attitude or emotions in check so you wouldn't get sucked into an emotional fray? If there was a conflict between you and a family member, did you think it was better to forgive, and mourn the person you wished he/she could be rather than mourn the fact that he/she is gone and your love came too late?

FINANCES

Were combined resources, gains through others or money-management emphasized? Did you make a perspicacious financial decision? Did money come through a partnership, corporation or legacy? Were there any unexpected advantages or cost cuts? If so, how or in what way?

PROBLEMS   The negative characteristics of a Scorpio type are obsessive behavior, possessiveness (or jealousy), vindictiveness, heaviness, resentment, rigidity, explosive rage.

    Did you see these traits in yourself or notice them in another? What troubles or disappointments were you experiencing?

GUIDANCE   Did you have a spiritual mentor? Was anyone guiding or counseling you? Were you attending any seminars or receiving guidance through a metaphysical source (tarot, psychics, astrology) or spiritual study? Did an intuitive response answer a prayer?

SUCCESS   Did you feel that it was better to try and fail than to attempt nothing and succeed? Did success come through your ability to make a favorable impression on others? Did someone want to market your idea, sell your product or give you the opportunity to utilize your skills or talents?

ACTION   Did you use your charm, persuasion or the resources that were available to you? Did obstacles make you better or bitter?

• **In light of your experience, what do you believe the Queen of Cups signified?**

- **What did you learn from it?**

- **If you drew the Queen of Cups in response to a question you asked, in what way did this card answer it?**

- **Now, take another look at your card. Is there anything that stands out about it you didn't notice before?**

- **If you were to make your own Tarot card, what words, pictures or symbols would you put on it?**

SOMETHING TO REFLECT UPON

The vine grows imperceptibly during the night. In the morning it looks the same as it did the morning before. And then there comes a morning when one sees that it has grown halfway up the tree. . . . How did it happen? It must have been growing all the while, because here it is, thick and strong, clinging so tenaciously that one can barely tear it away.

BELVA PLAIN, *Evergreen*

THE KING OF CUPS

Astrological Sign: Cancer

Cancer rules the fourth house and activities related to one's home environment (domestic affairs; property; family; relationship with one's parents, particularly the mother *); inherited tendencies (childhood conditioning, upbringing, habits and patterns, etc.); endings (or the conclusion of undertakings); and the awareness of a new-phase beginning.

> *Time frame:* June 21–July 22
> *Type:* Careful. Protective. Sensitive. Sentimental. Changeable. Intuitive. Malleable.
> *Thrust:* Emotional security. Conscientious action. Personal foundations. Responses to stimuli. The past.
> *Cornerstone:* To nurture and be nurtured
> *Life lesson:* Spiritual discernment

Cups represent emotions, pleasure seeking, intuition and spiritual awareness.

The King of Cups depicts one who is considerate, responsible and introspective, a humanitarian who, although empathetic, tends to be somewhat taciturn and emotionally reserved. This person is also described as a mentor, caregiver or guardian who dedicates his/her life toward uplifting others and upholding conventional values. Traditionally, Cups represent a person with light brown hair and hazel eyes.

Did you feel that you resembled this card type? Have you recently come in contact with someone who does?

• **What stood out the most in your experience of this card?**

In addition to your recollection, here are some other possibilities you might want to consider:

FOCUS   Did most of your activities center around your home, property or community? Were you more concerned with safety and security? Did

---

* Note: Some astrologers associate the father with the fourth house. How did *you* experience it?

you want a solid base of operation, something you could build your life around? Was there more emphasis on your feelings, personal life or spiritual growth?

DESIRES _____

Did you want to spend time with, make love to or share your life with someone and/or be financially independent or self-sustaining in the work that you do?

LOVE _____

Were you in a flirtatious mood or daydreaming about love and romance? Did those who tried to exercise a claim have to compete with your work or ideal lover? Were you with a man/woman who made you feel loved and cared for? Did you want to stay in the relationship you were in or were you looking for a way out?

OTHERS _____

Were you more retiring than at other times? Did you want/need/prefer more privacy? Did people seek you out for your services or guidance? Did others respond positively to you or your requests? Did you receive any good news? If so, what kind?

HOME _____

Were you more inclined to stay at home? Did you tend to eat, drink or cook more? Was anything new installed or established? Were you discussing a residential (or business) move? What were the conditions surrounding your home?

TRAVEL   Did you go on an extended trip or ocean voyage? Did you find that water rejuvenated you? Was your car in need of attention (tune-up, oil change, lube job)? Did you make a social call?

WORK   Vocations suited for a Cancerian type are doctor, metaphysician, priest, cook, caterer, restaurant owner, antique dealer, domestic worker, homemaker, gardener, conservationist, hotel manager, nutritionist, repairing home appliances.

Do any of these professions sound like something you're doing or would like to do? Did you speak to, or associate with, someone who worked in one of these trades?

Were you in business for yourself or working out of your home? Did you feel that you were in touch with who you were and what you really wanted to do? Were your talents being put to good use? Did your work curtail your romantic involvement? Were you easily distracted (or less ambitious) when others were around?

BODY/MIND   Health issues associated with a Cancerian type are breasts, stomach, uterus; gallbladder; gout; digestive disorders; poor circulation; esophageal reflex or lung trouble; flow of bodily fluids; immune deficiencies; hypochondria.

Have you experienced problems related to any of these areas recently? Has anyone close to you?

Were you prone to mood swings or emotional ups and downs? Did you feel that you were worn down or bombarded by external stimuli? Did you want/need to be nurtured? Were you more reflective than you normally are? Did you often reminisce about the past? Do you think your childhood conditioning influenced your outlook on life? Did you visit, or hear news from, someone in the medical profession? Did you feel more sensual? Were you more sexually active?

Were your intuitive faculties more pronounced? Did you enjoy tinkering with things, crafts or toy making? Was the blue bird of happiness found in your own backyard? What were you pleased about or grateful for?

SPIRIT

Was your family, especially your mother, more significant? Were you reviewing your past relationship with her? Was her influence more strongly felt? Did someone discuss coming to live with you or your living with them?

RELATIVES

Did you feel that it was important to get your finances in order or to make it your own way without compromising your integrity? Were you financially solvent? Was there something you should have paid closer attention to or discussed *before* you got started? Were you generous with your money? Is there anything you would have done differently?

FINANCES

The negative characteristics of a Cancerian type are being overly sensitive, touchy or cranky; moodiness; martyrdom; dishonesty; cruelty; penuriousness.
    Did you see these traits in yourself or notice them in another? What troubles or disappointments were you experiencing?

PROBLEMS

GUIDANCE _____   Did you believe that what you wanted or needed would come to you and you would be provided for?

SUCCESS _____   Were your home-based activities successful? Were any new projects in the works or being considered? Did anything (or anyone) augment your income? Did you receive a go-ahead in reply to a business query or financial matter? Was there still something missing?

ACTION _____   Did you refuse to accept less that what you knew was intrinsically right or to let your desires come between you and your higher purpose?

_____

• In light of your experience, what do you believe the King of Cups signified?

• What did you learn from it?

• If you drew the King of Cups in response to a question you asked, in what way did this card answer it?

• Now, take another look at your card. Is there anything that stands out about it you didn't notice before?

• If you were to make your own Tarot card, what words, pictures or symbols would you put on it?

SOMETHING TO REFLECT UPON

Getting what we want *when* we want it isn't necessarily a victory.

It's difficult to follow our Higher Self guidance when we want to move in a more expedient direction or our rationalizations would have us believe otherwise, but that is precisely what we need to do. Our reasoning mind can never take us beyond what it already knows, because that is its function, and if we hope to move beyond the ordinary, we must learn to depend on the extraordinary.

THE
SWORDS

YOUR QUERY SHEET

You can use this query sheet in addition to your weekly notes for questions you may have during the course of your workbook experience and in times to come.

Date:	Card:	Your Questions and Answers:
		Q:
		A:
		Q:
		A:
		Q:
		A:
		Q:
		A:
		Q:
		A:
		Q:
		A:
		Q:
		A:
		Q:
		A:
		Q:
		A:
		Q:
		A:
		Q:
		A:
		Q:
		A:
		Q:
		A:
		Q:
		A:
		Q:
		A:
		Q:
		A:
		Q:
		A:

◆   THE ACE OF SWORDS

Swords indicate action, discernment, struggle, sorrow, or sickness.

Aces represent new beginnings; they also signify a season. The Ace of Swords represents the winter months—December, January and February.

What season is it now? _____ What season does it *feel* like? _____

Numerologically, Aces correspond with the number 1, indicating fresh starts, invention, creativity, originality, independence, force and will. During the influence of the number 1, ideas, opportunities and new projects begin to flourish, and although one may know *what* one needs to do, it may take courage or daring to follow through.

Constructive: Confidence. Determination. Assuming responsibility. Strengthening one's abilities and sense of self. Singular effort.

Undermining: Willfulness. Unreasonable force. Fear of taking the initiative, promoting one's self or standing on one's own. Discouragement.

• **What stood out the most in your experience of this card?**

In addition to your recollection, here are some other possibilities you might want to consider:

Did you have a novel idea or begin something new? Were you thinking about a new product or venture? What was the overall feeling or general atmosphere? Was it positive, active and invigorating, or did it feel uncomfortable and agitating? Were communications or responses significant?   **FOCUS** _____

Did you want career satisfaction or personal gratification? What were your fondest hopes and wishes?   **DESIRES** _____

Did you get a call, proposition or unexpected response from someone who has a crush on you or loves you? Were there any declara-   **LOVE** _____ tions of love or affection? Did a new love take you by storm? Did you and your lover/mate think alike? Was he/she what you wanted in a partner? Was your love deepening or was the relationship on the rocks?

OTHERS

What, if any, impact did others have on you or vice versa? Were your friends and loved ones tense? Were there any conflicts? Did someone help you with an important project or problem? Were you more popular?

HOME

What was your home life like? Did anything occur that changed the status quo, your plans or your thoughts about the future? Did you have to make any compromises? Was there any extensive work or clean up done? Did a lover or representative from a company call on you? Did you hire new help?

TRAVEL

Were there any trips you just *had* to make? Did you travel to a new area? Was the weather unpredictable? Were you considering a trip or move to the north?

WORK

Did you have a new idea or revelation? Was it followed up with action? Were you assertive, driven or unwavering? Did someone express an interest in your work (or *you*)? Did you receive important news? Were you an overachiever?

Were your senses more acute? Did you feel focused, confident and decisive or touchy, edgy and explosive? If there were problems, were you determined to correct them? Was sex a hot topic?   **BODY/MIND**

Did good news or good fortune come through a lover, friend or admirer? Did you enjoy being active? What gave you the most pleasure? What positive changes were coming into your life?   **SPIRIT**

What impact did your family have on you? Was anyone upset? Did someone want or have to leave?   **RELATIVES**

Was there tension related to money matters? Was your income nominal? Were you equity rich but cash poor? Did your financial condition improve?   **FINANCES**

What disappointments, trouble spots or discouragements did you encounter? Were there any legal or ethical matters to be dealt with? Were you upset about a problematical work situation, trouble on the home front or an increase in your expenses? Was someone not paying you?   **PROBLEMS**

Was something or someone telling you to have faith in yourself, your work and your future, that no matter what the odds, you would ultimately have what you wanted?   **GUIDANCE**

SUCCESS ⎯⎯⎯⎯ What successes did you have? Were there any achievements you didn't give yourself credit for?

ACTION ⎯⎯⎯⎯ Were you determined to succeed?

⎯⎯⎯⎯

- In light of your experience, what do you believe the Ace of Swords signified?

- What did you learn from it?

- If you drew the Ace of Swords in response to a question you asked, in what way did this card answer it?

- Now, take another look at your card. Is there anything that stands out about it you didn't notice before?

- If you were to make your own Tarot card, what words, pictures or symbols would you put on it?

SOMETHING TO REFLECT UPON

Close your eyes and imagine a hand reaching out of the clouds offering you an opportunity to emerge into a new day of potentiality but with no promise of future success. . . . What would it feel like if you accepted it? Now ask yourself what would you feel like if you didn't.

◆   # THE TWO OF SWORDS

Swords indicate action, discernment, struggle, sorrow, or sickness.

Numerologically, the number 2 connotes assimilation, balancing polarities and dealing with unknowns. When the number 2 is present, partial success can be realized, but one may also find oneself having to repeat previous lessons or experiences in order to eliminate flaws or continue to progress. Reunions, reconciliations and an element of surprise could also be indicated.

Constructive: Patience. Tolerance. Cooperation. Nurturing, developing or refining what one has before commencing something new. Combined efforts. Personal interaction.

Undermining: Impatience. One-sidedness. Isolation. Lack of commitment or steady purpose.

• **What stood out the most in your experience of this card?**

In addition to your recollection, here are some other possibilities you might want to consider:

Was your energy on getting something accomplished? Had you attained some level of success but wanted to achieve more? Did further progress depend on influencing others or aligning yourself with the right people? Were there any surprises in your business or personal   **FOCUS** affairs? Did you have a decision to make that required insight or courage?

DESIRES ___ Did you want to get on with or improve something? Did you wish you had a business or romantic partner?

LOVE ___ Did you worry that you would never have that special someone or that love would pass you by? Did your prospects surprisingly change? Did you meet someone quite a bit older (or younger) than you? Was he/she charming, comforting or well-to-do? Were you wondering if you had a future together? Were you having mixed emotions? Was there a difficult choice to make?

OTHERS ___ Did you have to go through a few channels (or changes) before you reached the right person or got the answer you were waiting for? Was an offer accepted? Did you get the assistance, backing or support you wanted? Did a friend help you solve a problem? Was someone flirting with you?

HOME ___ Were you happy about a move that *didn't* take place? Were you considering a large purchase? Did a caller arrive bearing gifts?

TRAVEL ___ Did you receive news that led to an unplanned trip? Did you travel to a special restaurant? If so, was it by the sea? Did you go to a lake, river or pool? Were you saving money for a trip? Did an unexpected happening occur?

Was there a surprise meeting or encounter? Did you have a conversation with someone who liked your ideas and wanted to work with, or hire you? Was a tentative agreement reached? Was a new plan enacted? Did your business or profits take an upward swing?

WORK

Were you excited, anxious, worried and hopeful all at the same time? Was there something you needed to make peace with? Did your energy fluctuate between inexhaustible or none at all? Was your resistance low? Were you suffering from allergies or catching a cold or flu?

BODY/MIND

Did you feel grateful for something you weren't happy with before?

SPIRIT

Do you think you were neglecting someone? Were you inattentive, argumentative or impatient? If you and another had a row, did you declare a truce? Did you hear from a relative you hadn't spoken with in ages?

RELATIVES

Were you concerned about your financial future? Were you wondering how much money you were going to make or if you should force an issue that still wasn't resolved? Were there any ongoing negotiations?

FINANCES

PROBLEMS　　　　Were you unhappy that you didn't have the relationship you wanted or get the immediate result you expected? Were there problems that needed to be ironed out before you could progress?

GUIDANCE　　　　Did you hear a positive prediction about your future? Did a precognitive hunch pan out?

SUCCESS　　　　Was what you wanted within your reach? Did you attain something you thought was impossible to acquire?

ACTION　　　　Did you need to make the effort?

- **In light of your experience, what do you believe the Two of Swords signified?**

- **What did you learn from it?**

- **If you drew the Two of Swords in response to a question you asked, in what way did this card answer it?**

• Now, take another look at your card. Is there anything that stands out about it you didn't notice before?

• If you were to make your own Tarot card, what words, pictures or symbols would you put on it?

SOMETHING TO REFLECT UPON

Take the first step in faith. You don't have to see the whole staircase, just take the first step.

DR. MARTIN LUTHER KING, JR.

◆ THE THREE OF SWORDS

Swords indicate action, discernment, struggle, sorrow or sickness.

Numerologically, the number 3 indicates expressing one's self, creating, externalizing and relating. With the number 3, group activities or situations involving more than one person are usually emphasized. Although the 3 brings conditions to fruition, there may also be some delay. Growth of an inner, emotional nature is also indicated.

Constructive: Synthesizing. Conceptualizing. Becoming more selective or giving something your all. Embracing the lighter side of life. Keeping a positive, optimistic frame of mind. Allowing events to unfold.

Undermining: Ennui. Scattering energies. Overreacting or overindulging. Refusing to accept life on life's terms.

• **What stood out the most in your experience of this card?**

In addition to your recollection, here are some other possibilities you might want to consider:

FOCUS
Were you struggling with your life, relationships or work? Did you have problems with your health, home or family? Was there a clash between what you wanted to have, do or be and cold, harsh reality?

DESIRES
Were you wishing your lover/mate would return or that you could recover something that was lost?

LOVE
Did you and your lover/mate have an argument? Were you deserted, deeply hurt or left for another? Did you fear that what you cherished most would never happen, or was gone forever? If you thought your relationship was over, did you have a change of heart?

OTHERS
Was it difficult to enlist the assistance or support of others? Were people uncooperative or inconsiderate? Were you impatient or angry? Did you have trouble with sellers, lessors or business associates?

HOME
Did something need to be replaced or refurbished? Was your property run down, unkempt or in need of improvement? Were you vexed by, or having trouble with, (faulty?) equipment, insects or pesticides?

Did a trip (or someone returning) establish something better? If you traveled with a companion, did one of you become ill? Was the weather uncomfortable, cloudy or stormy? Were you given the wrong directions?

TRAVEL

Were you full of ideas but unable to find the words to express them or the way to put them into effect? If something new was proposed, were you reluctant to pursue or accept it?

WORK

Were you disillusioned, despondent or heartsick? Were you in physical or emotional pain? Did you feel fragmented or bested? Were you tempted to do something rash? Did you break out in a rash?

BODY/MIND

Was there a surprising twist in your business or love life? Did you receive a gift of love or an unexpected blessing?

SPIRIT

Did parenting issues need to be addressed? Did a little one act cranky, cause sadness or become ill?

RELATIVES

Did you receive money that was held up or delayed? Did gains come through friends, in-laws, investments or speculative ventures? Were there discussions about a property matter, rent reduction or inheritance?

FINANCES

PROBLEMS   Did personal insecurities create problems where there were none? Did you wallow in self-pity or negativity? Were you unwilling to deal with your feelings or let go of your resentment?

GUIDANCE   Were you getting the feeling that you needed to surrender something? Did you have trouble giving up or believing that a Divine Power could and *would* heal your pain, fear or difficulties on the material plane?

SUCCESS   Did delays, aborted attempts or what *looked* like a lost cause work in your favor?

ACTION   Were you able to get out of your own way? If not, what might you have done or said to take better care of yourself or make your experience a more positive one?

- **In light of your experience, what do you believe the Three of Swords signified?**

- **What did you learn from it?**

- If you drew the Three of Swords in response to a question you asked, in what way did this card answer it?

- Now, take another look at your card. Is there anything that stands out about it you didn't notice before?

- If you were to make your own Tarot card, what words, pictures or symbols would you put on it?

SOMETHING TO REFLECT UPON

Acceptance doesn't mean resigning one's self to things as they are; it means doing the best one can and then leaving the rest to God.

 # THE FOUR OF SWORDS

Swords indicate action, discernment, struggle, sorrow or sickness.

Numerologically, the number 4 connotes formation, stability and solidification. With the number 4, one's work and dreams are stressed, and although one's eyes may be on a bigger picture, or the promise of future reward, one must concentrate on what *is* and deal with the practical task(s) at hand.

Constructive: Deliberation. Constructive application. Down-to-earth practicality. Functionality and workability. Building solid, concrete foundations.

Undermining: Impractical dreaming. Pie-in-the-sky risk taking. Too much attention focused on the material aspects of life and not enough on the spirit.

• **What stood out the most in your experience of this card?**

In addition to your recollection, here are some other possibilities you might want to consider:

FOCUS   Were you engaged in activities related to printed material, social situations, financial matters or a business of your own? What were you planning, dreaming about or working toward?

DESIRES   Did you want a sign from the Universe that It supported your endeavors or to know if something you were about to do could be an answer to your prayers?

LOVE   Did you feel cut off or out of touch? Was your partner there for you? Were you determined to make a relationship work no matter what concessions you had to make? Did you go on a blind date or meet someone new? Were you clear about what you wanted in a partner?

OTHERS   Were you disturbed about or contesting a situation that didn't seem right or fair? Did you seek out a qualified professional, spiritual adviser or counselor? Were the people you encountered encouraging? Did you have friends in law enforcement, legal professions or the communications media?

Did someone you didn't expect to hear from phone or call on you? Did you profit through real estate or land ownership? If you worked from home, was it more productive than working in the field? **HOME**

Was travel, getting a passport or something "traveling" *to* you a hassle or disappointment? **TRAVEL**

Was your working environment tense or unpleasant? Did you speak with someone about being in business for yourself, incorporating or reinstating your position? If you were self-employed, was it more profitable than working for others? Did your job entail printing, graphics, drafting or books? **WORK**

Did you, or someone close to you, need glasses or medical attention? Were you treating yourself differently or looking at things from a different perspective? Did you need a respite (or vacation) before an activity could be resumed? **BODY/MIND**

What did you do to keep life from becoming boring or monotonous? What made it all worthwhile? **SPIRIT**

What was your experience with your family? Did you feel that your children were distant or slipping away from you? Was there news of a death or a "message" from someone who had passed on? **RELATIVES**

FINANCES   Was there a financial contention or discrepancy? Was money slow in coming? Were your worries soon over?

PROBLEMS   Were you having problems with the law, an official-type person, red tape or someone who's married?

GUIDANCE   What guidance were you receiving? *How* did it come to you? What phrase or thought were you hearing over and over again? What spoke to your heart?

SUCCESS   What did you need to retreat from or strengthen your position on? What was your greatest achievement?

ACTION   Did you ask or pray for what you wanted or needed and then continue to apply yourself to the work at hand?

- **In light of your experience, what do you believe the Four of Swords signified?**

• **What did you learn from it?**

• **If you drew the Four of Swords in response to a question you asked, in what way did this card answer it?**

• **Now, take another look at your card. Is there anything that stands out about it you didn't notice before?**

• **If you were to make your own Tarot card, what words, pictures or symbols would you put on it?**

SOMETHING TO REFLECT UPON

Have faith in your Father's love for thee and watch things turn out splendidly.

 # THE FIVE OF SWORDS

Swords indicate action, discernment, struggle, sorrow or sickness.

Numerologically, the number 5 indicates change, fluctuations in fate or fortune, conflict, experiential learning and the expansion of one's thinking. With the number 5, opportunities and challenges go hand in hand, and one must look to both the material and spiritual realm if one is to triumph or understand.

Constructive: Discrimination. Resourcefulness. Revision. Re-creation. Self-reliance. Inner conviction.

Undermining: Little faith in one's self or abilities. Panic. Distress. Rebellion.

• **What stood out the most in your experience of this card?**

In addition to your recollection, here are some other possibilities you might want to consider:

FOCUS   Were you working through difficult (astrological) challenges, arduous conditions or tedious tasks? Did you suffer from emotional fatigue or estrangement? Were you surprised by a sudden onslaught of problems or unprepared for the ordeal you had to go through once a course of action was decided upon?

DESIRES   Did you want to walk away from a conflict but felt that if the problem wasn't dealt with, you'd only take it with you? Were you resisting something you knew you had to do or work through? Did you wish you had more confidence?

LOVE   Were you feeling nostalgic over a relationship that ended badly? Were dreams shattered and promises broken? Were you sorry you acted the way you did? Did your heart ache when you were reminded of him/her? Were you having misgivings about someone? Was jealousy a problem?

OTHERS   Did people dismay or disappoint you? Were you cheated or taken advantage of? Did your depression cause you to withdraw from others? How did you treat your friends and loved ones?

Was a delivery delayed? Were there problems with machinery, communication devices or equipment? Did something cost more than you had intended to pay? Were you angry about a property matter? Did someone you were waiting for fail to show up or call? **HOME**

Did you travel for personal reasons or to help another? Did you have car or transportation problems? Was the weather bad? If you were contemplating a long-distance or overseas trip, did you decide not to go? **TRAVEL**

Were you frustrated with your work? Did unforeseen complications foil your plans? Were there far more problems than you anticipated? Did you have no recourse but to accept defeat and wait for conditions to improve? **WORK**

Were you troubled by a recurring problem? Did you get sick *again?* Were you taking more medication or vitamins? Did you need further treatment or an extended rest? Were you uncentered or at war with yourself (or your situation)? **BODY/MIND**

What was going *right?* What wins did you have? **SPIRIT**

Did a relative offer encouragement or give you something you wanted or needed? Were you concerned about a loved one's health or state of mind? Were you waiting for news about someone's (medical) test results? **RELATIVES**

FINANCES   Did you worry about your financial security? Were you shortchanged by an employer or company? Did you lose money through an oversight or an error in your judgment? If so, did it set you back or were you capable of sustaining yourself and, in reality, you were financially solvent?

PROBLEMS   Were you overcome by feelings of futility, failure or defeat? Were you tired of struggling with everything or fighting everyone?

GUIDANCE   Did it occur to you that if/when God wanted you to do something, He would give you the desire for it and the power to do it? Were you resisting your inner guidance? Did the thought cross your mind that even if you didn't see it, God had a plan?

SUCCESS   Did you succeed in some areas but fail in others?

ACTION   Did you have to *will* yourself to be strong? Were you able to push through your turbulent emotions and get to the other side?

- **In light of your experience, what do you believe the Five of Swords signified?**

- **What did you learn from it?**

- **If you drew the Five of Swords in response to a question you asked, in what way did this card answer it?**

- **Now, take another look at your card. Is there anything that stands out about it you didn't notice before?**

- **If you were to make your own Tarot card, what words, pictures or symbols would you put on it?**

SOMETHING TO REFLECT UPON

Sometimes physically distancing ourselves from our problems (even temporarily) is the only way to disengage emotionally long enough to clear our minds and gain a different perspective. When we finally give up, look within and pray for the solution instead of focusing on the problem, our answer comes.

Insanity is doing the same thing over and over, and expecting a different result.

ALBERT EINSTEIN

THE SIX OF SWORDS

Swords indicate action, discernment, struggle, sorrow, or sickness.

Numerologically, the number 6 indicates the need to make adjustments in one's thoughts, attitudes, behavior or condition. While this may feel burdensome, the number 6 also carries with it the ability to transcend difficulties and oftentimes serendipitously. Responsibilities, family and health may also be emphasized.

Constructive: Thoroughness. Resoluteness. Serving, giving or adapting to the needs of others. Love. Compassion.

Undermining: Indifference. Irresponsibility (toward self and others). Fixed opinions, beliefs or attitudes. Imbalance.

• **What stood out the most in your experience of this card?**

In addition to your recollection, here are some other possibilities you might want to consider:

FOCUS   Were you mainly concerned with getting something accomplished? Were partnerships, evaluations or opinions stressed? Were there important changes in your health, profession or relations with others? Who or what was steering *your* ship?

DESIRES   Did you want a relationship, business, or personal matter to be resolved?

LOVE   Did you meet a man/woman you felt you could relate to? Did he/she change your beliefs about love or your experience of loving? Were music, conversation or the arts instrumental in bringing the two of you together? Was the relationship consummated? If not, why?

OTHERS _____

Did you feel that you were at the mercy of others? Did people complain or yell at you? Was your only recourse to master the situation internally?

HOME _____

Did something broken, ripped or not working right need to be repaired? Were there any communication or mechanical breakdowns? Was it hard to get anything done? If you were considering a move or a change within your home, were you having second thoughts?

TRAVEL _____

Did you or another travel? If so, what were the reasons? Were you worried about someone who was traveling? Did news from a distance or a short trip change something for the better?

WORK _____

Did your work go well or did you feel as if you were doing twice as much and producing half the result? Did others make it difficult to pursue your goals? Were there any upsetting issues you had to deal with or confrontations you had to face?

BODY/MIND _____

Did ill health befall you? Were you suffering from stomach upsets, headaches or another affliction? Did complications with medical results or insurance papers arise? Was there a physical necessity you were ignoring? Did you need someone or something to take your mind off your work, routine or problems?

SPIRIT _____ Did you receive a compliment or flattering display of affection? Were there any other benefits? What gave you a sense of satisfaction, self-worth or well-being?

RELATIVES _____ Was there a rift between you and a family member? Did a relative take offense to something you said or the way you said it? Were you being harsh or defensive? Did someone need to make concessions? Did tensions ease off but the problem remain?

FINANCES _____ Were you broke, short of cash or only making a pittance? Did you have trouble collecting money that was owed to you? Did an illness, emotional issue or business disagreement cause a loss of earnings? Was there a fortunate adjustment in a relatively short time?

PROBLEMS _____ Did a promising situation turn out to be a disappointment? Did it seem as if you had a penchant for getting involved in problematical relationships or being attracted to unattainable people? Were you tired of hassles, complications or delays? Did you need to keep your cool or watch your tongue? If you realized that you were acting irrationally, did recognizing the problem keep it from escalating?

GUIDANCE _____ Were you getting the message (internally or through another) that you were heading in the wrong direction? Were you so wrapped up in your projects or the pursuit of your goal that you didn't hear it?

SUCCESS _____ Was the road to success not as smooth as you'd hoped for? Once your goal was in sight, did further obstacles become apparent?

What decisions did you make with regard to your wish? Did problems go away of their own accord or did you have to alter your stance and take action to correct them? Was it to your advantage to ease up, give yourself more time or pay more attention to your intuitive instincts?

ACTION

- In light of your experience, what do you believe the Six of Swords signified?

- What did you learn from it?

- If you drew the Six of Swords in response to a question you asked, in what way did this card answer it?

- Now, take another look at your card. Is there anything that stands out about it you didn't notice before?

- If you were to make your own Tarot card, what words, pictures or symbols would you put on it?

SOMETHING TO REFLECT UPON

Sometimes we must work hard to achieve results but other times we need to cease effort-ing and simply rest.

Ask yourself: "What is the worst that can happen if I stop worrying, pushing or re-acting?"

Now, take a deep breath and imagine that your Higher Power is in control . . . that you are being led into still waters. . . . Let the calming sensation soothe your soul . . . *feel* how good it feels to just let go. . . .

 # THE SEVEN OF SWORDS

Swords indicate action, discernment, struggle, sorrow, or sickness.

Numerologically, the number 7 indicates a period of introspection, analysis or soli-tude. During the influence of the number 7, one's psychological and spiritual resources are expanded and faith in what can't be seen, but nevertheless exists, is demanded.

Constructive: Evaluation, research or investigation. Experimenting and being willing to look at things differently. Waiting for what you want to come to you. Trusting your in-tuition and Higher Self.

Undermining: Pessimism. Separatism. Perfectionism. Living in one's head.

• **What stood out the most in your experience of this card?**

In addition to your recollection, here are some other possibilities you might want to consider:

FOCUS   Were you having trouble applying yourself, making plans or sticking to schedules or appointments? Were you concerned about your health (or the well-being of another)? Was there a problem you were trying to correct or get an answer to? Were conditions unsettled or unstable?

DESIRES

Were you wishing you could sneak away from your work or responsibilities or hoping that someone would call?

LOVE

Did an exciting new romance (or call from a lover) make you feel giddy? Were you involved with, or attracted to, someone you never thought you would be? Was he/she rich, famous or in a much higher (or lower) station in life? Were you facing a situation you felt might put you in a compromising position?

OTHERS

Were you trying to reach someone but not having any luck? Did business people keep you on hold? Were you surprised by the sudden appearance of an old friend or business associate? Did a friend, doctor or acquaintance help you with a problem or steer you in the direction of someone who could?

HOME

Were you feeling pushed or pulled? Did you need to have a talk with your gardeners, maintenance people or groundskeeper? Was a shipment or work order delayed?

TRAVEL

Did you want to take a vacation? Was there tension (or resistance) related to travel plans, scheduling or transportation? Did you or another have to travel alone or sooner than expected?

WORK

Was your work difficult to resolve or conclude? Did you want to get away but something kept pulling you back? Were you a workaholic or too much of a perfectionist? Was it to your advantage to continue applying yourself? If you *weren't* working, what did (or would) you do?

BODY/MIND

Were you dreading a doctor visit or a health matter you had to attend to? Were you (or a relative) having a problem with your breasts or chest? Was your neck stiff or your head aching? Did a muscle relaxer or respite help? Was there a pattern of thinking you were trying to change?

SPIRIT

Did you enjoy being in the company of others? Did something put a smile on your face and a song in your heart? Was a gift of wine, food or music given or received?

RELATIVES

Did a loved one want to be alone for awhile? Did you let him/her know you cared but respected his/her need for space? If there were times when you were at odds with each other and you struggled or argued, deep down, did you love your family and have its welfare at heart?

FINANCE

Did you want to stabilize your finances but have trouble doing it? Were you anxious about money that was delayed or a check you thought was lost? Were you annoyed by little "reminders" or rising (medical) expenses? Did you need to get a second opinion or another estimate? Were there any lucky financial breaks or surreptitious advantages?

Was something bothering you that you just didn't want to contend **PROBLEMS**
with? Were you disappointed in a business associate, lover or friend
who let you down? Do you think you were overlooking something
obvious? Did you need to be more discerning?

    What did you do about it?

Were you beginning to see that there were other ways of looking at **GUIDANCE**
things? Was something (or someone) telling you that you were too
critical of yourself or being too demanding? Did that realization extend to others as well?

Did success come in unexpected ways? Who, what or where did it **SUCCESS**
come from?

Were you able to put things in their proper perspective? Did being **ACTION**
more relaxed about life solve problems faster than struggling with
them? Did you finish what needed to be done and do what you had
to do?

- **In light of your experience, what do you believe the Seven of Swords
  signified?**

- What did you learn from it?

- If you drew the Seven of Swords in response to a question you asked, in what way did this card answer it?

- Now, take another look at your card. Is there anything that stands out about it you didn't notice before?

- If you were to make your own Tarot card, what words, pictures or symbols would you put on it?

SOMETHING TO REFLECT UPON

It's good to set deadlines . . . it's also okay to extend them.
It's good to have goals in life . . . it's also okay to change them.
It's good to strive for perfection . . . it's also okay to be imperfect and make mistakes.
It's good to know our limitations . . . it's also okay to forget them.

THE EIGHT OF SWORDS

Swords indicate action, discernment, struggle, sorrow, or sickness.

Numerologically, the number 8 connotes the potential for success, accomplishment or recognition and the capacity to achieve one's goals, but unless one seeks the Power Within, these may not be easily attained. Although a positive change of mind or status almost always accompanies the number 8, moral integrity, fortitude and emotional equilibrium will also be required.

Constructive: Attending to business, finance and material matters. Asserting one's self or one's authority. Enacting daring plans. Becoming proficient.

Undermining: Strain. Overemotionalism. Oppression. Careless disregard for the spiritual or material realities of life.

• **What stood out the most in your experience of this card?**

In addition to your recollection, here are some other possibilities you might want to consider:

Were you feeling trapped in a situation you couldn't see your way out of or exert any influence over? Did you feel as if you were suddenly plunged into darkness? Were there any losses through (hidden) enemies or unforeseen dangers? **FOCUS**

Did you want to be liberated from an oppressive situation? **DESIRES**

Were you tired of being alone or of having to live without the love you needed in your life? Did you feel boxed in? Were these walls of your own making? Did you have work to do that having a relation- **LOVE** ship might interfere with? Was someone gratifying his/her needs at your expense? Were you tired of being a caretaker?

OTHERS

Did someone say or do something that threw you off balance? Were you upset about what someone *didn't* say or do? Were people working against you? Was there an oppressive (or abusive) person you wanted to get away from? Did you need to be more discriminating in your choice of friends?

HOME

Did you have plumbing or electrical problems? Were there any disturbing incidents? Did you install any safety devices? Did a guest, lover or admirer arrive? If you wanted to sell your house or property, did you get an offer?

TRAVEL

Were your travels extensive? Did you go to a different environment? Were there dangers on the road, near misses or accidents? Was your excursion fortunate in any way?

WORK

Did you dislike your job or feel that your work wasn't going well? Were you feeling stuck or deadlocked? Did you wish you could take some sick leave or walk away from it? Did you have to abandon a project?

BODY/MIND

Were you in mental, physical or emotional distress? Did you need to watch your health or be more cautious? Were sharp objects or electrical gadgets a hazard? Were you a prisoner of your heart or mind?

Did an opportunity come right to your door? Were there any surpris-   **SPIRIT**
ing, positive developments in your business or social life? Did you
have a conversation that lifted your spirits or soothed your soul? Did
a little romance work wonders? Was it with someone new?

Was a friend or family member going through a crisis? If not, was   **RELATIVES**
someone helping you through *yours?* Was somebody (you?) feeling
or acting helpless?

Were you feeling strapped? If you lost money in one area was it made   **FINANCES**
up in another? Did gains come through an investment, profit sharing
or return?

Were you creating difficulties? Were your biggest hurdles your resist-   **PROBLEMS**
ance to what was happening or your fear of what *might* happen?
Were you beginning to see that *events* weren't your worst problem,
your *reaction* to them was?

Did you turn within for strength or guidance? Were you *given* the   **GUIDANCE**
power to overcome your fears or problems? What messages were you
receiving from your Inner Self?

Was there a positive turn of events? If so, what caused it? What gave   **SUCCESS**
you (or *could* give you) the feeling of success? What did (or could)
you give yourself credit for?

ACTION _____   Did you practice inner listening in times of trouble and try to let go of your exacting standards or limiting beliefs about yourself or your abilities? Did you eventually realize that what "shoulda," "woulda," "coulda" been didn't matter? Did you say "no more" and walk away?

_____

- **In light of your experience, what do you believe the Eight of Swords signified?**

- **What did you learn from it?**

- **If you drew the Eight of Swords in response to a question you asked, in what way did this card answer it?**

- **Now, take another look at your card. Is there anything that stands out about it you didn't notice before?**

- **If you were to make your own Tarot card, what words, pictures or symbols would you put on it?**

SOMETHING TO REFLECT UPON

Neither life nor the people in it are predictable, perfect or always fair. Some things will inevitably go wrong or be painful experiences for us.

Experience is a hard teacher because it gives us the test first, the lesson later.

 # THE NINE OF SWORDS

Swords indicate action, discernment, struggle, sorrow, or sickness.

Numerologically, the number 9 stands for completion, arrival, integration and realization. When a number 9 surfaces, it marks a transition between what was and what is to come, a parenthesis in time as one pauses to reflect on all that went before and the unknown potential of that which is yet to be.

Constructive: Broadness of viewpoint, perspective and understanding. Having faith in one's source of supply. Discard. Detachment. Impersonal interaction.

Undermining: Self-centeredness. Dissipation. Suffering.

• **What stood out the most in your experience of this card?**

In addition to your recollection, here are some other possibilities you might want to consider:

Were you grieving over a loved one, going through a crisis or distressed about your future? Did you suddenly feel thwarted when previously things were going well? Did you fear that a cherished plan might be aborted?

FOCUS

DESIRES

Did you wish that something would work out or that you could stop feeling a certain way?

LOVE

Were you in an on-again-off-again relationship? Were you lied to about another woman or man? Was there an uncontrollable separation or breakup? If so, was it caused by an affair? Did you eventually get back together or was the heartbreak so damaging, it could never be repaired? Was your relationship (or relationship status) entering a new phase?

—

OTHERS

Was someone upset about a plan that was canceled? Were you able to count on others when the going got tough?

HOME

Did anything occur that seemed like an omen? Did someone tell you that he/she might be moving in or going away? Was an offer rescinded? Did you need to fix a cooler, waterline or power source? Did someone arrive you were happy to see?

TRAVEL

Were you missing someone who has gone out of your life? Did a person you love go on a trip and leave you behind? Were you hoping that in your travels you'd run into an old flame? Were there problems with airplane tickets or dangers in the air?

WORK

Did something cause you to worry that what you were doing wasn't going to be accepted? Were old ideas reworked? Did a new concept prove to be a life-changing and/or very lucrative idea?

Were you inconsolably depressed? Did you suddenly become ill, sick **BODY/MIND**
to your stomach, perhaps? Did a blood test or work-up turn out to be
negative? Were you an expert at taking care of everyone and everything but yourself? Did your anguish continue?

Did a glimmer of hope or inspiration pierce the darkness? Did you **SPIRIT**
get, accomplish or hear something that brought relief or joy? Were
you surprised by a stroke of good luck? Did most of your fears turn
out to be unfounded?

Did an illness, loss or tragedy befall a friend, loved one or pet? Did a **RELATIVES**
relative (or friend) help you out emotionally or financially?

Were you worried that a source of income was running out? Were **FINANCES**
you upset when bills came or you had expenses you hadn't planned
on? Was money from a new venture or direction coming in? Did your
financial position improve considerably?

Were you trying to understand *why* things were happening as they **PROBLEMS**
were? Did something you said, did or thought come back to haunt
you? Were you filled with despair or regret? Did you wish you could
have a second chance?

Was something or someone telling you to wait and let time take its **GUIDANCE**
course? Were you reminded of a previous event that felt like a failure or
loss but proved to be an opportunity for growth and greater reward?

SUCCESS　　Did new avenues or resources spring from old? Was your wish fulfilled? Did your product or presentation bring substantial gains and supreme success?

ACTION　　What stance did you take?

- In light of your experience, what do you believe the Nine of Swords signified?

- What did you learn from it?

- If you drew the Nine of Swords in response to a question you asked, in what way did this card answer it?

- Now, take another look at your card. Is there anything that stands out about it you didn't notice before?

- If you were to make your own Tarot card, what words, pictures or symbols would you put on it?

SOMETHING TO REFLECT UPON

You may want to record this guided meditation and play it back with your eyes closed.

Imagine that you are sitting in a dark room. . . . Cover your eyes with both hands and focus all of your attention inward . . . the past is now gone and the future is yet to be . . . as you contemplate the stillness, you realize that you are uncomfortable sitting in the darkness. "What is behind me?" you wonder . . . . "What is before me that I can't see?" . . . and as you continue to sit in the silence, you become aware of your breathing . . . the rise and fall of your chest . . . and you realize that you must be in this room to conquer a fear . . . "what am I so afraid of?" you ask yourself . . . "what is causing so much anxiety?" . . . "why does this darkness feel so heavy?" As you ponder these thoughts, a picture the size of an 8 x 10 photograph begins to materialize before you, and you instinctively know that the image beginning to take shape is the outward projection of your fear . . . all of your attention is fixed on this murky image, and as you continue to observe it, the picture becomes sharper and sharper until it's fully in sight. As you look at the image, what do you see? What does your fear look like? What is being revealed to you? Allow yourself to see this clearly, to become aware of every minute detail. . . . And now, as you recognize the full scope of your fear, take your hands away from your face and imagine that they are reaching for the photograph . . . and as your hands come together toward the middle, tear the picture up . . . keep tearing until all the pieces have fallen into the wind and nothing remains but a sigh of relief . . . notice that the room is becoming brighter . . . the walls are disappearing and it doesn't feel as heavy anymore . . . let the lightness come in . . . see the room getting brighter and brighter . . . feel the sense of release . . . the lightness of spirit . . . allow yourself to breath freely for a moment or two, and then, when you are ready, open your eyes. . . .

Man stands in his own shadow and wonders why it's dark.
COMMENTARY ON DOGEN'S KYOJUKAIMON
BY THE REVEREND MASTER JIYU-KENNETT

THE TEN OF SWORDS

Swords indicate action, discernment, struggle, sorrow or sickness.

The 10 in the Tarot marks the end of one phase and the beginning of another. Although it has the same basic meaning as the number 1, it also signifies a time when one may have to come to terms with something that was previously overlooked, unfinished or avoided.

• **What stood out the most in your experience of this card?**

In addition to your recollection, here are some other possibilities you might want to consider:

FOCUS   Had neglected duties, unresolved issues or avoided responsibilities piled up to such an extent that you couldn't move forward until you dealt with them? Did it seem like nothing you did was turning out the way you wanted it to?

DESIRES   Did you hope for the best but fear the worst?

LOVE   Did you realize that you were wasting your time second-guessing your lover's motives, that relationships are hard enough when *both* people are trying? Did you feel that love is like champagne, intoxicating and effervescent, but if shaken up too much it just goes flat? Had you had enough? Were you finally over him/her?

Did someone insult you or burst your bubble? Did you outgrow a **OTHERS**
friendship? Was a conversation you had with someone, or something
somebody did, going over and over in your mind?

Did it seem as if you were always fixing, revising or repairing some- **HOME**
thing? Did bad news come in the mail?

Were your travels uplifting? Did being in different surroundings **TRAVEL**
bring positive changes or a happier outlook?

Did you and another constantly argue? Were there power plays at **WORK**
work? Were you tired of problems, back stabbing or inconclusive
answers? Did you quit? Were you demoted or fired? Was a proposal
declined?

Were you drained by the strain of your work, family or love life? Did **BODY/MIND**
your head or body ache? Did exercise or meditation relieve the tension? Were tears a catharsis?

Did you receive an unexpected gift? What did you take pleasure in? **SPIRIT**

Did you spend money on a relative or help him/her out financially? **RELATIVES**
Was someone always footing the tab?

FINANCES   Was money a sore spot? Did you fear poverty or ruin? If you were in debt or had bad credit, did the problem finally get resolved? Did you receive good news or a gratifying financial surprise?

PROBLEMS   Did events convene in such a way that you were suddenly facing the very thing you hoped to avoid? Did something occur that enabled you to effect changes that were inconceivable before?

GUIDANCE   Did you feel that you weren't always aware of your inner guidance and, consequently, missed important messages or cues? Did you deny the Voice within? Did negative thinking drown it out?

SUCCESS   Did you fear that success would be a long time coming or might not come at all? Once the worst was over, did a new reality begin to dawn?

ACTION   Did you have no recourse but to accept your current predicament and work on changing yourself?

• **In light of your experience, what do you believe the Ten of Swords signified?**

- What did you learn from it?

- If you drew the Ten of Swords in response to a question you asked, in what way did this card answer it?

- Now, take another look at your card. Is there anything that stands out about it you didn't notice before?

- If you were to make your own Tarot card, what words, pictures or symbols would you put on it?

SOMETHING TO REFLECT UPON

Thomas A. Edison was quoted as saying, "I am not discouraged, because every wrong attempt discarded is another step forward."

In our darkest hour, when our dreams are crushed and our efforts have failed, that is when we need to trust ourselves and our God the most. No matter what the appearance, our experience today *is* preparing us for a brighter tomorrow. We may have the right dream, but the wrong person; or we might need to create a bigger dream, or our timing could simply be off. Whatever the case, we need to remember that even though we think we know what the future holds, God's works are like a puzzle and we can't see the whole picture until all the pieces are in.

THE PAGE OF SWORDS

Astrological Sign: Taurus

Taurus rules the second house and activities related to one's finances and personal resources (income, earning capacity, how one meets obligations, hidden talents); possessions and whom or what one values; material security, and the desire for emotional
stability through people and things. (Note: Because the element associated with the suit of
Swords is air, Aquarius is also attributed to this card. How did *you* experience it?)

Time frame: April 20–May 20

Type: Patient. Persevering. Deliberate. Determined. Methodical. Diligent. Sensual.

Thrust: The physical world. Grounding. Practicality. Protecting assets. Preserving
the status quo.

Cornerstone: To have and hold

Life lesson: Detachment and/or adaptability

Swords indicate action, discernment, struggle, sorrow or sickness.

Pages are commonly referred to as messengers, children or youths, but they can also represent one's maturing self, lovers or problems.

The Page of Swords connotes a person who is bright, perceptive and thoughtful.
He/she may show little emotion on the surface but feels things deeply and genuinely cares
about the welfare of others. Albeit a little naive, this Page can *grow* into brilliance and
eventually have it all. Traditionally, Swords represent a person with brown or black hair
and brown eyes.

Did you feel that you resembled this card type? Have you recently come in contact
with someone who does?

• **What stood out the most in your experience of this card?**

In addition to your recollection, here are some other possibilities you might want to
consider:

Were you struggling to achieve your goals? Did you worry about what tomorrow may bring or your ability to handle something you sensed you were going to have to deal with? Was your self-esteem determined by the things you possessed, the people you were involved with or the job title you held? Was *how* obligations were met, ends were achieved or resources were utilized important to you?

FOCUS

Did you wish you could walk away from or forget a painful relationship or *make* something that wasn't working, work?

DESIRES

Were you or your lover having problems coping with the feelings the relationship was stirring up? Was someone torn between love or money? Was the truth about a situation revealed? If you were on the verge of breaking up, did the relationship end or did the two of you make up? Were there any surprising changes or positive developments?

LOVE

Did you stay cool, calm and collected when people or conditions opposed you, or did you get upset and lose your temper? Did you resent anyone who tried to change you or force you to alter your plans? Were there unexpected complications in your business or personal affairs? Was a significant adjustment made? Did the pressure ease off?

OTHERS

Were you preparing to travel or returning from a trip? Did anything significant occur when you arrived or returned home? Were you considering a roommate or thinking about renting your house? Did being at home (or having your own home) make you feel more secure? Did an old friend stop by or drop you a line? Did a message, phone call or the return of a lover change things for the better?

HOME

TRAVEL   Was someone traveling to see you? If you planned an outing, did an unexpected event delay your departure? Did weather conditions change and suddenly become cold? Did something disturb or disappoint you? Was there danger near water?

WORK   Vocations suited for a Taurean type are anything related to comfort, beauty, art or finances; interior decorator; realtor; plastic surgeon; wine or food merchant; banker; fund-raiser; ecologist; geologist; commercial artist; singer; musician; art dealer; florist.

Do any of these professions sound like something you're doing or would like to do? Did you speak to, or associate with, someone who worked in one of these trades?

Did you want cooperation in business or to be more successful, effective, or productive? Did emotional or relationship problems interfere? If your work wasn't motivating, cost-effective or inspiring, did you drop it or not show up, or did you stick it out and finish what you started?

BODY/MIND   Health issues associated with a Taurean type are throat, neck and thyroid gland; vocal cords; laryngitis; tonsillitis; weight; ears; lower jaw; chin; mumps; abscesses.

Have you experienced problems related to any of these areas recently? Has anyone close to you?

Did your throat, jaw or gums bother you? Were you concerned about your weight? If you were craving sweets, did you need more sweetness (love and tenderness, etc.) in your life? Were you more tac-

tile, sensual or overtly sexual than usual? Did you consider yourself
to be a healthy person?

SPIRIT

Did you enjoy working on creative (or expressive) projects, buying
extravagant gifts or flirting with others? If you needed practical or
emotional support, did you receive it? Did you experience a new beginning or have a new lease on life? If so, what caused it?

RELATIVES

Was someone in your family traveling or living abroad? Did spending
time with your relatives help you understand yourself? Did someone
buy you a gift or do something thoughtful for you? Were you proud
of a family member, child or pet?

FINANCES

Did it seem as if there was never enough money to go around? Did
you wish you were rich? Did you live within your means? Were you
concerned about your (or someone else's) financial condition or earning capacity? If your affairs were unsettled, did they get straightened
out?

PROBLEMS

The negative characteristics of a Taurean type are possessiveness,
jealousy, laziness, stubbornness, superficiality (or identifying with
the wrong things), sudden bursts of anger or anger that is hard to ap-
pease.

Did you see these traits in yourself or notice them in another?
What troubles or disappointments were you experiencing?

GUIDANCE   Did you trust that what you couldn't see or understand would be revealed to you? If you heard or thought something negative, did someone or something tell you not to believe it?

SUCCESS   Did attaining your goal(s) come through deliberate effort, workable ideas or the gradual wearing down of obstacles? Were successful conclusions reached?

ACTION   Did you make choices that promoted self-growth, self-esteem or productivity even if your heart wasn't in it or you were not inspired? If you didn't like the position you were in, did you do something to change it?

• In light of your experience, what do you believe the Page of Swords signified?

• What did you learn from it?

• If you drew the Page of Swords in response to a question you asked, in what way did this card answer it?

- Now, take another look at your card. Is there anything that stands out about it you didn't notice before?

- If you were to make your own Tarot card, what words, pictures or symbols would you put on it?

SOMETHING TO REFLECT UPON

Take a moment and think about the problem, behavior or condition you can't seem to release. . . . Once it's clear in your mind, ask yourself: "How is this (pain, pessimism, fill in the blank) serving me? What am I getting out of it?" Then ask yourself: "What would happen if I no longer had this problem, behavior or condition?"

The intellect has little to do on the road to discovery. There comes a leap in consciousness, call it intuition or what you will, and the solution comes to you and you don't know how or why.

ALBERT EINSTEIN

 # THE KNIGHT OF SWORDS

Knights symbolize comings or goings, beginnings or endings and direction of thoughts or energy. When a Knight appears, long-term conditions will change.

There is no astrological or numerological correlation to the Knights.

Swords indicate action, discernment, struggle, sorrow or sickness.

- What stood out the most in your experience of this card?

In addition to your recollection, here are some other possibilities you might want to consider:

FOCUS   Did you feel that your reality had changed? Were you moving into a more active or productive period? Who or what was *rushing* into your life? Were there any agitating influences?

DESIRES   Did you establish a link with someone (or something) and want the chain of events to continue?

LOVE   Was there a new (or renewed) romance in your life? Were you swept up in a powerful love affair or seduced by a charming, disarming admirer who won you over with his/her persistence, tenderness or generosity? Were *you* the seducer? Did you ask someone out? Was there a meeting of hearts and minds? Were you happier or more at peace with yourself when you were loved? Did you think your relationship was (or could be) an enduring one?

OTHERS   Were you primarily involved with professional people? Did others rush to your aid? Did you meet someone who could subsidize you, manage your affairs or make you successful? Did you hear of an illness or death?

HOME   Did a service person, policeman or lover come to your home? Were you waiting for important news or for the arrival of someone? Did you do more entertaining? Were you away from home a great deal of the time? Was there a positive change in your environment?

Did you have several short trips to make or errands to run? Did you travel with a sweetheart? Did a lover or loved one return from a trip and call on you?

TRAVEL

Did you receive good news about your work? Were you rising from obscure status to a more prominent position? Did you begin a new venture, start a new job or connect with someone who could further your career goals?

WORK

Were you feeling positive and optimistic? Did the intervention of another bring these feelings about? Did you make any impulsive decisions? Did your sex life change?

BODY/MIND

Did someone (or something) cause your spirits to soar? Were you lucky in love or money matters?

SPIRIT

Were you and a family member discussing a matter of grave importance? Were you trying to sort out your feelings regarding one of your relatives or wondering what to do?

RELATIVES

Did you feel that you were prospering? Did your earnings or assets increase? Was there a substantial improvement? If so, who or what caused it?

FINANCES

PROBLEMS   Were you apprehensive about something? Did you worry that you wouldn't reach your destination or somebody wasn't going to follow through? Was someone going (or about to go) out of your life? Did your concerns cause you to seek guidance or advice? Did you receive a clear answer or direction?

GUIDANCE   Were you more in tune with your inner Self? What were you doing to make your connection stronger? Did you recently learn something you were putting into practice? What insights did you have?

SUCCESS   Were you experiencing a time of increased awareness, prosperity or influence? Was there an exciting turn of events in your love life, profession or lifestyle? Did you gain influence, support or esteem? Were you suddenly making great strides? Did you feel as though you attracted success?

ACTION   Did you proceed confidently and determinedly?

- **In light of your experience, what do you believe the Knight of Swords signified?**

- **What did you learn from it?**

- If you drew the Knight of Swords in response to a question you asked, in what way did this card answer it?

- Now, take another look at your card. Is there anything that stands out about it you didn't notice before?

- If you were to make your own Tarot card, what words, pictures or symbols would you put on it?

SOMETHING TO REFLECT UPON

Expect the best. Your prayers have already been answered; you just don't know it yet.

◆   # THE QUEEN OF SWORDS

Astrological Sign: Virgo

Virgo rules the sixth house and activities related to one's work (performance, working conditions, obtaining or holding a job, relationship with coworkers); service (giving of self, usefulness, the way one treats those who serve); health (physical needs, attitude toward, how one copes with challenges). (Note: Because the element associated with the suit of Swords is air, Libra is also attributed to this card. How did *you* experience it?)

    Time frame: August 23–September 22
    Type: Vigilant. Logical. Serious. Reserved. Meticulous. Discriminating. Self-reliant.
    Thrust: Efficiency. Service. Dissecting the nature of things. Improving. Discarding.

Cornerstone: To analyze and perfect
Life lesson: Tolerance
Swords indicate action, discernment, struggle, sorrow or sickness.

The Queen of Swords depicts one who is strong in character, intensely perceptive and wise beyond her/his years. Although this Queen has great depth, her/his complex personality makes her/him difficult to fathom. This is a person who has known exquisite happiness but may currently be suffering a great loss. The Queen of Swords is also referred to as one who is childless, widowed or divorced. Traditionally, Swords represent a person with brown or black hair and brown eyes.

Did you feel that you resembled this card type? Have you recently come in contact with someone who does?

• **What stood out the most in your experience of this card?**

In addition to your recollection, here are some other possibilities you might want to consider:

FOCUS   Was your energy on any of the sixth house activities listed? Were you taking stock of your life or examining the way you've dealt with adversity? Were you becoming more aware of the growth process and the importance of detachment? Did you recently have a spiritual awakening? Were you maturing through experience?

DESIRES   Were you hoping you could keep the faith or continue to trust the process?

LOVE   Were you mourning the loss of someone you loved? Were you worried that he/she was everything you ever dreamed of, and you'd never find someone like him/her or love that way again? Did you prefer to remain single rather than lower your standards? Did the thought cross your mind that change or alone time was necessary for you to devote more attention to your spiritual development or to raise your present relationship experience to a higher, healthier or more accepting level?

OTHERS

Were you drawn to people who were intellectually stimulating? Did you feel alone even when you weren't? Was there news of a separation, illness or death? Did you and another have a discussion about dying? How did you treat others?

HOME

Did you live alone? Were you self-sufficient? If something needed to be done, could you do it on your own? Was something repaired at a minimal price or no (extra) cost to you?

TRAVEL

Were your journeys inner ones? If you made travel plans, were there any detours or changes? Could you write off your travel expenses? Was a loved one considering a job change that meant leaving you alone or moving to another state?

WORK

Vocations suited for a Virgo type are anything relating to health, medicine or analysis; dietitian; (massage) therapist; metaphysician (astrologer, numerologist, yoga teacher, etc.); librarian; veterinarian; scientist; researcher; critic; computer operator, programmer or technician; secretary.

Do any of these professions sound like something you're doing or would like to do? Did you speak to, or associate with, someone who worked in one of these trades?

Did you want your job to serve a useful purpose? Did you feel that you needed to work in order to justify your existence? Did you tend to take on more than you could safely manage? Did simple tasks turn into Cecil B. DeMille productions? Were you looking for a new line of work or waiting for something to arrive or develop?

BODY/MIND

Health issues associated with a Virgo type are intestines, bowels, stomach, solar plexus, colitis, hands, skin eruptions, food intake and assimilation, diarrhea, nervous disorders, anorexia nervosa or bulimia.

Have you experienced problems related to any of these areas recently? Has anyone close to you?

Were you more concerned with your health, diet, nutrition, hygiene, etc.? Did a health problem interfere with your ability to function effectively? Were you happy with your physical appearance, age or professional status? Do you think you were undemonstrative? Did you feel sexually inhibited or repressed?

SPIRIT

Did you feel that frivolous activities were a waste of time or money? Did you enjoy your own company? Did you like doing things alone? Did you receive guidance through your dreams?

Were you and your family close or were you on your own? Did you feel that you had become your mother? Were there any problems or losses with regard to children, childbearing or pets? **RELATIVES**

Were you keeping a record of your expenses? Did anyone owe you money? Were agreements being honored? What were your thoughts or feelings regarding your financial condition? **FINANCES**

The negative characteristics of a Virgo type are skepticism; lack of faith; worrying; being overly critical, finicky or picky; insecurity; strain. **PROBLEMS**
    Did you see these traits in yourself or notice them in another? What troubles or disappointments were you experiencing?

Were you seeking a higher understanding or learning to discern the difference between true guidance (the intuitive voice that gently persists, calms and reassures) and "should" guidance (the voice that shouts, nags, argues and creates inner unrest)? Did you have faith when appearances told you not to? **GUIDANCE**

Were your accomplishments great? Through faith and perseverance, did success finally come? **SUCCESS**

Did you feel that even though you were going with the flow, sometimes you had to paddle a little harder to keep from sinking? **ACTION**

- In light of your experience, what do you believe the Queen of Swords signified?

- What did you learn from it?

- If you drew the Queen of Swords in response to a question you asked, in what way did this card answer it?

- Now, take another look at your card. Is there anything that stands out about it you didn't notice before?

- If you were to make your own Tarot card, what words, pictures or symbols would you put on it?

SOMETHING TO REFLECT UPON

Faith is like a muscle; the more we exercise it the stronger it gets.

THE KING OF SWORDS

Astrological Sign: Libra

Libra rules the seventh house and activities related to partnerships (marriage, personal and business); interactions with the public (social awareness, the effect others have on one's emotional stability); contracts, agreements, legal affairs or the law (including the law of cause and effect, reaping what one sows, etc.).

Time frame: September 23–October 22

Type: Charming. Easygoing. Agreeable. Humanitarian. Sensitive. Sentimental. Selfless.

Thrust: Justice. Fairness. Compassion. Relationships. Teamwork. Distilling experiences. Peace and harmony.

Cornerstone: To balance

Life lesson: Courage and/or decisiveness

Swords indicate action, discernment, struggle, sorrow or sickness.

The King of Swords represents an authority figure whose high-minded ideas, sense of fair play and controlled reactions make him/her a person others look up to. He/she seems dualistic in nature because while he/she craves companionship, friends and gaiety, his/her hardworking, serious approach to life leaves little room for romance and pleasure. Although he/she appears to be cold, unbending or severe, this is a person who can be easily hurt by others and may not be as confident as one might think. Traditionally, Swords represent a person with brown or black hair and brown eyes.

Did you feel that you resembled this card type? Have you recently come in contact with someone who does?

• **What stood out the most in your experience of this card?**

In addition to your recollection, here are some other possibilities you might want to consider:

Were you dealing with government matters, legal issues or an au- **FOCUS** thority figure? Were you experiencing inner or external conflicts? Did you worry about making a living or getting ahead in life? Were you learning to be more open, loving, trusting or compassionate? Were you contemplating your effect upon others or how your attitude shapes your world?

DESIRES

Did you wish you had a more peaceful home life or relaxed working environment? Were you looking for a life mate or sponsor? Did you want to see things differently or gain a new perspective?

LOVE

Were you dating or married to someone in a legal, government or military profession? Was your relationship sustaining or was it incapable of quenching little more than your thirst for romance or companionship? If you were having difficulties, do you think that you may be blind to the truth about the situation or living in a dream world?

OTHERS

Did you have more contact with the public? Were you enlarging your circle of friends or analyzing your interactions with them? Did you need to feel that you belonged or that you were part of the group? Were you emotionally guarded or so caught up in defending your position that you failed to notice how others felt? Did you incur any losses through thieves, opportunists, unscrupulous business partners or fraudulent contracts?

HOME

Were you uncomfortable in an inharmonious or unkempt environment? Were you thinking of moving in with someone, getting a roommate or doing something to reduce your expenses?

Did you need to be more cautious in your travels? Was someone tail-gating you? Were there any roadblocks or traffic jams? Did you have to find an alternate route? Did you forget something? Were you trying to?   **TRAVEL**

Vocations suited for a Libra type are anything related to people, beauty, the military or the law; marriage counselor; diplomat; medi-ator; hostess; employment agent; artisan; jeweler; cosmetologist; sound engineer; set designer; soldier; lawyer; judge; policeman.   **WORK**

   Do any of these professions sound like something you're doing or would like to do? Did you speak to, or associate with, someone who worked in one of these trades?

   Were you apprehensive about your work? Did you feel that you were going to have to work long and hard before your efforts panned out? Were your sales, presentations or job interviews going well? Was your working environment austere?

Health issues associated with a Libra type are kidneys, ovaries, loins, lower back, knees, urinary tract, skin disorders or rashes, stomach or colon, diabetes.   **BODY/MIND**

   Have you experienced problems related to any of these areas re-cently? Has anyone close to you?

   Did you crave starchy foods or fruits? Did you have a low-grade infection or virus? Were you taking anti-inflammatory drugs? Did you tend to worry a lot? Were you fighting to overcome a fear or a sense of foreboding? Were you overly concerned about your health or the health of another? Were you more perceptive than you were at other times?

SPIRIT

Did you have a change of heart or perspective? What brought you the most enjoyment?

RELATIVES

Was there friction between you and a family member? Did you have a difficult time getting a relative (or child) to do what you wanted him/her to do? Were you able to get the help or cooperation you sought? Did you have a discussion about money? Did a relative (or pet) who's been contrary or indifferent become more kind or loving?

FINANCES

Were you troubled by a delay in a legal or financial matter? Did you worry about making ends meet, the credibility of another or the IRS?

PROBLEMS

The negative characteristics of a Libra type are indecisiveness, insincerity, self-indulgence, fickleness, snobbishness, intolerance, uncooperativeness.

Did you see these traits in yourself or notice them in another? What troubles or disappointments were you experiencing?

GUIDANCE

Did you feel that you were in touch with your Higher Power? If you were ignoring your intuition or gut feelings, did doing so prove to be a time-consuming or costly mistake? Did you get the impression that more inner work needed to be done before you'd have the relationship you wanted or you were more effective in the world?

SUCCESS

Did attaining success feel like an uphill battle?

Did you carry on despite the trials or difficulties you had to endure?   **ACTION**

• In light of your experience, what do you believe the King of Swords signified?

• What did you learn from it?

• If you drew the King of Swords in response to a question you asked, in what way did this card answer it?

• Now, take another look at your card. Is there anything that stands out about it you didn't notice before?

• If you were to make your own Tarot card, what words, pictures or symbols would you put on it?

SOMETHING TO REFLECT UPON

Imagine that you were just told that you were an angel and your mission in life was to uplift others and help to bring peace and harmony into their lives. . . . How would you go about it? How would you touch their hearts? What kind of an angel would you be?

Close your eyes and think back on the people you met during your day or week; what might you have done differently? How would you have felt about yourself knowing you were *really* an angel?

THE
PENTACLES

YOUR QUERY SHEET

You can use this query sheet in addition to your weekly notes for questions you may have during the course of your workbook experience and in times to come.

Date:	Card:	Your Questions and Answers:
		Q:
		A:
		Q:
		A:
		Q:
		A:
		Q:
		A:
		Q:
		A:
		Q:
		A:
		Q:
		A:
		Q:
		A:
		Q:
		A:
		Q:
		A:
		Q:
		A:
		Q:
		A:
		Q:
		A:
		Q:
		A:
		Q:
		A:
		Q:
		A:
		Q:
		A:

THE ACE OF PENTACLES

Pentacles deal with tangibles and issues involving money, manifestation, values or power.

Aces represent new beginnings; they also signify a season. The Ace of Pentacles represents the spring—March, April, May.

What season is it now? _____ What season does it *feel* like? _____

Numerologically, Aces correspond with the number 1 indicating fresh starts, invention, creativity, originality, independence, force and will. During the influence of the number 1, ideas, opportunities and new projects begin to flourish, and although one may know *what* one needs to do, it may take courage or daring to follow through.

Constructive: Confidence. Determination. Assuming responsibility. Strengthening one's abilities and sense of self. Singular effort.

Undermining: Willfulness. Unreasonable force. Fear of taking the initiative, promoting one's self or standing on one's own. Discouragement.

• **What stood out the most in your experience of this card?**

In addition to your recollection, here are some other possibilities you might want to consider:

Was your focus on investments of time or money, potential partnerships, love affairs or pleasure? Were new things replacing old? Did you feel as though you were moving into a brand new arena of untapped potentiality? Were ideas becoming tangible realities?

FOCUS _____

Did you want something that was cut off, cut back or completely severed to "spring" back to life or be replaced by something better?

DESIRES _____

Were your thoughts turning to romance? Did you want to have a significant love affair? Did you meet someone who piqued your inter-

LOVE _____

est? Was there something different about him/her? If you were in a committed relationship, did you wish your partner would be more responsive? Did you think about getting involved with someone else? If you thought you were at the end of your rope, did conditions take a turn for the better? Did a relationship you thought was over start up again?

OTHERS

Did you hear from or call on an old friend or acquaintance? Did you make new friends easily? Were you unwilling to spend your time with people who didn't support the way you wanted to feel about yourself? Were you invited to a social event, dinner party or fund-raising benefit?

HOME

Did you purchase (or were you enjoying) an entertaining commodity, something you couldn't afford before or a new house? Did you have a happy home life? Were you content?

TRAVEL

Did money, or good news about money, come from afar? Were you considering a trip or move to the South?

WORK

Were you feeling confident about your work? If you'd been in a lull, was there a new beginning or sudden surge of activity? Did you embark on a new enterprise or start a company of your own? What paths were open to you?

BODY/MIND

Were you a positive thinker? Were you in great shape? Did you experiment with any new age, natural or herbal treatments? If you were previously in poor health, were you on the road to recovery?

SPIRIT

Did you do things just for the heck of it or take time out to play and enjoy yourself? Did a guru visit you in a dream? What was enriching your life?

RELATIVES

Were you and your family experiencing better times, better health and improved conditions? What did you cherish most?

FINANCES

Did you receive a substantial sum of money? Was it through a time investment, something stemming from the past or a contractual agreement? Did you spend more freely? Were you a Wall Street whiz or a shrewd barterer? What financial opportunities were presented to you?

PROBLEMS

Were you experiencing a time of material or financial reversals? Did you need to redo something that wasn't done right the first time? If you came to a dead end, was it because you ignored your intuition, lacked sufficient knowledge or needed to be more patient?

GUIDANCE

Were you becoming more aware of the power of your mind? Did you notice that the things you thought or said were producing a corresponding material response? If you were thinking or saying negatives like "give me a break" or "I'm sick of (fill in the blank)," did machinery coincidentally break down? Did you become physically ill?

SUCCESS _____   Did success come through pleasurable pursuits and profitable investments of your time, money or energy? Did a long shot pay off?

ACTION _____   How were you demonstrating your power? Were you growing flowers or weeds?

_____

- In light of your experience, what do you believe the Ace of Pentacles
signified?

- What did you learn from it?

- If you drew the Ace of Pentacles in response to a question you asked, in what
way did this card answer it?

- Now, take another look at your card. Is there anything that stands out about
it you didn't notice before?

- If you were to make your own Tarot card, what words, pictures or symbols
would you put on it?

SOMETHING TO REFLECT UPON

Sitting quietly, doing nothing, spring comes and the grass grows by itself.
ZEN MASTER, ZENRIN

◆ THE TWO OF PENTACLES

Pentacles deal with tangibles and issues involving money, manifestation, values or power.

Numerologically, the number 2 connotes assimilation, balancing polarities and dealing with unknowns. When the number 2 is present, partial success can be realized, but one may also find oneself having to repeat previous lessons or experiences in order to eliminate flaws or continue to progress. Reunions, reconciliations and an element of surprise could also be indicated.

Constructive: Patience. Tolerance. Cooperation. Nurturing, developing or refining what one has before commencing something new. Combined efforts. Personal interaction.

Undermining: Impatience. One-sidedness. Isolation. Lack of commitment or steady purpose.

• **What stood out the most in your experience of this card?**

In addition to your recollection, here are some other possibilities you might want to consider:

Were you experiencing emotional tribulation due to business ordeals **FOCUS**
or ineffective personal, verbal or written efforts? Was your schedule

difficult to manage? Were you trying to maintain balance in the midst of uncertainty?

DESIRES

Did you want a material thing or a solution to a dilemma?

LOVE

Did you feel star-crossed in matters of the heart or want more from a relationship than you were getting? Were your desires and what you knew you *had* to do creating conflict? Did you have a romantic change of heart? If so, did a new element (or person) bring the change about?

OTHERS

Were you waiting to get word from someone you were having an ongoing discussion with? Were your initial impressions right? Did a female help when others couldn't?

HOME

Did activities at home or work occupy most of your time? Did your plans seem to go awry? Were you wondering if you should give up your apartment or put your house on the market?

TRAVEL

Did you get a job assignment that required you to travel? Did you have an expense account? Were you up in the air about a trip? Did you entertain the thought of buying a new car?

WORK

Were you discouraged by a project that wasn't moving as fast as you thought it should or producing the result you wanted? If you were losing your incentive, did something happen to renew your enthusiasm?

Did you feel as if you were between a rock and a hard place? Did you **BODY/MIND**
have a difficult time keeping your emotions on an even keel? Were you
trying to keep your weight down but snacking was keeping it up? Were
you experiencing "brain drain" or tension-related problems (shortness of breath, stiffness in your shoulders, grinding your teeth, etc.)?

Did you have a dream that came true? Did a gift completely change **SPIRIT**
your perspective or win over the heart of the person you gave it to?
Did you believe that "what goes around comes around"?

Did you spend quality time with your loved ones or were you too **RELATIVES**
busy or preoccupied?

Were you lucky in financial matters? Did a favorable outcome hinge **FINANCES**
on your ability to persuade others or negotiate a deal or settlement
that was agreeable to all? If you applied for credit, did you get it? Did
you have a sudden impulse to go shopping? Did you want to buy
music, cassettes, CDs or video equipment?

Was something you wanted delayed? Were you frustrated by the fact **PROBLEMS**
that the news you were waiting for didn't arrive or you weren't able
to connect with the one you wanted to see or talk to? Was an agreement broken? Was legal action taken over a breach of contract?

If you had a need did you ask for assistance? Did God help you when **GUIDANCE**
you helped yourself?

SUCCESS   Were you able to manifest the results you wanted? Did good prevail?

ACTION   Was it more important to focus on what was done or that which
                         could be seen or touched rather than what was said or implied? Did
                         you make a decision?

- In light of your experience, what do you believe the Two of Pentacles
  signified?

- What did you learn from it?

- If you drew the Two of Pentacles in response to a question you asked, in what
  way did this card answer it?

- Now, take another look at your card. Is there anything that stands out about
  it you didn't notice before?

- If you were to make your own Tarot card, what words, pictures or symbols
  would you put on it?

SOMETHING TO REFLECT UPON

Nothing can be gained by worrying as it will only cause distress. What if more could be attained by putting your mind to rest?

> *Consider the lilies of the field, they neither toil nor spin.*
> MATTHEW 6:28

 # THE THREE OF PENTACLES

Pentacles deal with tangibles and issues involving money, manifestation, values or power.

Numerologically, the number 3 indicates expressing one's self, creating, externalizing and relating. With the number 3, group activities or situations involving more than one person are usually emphasized. Although the 3 brings conditions to fruition, there may also be some delay. Growth of an inner, emotional nature is also indicated.

Constructive: Synthesizing. Conceptualizing. Becoming more selective or giving something your all. Embracing the lighter side of life. Keeping a positive, optimistic frame of mind. Allowing events to unfold.

Undermining: Ennui. Scattering energies. Overreacting or overindulging. Refusing to accept life on life's terms.

• **What stood out the most in your experience of this card?**

In addition to your recollection, here are some other possibilities you might want to consider:

FOCUS

Did the focus of your activities revolve around communications, meetings, groups and career goals? Were you discovering, completely absorbed in or carried away by something new?

DESIRES

Were you seeking agreement or financial backing? Did you want to improve the quality of your work, relationship with another or your spiritual life?

LOVE

Were you open to love or new opportunities? Were you involved with someone who met your relationship needs? If so, did he/she feel the same about you? Were you both ready to make a commitment? Did you discuss living together? Were you making plans for your future?

OTHERS

Did you have caring friends and associate with interesting people? Did you attend any community meetings or public gatherings? Did an emissary from a group or company call on you? Who did you want to spend your time or share your accomplishments with?

HOME

Were you engrossed in your work or pursuing pleasurable activities you could do from, or close to, home?

TRAVEL

Did you take a short trip or leave home (or a vacation) sooner than you would have preferred? Did someone from another city or state travel to see you? Did your environment promote your objectives?

Were you a seasoned communicator or artisan? Were you dedicated to your craft? Did good news arrive concerning a business venture or proposal? Were there any revisions or concessions you had to make? Did (or could) you market what you created, invented or wrote? Were you proud of your work and achievements?

WORK

Were you feeling happier or more sociable than usual? Was there an absence of inner conflict or discord? How were you growing? What part of you was still evolving?

BODY/MIND

Did you love your work and your life? What did you most enjoy doing?

SPIRIT

Did a relative help you in your business? Was anyone seeking counsel, credit or legal aid? Were you happy when your family was happy? Did you go into something new together or work toward a common goal?

RELATIVES

Did you spend more money or buy office equipment, business staples or art supplies? Was a check due to arrive shortly? Were you hoping for long-term profits? Was an investment paying off? Did your stock(s) go up (or down)?

FINANCES

Were you troubled by a meeting or conversation you had with another? Were you lazy, easily sidetracked or unfocused? Did you eat,

PROBLEMS

drink, smoke or work too much? If so, was it to compensate for a lack you were feeling?

GUIDANCE

Did you wish you were more aware of your Inner Guidance, or that the still small voice within was a bit (a lot) louder?

SUCCESS

Were your activities productive and your discussions profitable? Were you given something you felt was a godsend?

ACTION

Were you determined to do whatever it took to accomplish your goal, sell your idea(s) or get your point across? Was what you wanted to achieve worth the effort you put into it or the compromises you had to make?

• **In light of your experience, what do you believe the Three of Pentacles signified?**

• **What did you learn from it?**

- If you drew the Three of Pentacles in response to a question you asked, in what way did this card answer it?

- Now, take another look at your card. Is there anything that stands out about it you didn't notice before?

- If you were to make your own Tarot card, what words, pictures or symbols would you put on it?

SOMETHING TO REFLECT UPON

Being more spiritual doesn't mean that our heads are in the clouds, our feet no longer touch the ground and we abandon our earthly pursuits. On the contrary, it means bringing heaven down to earth by tuning in to the God in us and becoming more aware of our intuitive guidance and inner resources.

We don't have to drive to a church or a temple or an ashram to feel closer to our God; we can create a hallowed space at home. Whether it's a candle burning atop a table or a chair in the kitchen, wherever we seek Him *becomes* a sacred place. God doesn't care *where* we are, what religion we belong to or what condition we come to Him in; He cares only that we come. . . . And the more *we* commune with Him, the more active our awareness of His presence in our lives becomes.

Thou wouldst not seek Me if thou hadst not already found Me.
                                                    BLAISE PASCAL

THE FOUR OF PENTACLES

Pentacles deal with tangibles and issues involving money, manifestation, values or power.

Numerologically, the number 4 connotes formation, stability and solidification. With the number 4, one's work and dreams are stressed, and although one's eyes may be on a bigger picture, or the promise of future reward, one must concentrate on what *is* and deal with the practical task(s) at hand.

Constructive: Deliberation. Constructive application. Down-to-earth practicality. Functionality and workability. Building solid, concrete foundations.

Undermining: Impractical dreaming. Pie-in-the-sky risk taking. Too much attention focused on the material aspects of life and not enough on the spirit.

• **What stood out the most in your experience of this card?**

In addition to your recollection, here are some other possibilities you might want to consider:

FOCUS   Were financial matters, accretion or career goals a focal point? Did every penny or action count? Was personal performance or effectiveness an issue? Were you thinking about, or affected by, a new relationship or partner?

DESIRES   Did you hope that the people you dealt with would be congenial or that something you had begun would work out, last or succeed?

LOVE   Were there obstacles to circumvent (logistics, business, geography, other priorities)? Were you detached or uncommitted? Did your heart belong to someone (or some*thing*) else?

Did the important people in your life respond as soon as, or in the way that, you hoped they would?   **OTHERS** _____

Did you think you needed to get out more? Did you make any long-distance phone calls? Did anything significant occur?   **HOME** _____

Did you take any short trips or travel for financial reasons? Were papers involved? Did you buy a car or something for your car?   **TRAVEL** _____

Was your heart in your work? If not, why? Did you continue anyway? Were any improvements or professional advancements made?   **WORK** _____

Did you think you needed to steer your energy into more positive, constructive or emotionally-gratifying channels? Did a health condition (mental or physical) halt any of your activities? If so, was it of a long duration? Did you need to consult a physician?   **BODY/MIND** _____

Did you give, receive or exchange a gift? Was luck with you in getting what you wanted? What were you pleased about? Did being generous with your money or possessions make you happy?   **SPIRIT** _____

Did your family assist you or champion your cause? Were you thinking about (or mourning) the death of a loved one or pet?   **RELATIVES** _____

FINANCES   Were you bartering, trading or looking for investors? Did someone assist you or come to your aid? Did you get the money or product you wanted?

PROBLEMS   Were you troubled by something that wasn't working out the way you thought it should or as soon as you wanted it to? Was money delayed or held up by a bank, company policy or lender? Were you and your lover/mate (sexually) incompatible?

GUIDANCE   Did it occur to you that the results you wanted depended upon your priorities and the value you put on yourself? How much do you think you, your time or what you want are worth?

SUCCESS   Were you able to take something unworkable, useless or mediocre and turn it into something useful, valuable or profound? Were your business transactions successful? Did you succeed in forming a new partnership?

ACTION   What position did you take?

- **In light of your experience, what do you believe the Four of Pentacles signified?**

- **What did you learn from it?**

- **If you drew the Four of Pentacles in response to a question you asked, in what way did this card answer it?**

- **Now, take another look at your card. Is there anything that stands out about it you didn't notice before?**

- **If you were to make your own Tarot card, what words, pictures or symbols would you put on it?**

SOMETHING TO REFLECT UPON

Close your eyes and imagine that you had become rich overnight, that you had just won the lottery and you were sitting on top of a pile of your millions. . . . Would your feelings, actions or decisions have been the same? Would you continue to do what you're currently doing? What would be different? Can you apply this awareness now?

> *If you put a small value upon yourself, rest assured that the world will not raise your price.*
>
> ANONYMOUS

THE FIVE OF PENTACLES

Pentacles deal with tangibles and issues involving money, manifestation, values or power.

Numerologically, the number 5 indicates change, fluctuations in fate or fortune, conflict, experiential learning and the expansion of one's thinking. With the number 5, opportunities and challenges go hand in hand, and one must look to both the material and spiritual realm if one is to triumph or understand.

Constructive: Discrimination. Resourcefulness. Revision. Re-creation. Self-reliance. Inner conviction.

Undermining: Little faith in one's self or abilities. Panic. Distress. Rebellion.

• **What stood out the most in your experience of this card?**

In addition to your recollection, here are some other possibilities you might want to consider:

FOCUS   Did you feel financially sound but spiritually impoverished? Were you encountering the dark side of the human experience or going through "a dark night of the soul"? Were you dealing with issues you didn't want to confront or facing your biggest fears?

DESIRES   Did you wish you weren't alone, or that you had a more direct experience of God in your life and affairs?

LOVE   Were your romantic desires unfulfilled? If love was offered, was your heart still mourning a breakup or longing for something else? Did a relationship falter because of a lack of communication, misunderstanding or sexual problem? If so, were the difficulties eventually overcome or were your paths and destinies too different and there was no alternative but to part?

Were you disappointed in people who let you down, didn't follow through or were irresponsible in their ethical or financial responsibility to you? Did you join a support or recovery group? Were you in contact with people whose experience was similar to yours? Were you saddened by a tragedy, misfortune befalling another or man's inhumanity to man? **OTHERS**

Were you going through a tremendous upheaval? Was it difficult to find solace? **HOME**

Were you contemplating a journey? Did you have to spend money on car repairs? Were there any other problems related to cars, transportation or travel? **TRAVEL**

Was there tension in your working environment? Were people difficult to cope with or deal with? Was there dissension among employees? Did someone quit? Was a job lost? Were you having a love/hate/stalemate relationship with your work? Were there any heated debates? Did problems escalate until you could no longer ignore them? Were you forced to take a hiatus? Once you accepted the setback and returned to work, did a greater comprehension emerge? **WORK**

Were your material ambitions making you a miserable person, no good to yourself or others? Did you have serious doubts about your **BODY/MIND** abilities, your work or God? Did the future look hopeless? Did masking the pain you were feeling cause your health to suffer? Did it occur to you that your difficulties were signaling a deeper problem?

SPIRIT

Were your dreams instructional? Were you lucky in financial matters?

RELATIVES

Was a relative having (financial?) problems? Were you too upset or exhausted to be of much help? Were there any quarrels? Were feelings finally heard and soothed or were they stomped on and suppressed?

FINANCES

Was your economic position improving? Was money spent on, or received for, spiritual or metaphysical work? Did you get an unexpected bonus or promotion? Did money come through what appeared to be an unfortunate experience?

PROBLEMS

Did problems crop up you didn't anticipate? Was it becoming painfully evident that no matter how hard you tried, you couldn't rise above the hardships you were experiencing? Did you fail to recognize the signs and symptoms of physical or emotional neglect? Did you *know* you were pushing yourself beyond your limits but you did it anyway?

GUIDANCE

Were you praying for help and understanding? Did soul searching or reading spiritual material provide insights or comfort? Do you think you were becoming a more compassionate, conscientious or resourceful person as a result of your suffering?

Did your greatest achievement come through a spiritual deliverance? **SUCCESS**
Were you successful in adopting a new method of operation that
proved to be an asset in your work, or in processing what you learned
and turning it into a psychology of being?

Did you have to struggle to fulfill your obligations or your responsi- **ACTION**
bility to yourself? What enabled you to continue on?

- **In light of your experience, what do you believe the Five of Pentacles signified?**

- **What did you learn from it?**

- **If you drew the Five of Pentacles in response to a question you asked, in what way did this card answer it?**

- **Now, take another look at your card. Is there anything that stands out about it you didn't notice before?**

- If you were to make your own Tarot card, what words, pictures or symbols would you put on it?

SOMETHING TO REFLECT UPON

God wishes us to recognize the problem(s) He's about to remove because He wants us to *feel* His presence in our lives and hearts, not just to know Him vicariously.

◆   # THE SIX OF PENTACLES

Pentacles deal with tangibles and issues involving money, manifestation, values or power.

Numerologically, the number 6 indicates the need to make adjustments in one's thoughts, attitudes, behavior or condition. While this may feel burdensome, the number 6 also carries with it the ability to transcend difficulties and oftentimes serendipitously. Responsibilities, family and health may also be emphasized.

Constructive: Thoroughness. Resoluteness. Serving, giving or adapting to the needs of others. Love. Compassion.

Undermining: Indifference. Irresponsibility (toward self and others). Fixed opinions, beliefs or attitudes. Imbalance.

- **What stood out the most in your experience of this card?**

In addition to your recollection, here are some other possibilities you might want to consider:

Was your energy on tangible acquisitions and improving your status, **FOCUS**
capital or material well-being? Were you drawing comparisons or
analogies? What projects, causes or activities were you involved in?
Were there any promising opportunities or token starts?

Did you want what was rightfully yours, or to know if you'd have or **DESIRES**
make enough money?

Were you feeling a sense of separateness? Was the distance between **LOVE**
you and another increasing? If so, what was the reason? Did money,
position or status come between you? Was there an *adjustment* you
could make?

Did a business proposal need to be decided or firmed up? Was there a **OTHERS**
problem with your phone, fax, computer or other communication
lines? Were you concerned about a friend?

Did anything out of the ordinary occur? Did you injure yourself or **HOME**
experience a life-threatening situation? Were you so socked into your
work or project(s) you couldn't relax?

Did you travel for business reasons, social calls or group activities? **TRAVEL**
Did a favor, special occasion or financial matter require travel?

WORK   Were you uncertain about the success of a new venture, or not yet established? Was there an undercurrent of unfinished business? Were you getting the impression that it might be better to change your thinking than your job, location or employer?

BODY/MIND   Were you in a positive mood? What values did you base your happiness upon? Were you attending to your health, diet or weight? Did you need to rest, slow down or unwind? Were you considering a different insurance plan?

SPIRIT   Were you given a gift or token of love? Did someone surprise you with a charitable act, sponsor you or give you a discount? Were *you* charitable?

RELATIVES   Did a relative want to travel or move? Were you planning a trip or rendezvous? Was anyone unhappy or ill? How much time or consideration was devoted to your family?

FINANCES   Were you waiting for money or supporting anyone? If so, what were your feelings with regard to that? Was your patience wearing thin? Did your income and outflow balance out? Did you come up with any moneymaking ideas?

Were you having trouble making the right connections? Were you disappointed in something that didn't turn out the way you thought it would, or wasn't all that it was cracked up to be? Were you envious of those who were younger, older, thinner, brighter or more successful than you?   **PROBLEMS**

Did you have a realization that altered your experience? Did new information make something impossible suddenly possible? Were the answers you needed available? Were you advised to keep an open mind? What insights did you have?   **GUIDANCE**

Did success come through educational resources or asking the right questions? If you reworked a previous project, did the new effort surpass the old? Did you accomplish more than you thought you were capable of? If you were preoccupied with money or security, did it cease to be an issue?   **SUCCESS**

Did you revert to, or follow through with, an original plan or decision? Were you willing to defer instant gratification?   **ACTION**

• **In light of your experience, what do you believe the Six of Pentacles signified?**

- **What did you learn from it?**

- **If you drew the Six of Pentacles in response to a question you asked, in what way did this card answer it?**

- **Now, take another look at your card. Is there anything that stands out about it you didn't notice before?**

- **If you were to make your own Tarot card, what words, pictures or symbols would you put on it?**

SOMETHING TO REFLECT UPON

If you were told you only had a week to live, what would you do differently?
How would you live *this* day if you thought it was your last?

THE SEVEN OF PENTACLES

Pentacles deal with tangibles and issues involving money, manifestation, values or power.

Numerologically, the number 7 indicates a period of introspection, analysis or solitude. During the influence of the number 7, one's psychological and spiritual resources are expanded and faith in what can't be seen, but nevertheless exists, is demanded.

Constructive: Evaluation, research or investigation. Experimenting and being willing to look at things differently. Waiting for what you want to come to you. Trusting your intuition and Higher Self.

Undermining: Pessimism. Separatism. Perfectionism. Living in one's head.

• **What stood out the most in your experience of this card?**

In addition to your recollection, here are some other possibilities you might want to consider:

Were you reevaluating your goals, your life or your relationship(s)? Did progress appear to be at a standstill? Were results slow in coming? Did not being productive or having to wait for what you wanted cause you to become anxious, disheartened or depressed? **FOCUS** _____

Did you want to succeed but wonder if you would or could? **DESIRES** _____

Did you resign yourself to the likelihood of either continuing a non-fulfilling relationship or having to go through life alone? Were you waiting for your lover to finish something (his/her previous relationship, getting over being angry, lack of financial security, etc.) so that you could be together or he/she would come back to you? Did mat- **LOVE** _____ ters of the heart take a dramatic turn for the better? Was it because of a newfound love or romance? Were you wondering if a relationship was what you really wanted?

OTHERS

Were you getting the support you needed? Were you disappointed in the business response you received (or the lack thereof)? Was someone ignoring you or putting you off? If you were waiting for a call did it come? Was a long-distance conversation beneficial?

HOME

Were you having a difficult time at home? If so, what was causing it? Did you meet or entertain a (new) neighbor?

TRAVEL

Did you want or need to get away for awhile? If you traveled, did you have a good time? Was the weather hot and sticky?

WORK

Were you dissatisfied with your (life's) work or unhappy with the progress you were making? Did you worry about completing it? Were you beginning to wonder if it was even *worth* pursuing? Did someone steal your ideas?

BODY/MIND

Were you suffering from depression or anxiety? Did you need to cease your current activities (or the hammering of your thoughts)? Did you have to go to the doctor or take medication? Was what you were doing (or contemplating) in your best interest?

Were you pleased with a new possession or discovery?   **SPIRIT**

Were you impatient or abrupt? Did your family sense your inner frustration? Were you rethinking your conduct?   **RELATIVES**

Did you want to have or make more money? Did an important decision hinge on money or your partner's earning capacity? Did you worry about your finances or going into the red? Were you keeping an eye on your expenses? Did you scrutinize receipts and document your expenditures? Was there a slight or big improvement? Did good news (or a check) arrive?   **FINANCES**

Were you disappointed in the time it would take for your goals to be realized? Was fear your worst enemy? Was the fate you felt trapped in only in your mind?   **PROBLEMS**

Was something (or someone) telling you to be patient, that you would eventually succeed? What special guidance were you receiving?   **GUIDANCE**

Was it hard to get established? Did anything reinforce your determination? Was something of value learned, earned or acquired?   **SUCCESS**

ACTION   Did you realize that you didn't have to strive or suffer, but to discover?

- In light of your experience, what do you believe the Seven of Pentacles signified?

- What did you learn from it?

- If you drew the Seven of Pentacles in response to a question you asked, in what way did this card answer it?

- Now, take another look at your card. Is there anything that stands out about it you didn't notice before?

- If you were to make your own Tarot card, what words, pictures or symbols would you put on it?

SOMETHING TO REFLECT UPON

To everything there is a season,
and a time for every purpose under heaven:

A time to be born, and a time to die;
a time to plant, and a time to pluck up that which is planted;

A time to kill, and a time to heal;
a time to break down, and a time to build up;

A time to weep, and a time to laugh;
a time to mourn, and a time to dance;

A time to cast away stones, and a time to gather stones together;
a time to embrace, and a time to refrain from embracing;

A time to get and a time to lose;
a time to keep, and a time to cast away;

A time to rend, and a time to sew;
a time to keep silence, and a time to speak;

A time to love, and a time to hate;
a time of war, and a time of peace.

Ecclesiastes 3:1

◆ THE EIGHT OF PENTACLES

Pentacles deal with tangibles and issues involving money, manifestation, values or power.

Numerologically, the number 8 connotes the potential for success, accomplishment or recognition and the capacity to achieve one's goals; but unless one seeks the Power Within, these may not be easily attained. Although a positive change of mind or status almost always accompanies the number 8, moral integrity, fortitude and emotional equilibrium will also be required.

Constructive: Attending to business, finance and material matters. Asserting one's self or one's authority. Enacting daring plans. Becoming proficient.

Undermining: Strain. Overemotionalism. Oppression. Careless disregard for the spiritual or material realities of life.

• **What stood out the most in your experience of this card?**

In addition to your recollection, here are some other possibilities you might want to consider:

FOCUS   Were you diligently applying yourself to your work, career goals and activities related to finance and profit? Did you need assistance or backing? Were friendships, romance and social get-togethers highlighted? Were you making the most of what you had? What was changing in your life?

DESIRES   Did you hope your plans would turn out well and your enterprises would be successful?

Did you attract admirers? Were you captivated by an artist, crafts-man, designer or actor? Did a new relationship begin? If so, did you think it was practical, workable or realistic?

LOVE

Did you do something that nourished others? Did people tell you that you made a difference in their lives? Did you meet someone who changed the course of your romantic or financial experience? Did anyone assist, train or back you?

OTHERS

Were you looking for a solution to a problem or trying to figure out how you could make better use of your time or money?

HOME

Did you travel for practical or financial reasons? Were you hoping to meet, or travel with, someone special? Did the traffic or weather make you nervous?

TRAVEL

Was what you were doing or selling profitable? Did you have the op-portunity to diversify your skills or practice a new one? Were you sat-isfied with your achievements? Did someone offer to subsidize you? What tools were you working with?

WORK

Were you more conscious of your physical presence and emotional needs? Did too much of anything—work, food, sun, drink—make you ill? Were you losing weight or your appetite? Were you begin-ning to recognize the limits of your energy and the importance of maintaining balance in your life?

BODY/MIND

SPIRIT — Were you in good spirits? Did someone or something light up your life? What made you laugh or sing?

RELATIVES — Did you want/need to spend more time with your family? Were you trying to schedule an outing together?

FINANCES — Were you more mindful of your investments and securing your financial future? Did you think you could have made more money if you had been more savvy or had a better head for business?

PROBLEMS — Were you disappointed in love or discouraged by the effort it took to accomplish your goals? Did you feel pressured into accepting something you really didn't want?

GUIDANCE — Were you getting the impression that it was not a time to assert yourself, that you alone did not have the energy, wisdom or wherewithal to attain what you were after?

SUCCESS — Did you have small successes but not big ones?

ACTION — Did you have to work harder and longer to achieve the same ends? Did you need to look to the past to find answers in the present?

- In light of your experience, what do you believe the Eight of Pentacles signified?

- What did you learn from it?

- If you drew the Eight of Pentacles in response to a question you asked, in what way did this card answer it?

- Now, take another look at your card. Is there anything that stands out about it you didn't notice before?

- If you were to make your own Tarot card, what words, pictures or symbols would you put on it?

SOMETHING TO REFLECT UPON

The times we least feel like turning within and seeking spiritual assistance are when we need to the most.

THE NINE OF PENTACLES

Pentacles deal with tangibles and issues involving money, manifestation, values or power.

Numerologically, the number 9 stands for completion, arrival, integration and realization. When a number 9 surfaces, it marks a transition between what was and what is to come, a parenthesis in time as one pauses to reflect on all that went before and the unknown potential of that which is yet to be.

Constructive: Broadness of viewpoint, perspective and understanding. Having faith in one's source of supply. Discard. Detachment. Impersonal interaction.

Undermining: Self-centeredness. Dissipation. Suffering.

• **What stood out the most in your experience of this card?**

In addition to your recollection, here are some other possibilities you might want to consider:

FOCUS   Were you primarily concerned with business, (corporate) enterprise and mergers? Were you given the opportunity to make more money or better your material position? Did a new plateau await you?

DESIRES   Did you want to promote yourself, form a new partnership or resolve unfinished business?

LOVE   Did love come through work, service-type people or public meeting places? If you were separated from a loved one, was it only a temporary condition? Were you content with your relationship or relationship status?

Were your interactions mostly business oriented? Did you receive a   **OTHERS**
letter of gratitude or commendation? Did you make a positive difference in the lives of others?

Were you working from home or taking your work home? Did you   **HOME**
need more space or think about adding on, or converting, a room?

Were you traveling for business reasons or waiting for news or a   **TRAVEL**
package to come from a distance?

Did someone offer you a job or pay you for your services? Were   **WORK**
negotiations conducted over the phone? Did being busy compensate
for a lack you were feeling in another area of your life?

Were you in good health and free of cares or worries? Did someone   **BODY/MIND**
you know have a substance-abuse problem?

What did you do to make your life richer and more satisfying?   **SPIRIT**

Did a little one or pet bring joy into your world? Was your family   **RELATIVES**
generous or accommodating? Were you able to make them happy?

FINANCES   Were you experiencing better financial conditions? Were you compensated for your efforts, work or services? Did you feel prosperous?

PROBLEMS   Were you worried that a deal was blown, or a business was about to fold? Did a partnership look as though it wasn't going to get off the ground, or that it might be severed? Did you distrust yourself or your decision-making ability?

GUIDANCE   Were you getting the message to go for it; that a bird in the hand was worth two in the bush?

SUCCESS   Were your negotiations successful? Were you satisfied with your accomplishments? Did you attain the cooperation you sought? Was your wish for a union fulfilled? Did a plan that looked iffy go through after all?

ACTION   What did you need to eliminate or give more thought to? Did you have to take the initiative in order for your material, romantic or partnership desires to be realized?

- **In light of your experience, what do you believe the Nine of Pentacles signified?**

• **What did you learn from it?**

• **If you drew the Nine of Pentacles in response to a question you asked, in what way did this card answer it?**

• **Now, take another look at your card. Is there anything that stands out about it you didn't notice before?**

• **If you were to make your own Tarot card, what words, pictures or symbols would you put on it?**

SOMETHING TO REFLECT UPON

Not in the stars but in ourselves lies our destiny.
JULIUS CAESAR

 # THE TEN OF PENTACLES

Pentacles deal with tangibles and issues involving money, manifestation, values or power.

The 10 in the Tarot marks the end of one phase and the beginning of another. Although it has the same basic meaning as the number 1, it also signifies a time when one may have to come to terms with something that was previously overlooked, unfinished or avoided.

- **What stood out the most in your experience of this card?**

In addition to your recollection, here are some other possibilities you might want to consider:

FOCUS — Did your world revolve around your family, friends and day-to-day living or were your sights set on building your career or increasing your worldly status? Was your workplace or community emphasized? Were traditions, groups or negotiations important?

DESIRES — Were you hoping to succeed with a plan or proposal or to establish better relations with others?

LOVE — Was love an important part of your life? Did you wish it were? Were you able to spend time with the one you wanted to be with or to cement the type of relationship you wanted to have?

OTHERS — Did you feel valued or appreciated? Were your business associates fair, reliable or trustworthy? Were you involved with any specialized groups? Did someone offer support, bolster your confidence or boost your morale?

HOME — Did your home reflect your inner growth or your worldly accomplishments? Were you living within your means? Did anything need maintenance or repair? Did you redecorate or remodel? Did your living arrangements or activities change?

Did a relative come to visit? Were you planning a trip or family af-   **TRAVEL**
fair? Were there any requirements you needed to take care of concerning your means of transportation?

What was your career status? Were projects a go or were they diffi-   **WORK**
cult to launch? Was your job relatively easy or had it suddenly become a chore? Was your work motivated by a sense of purpose or did
you do it only for the money?

Were you enjoying the fruits of your labor or were you feeling   **BODY/MIND**
bogged down by work or responsibilities? Did a family member or
pet need shots, grooming or looking after? Were you in good health?

What made you happy? Did something happen to make life more in-   **SPIRIT**
teresting? When was the last time you really enjoyed yourself? What
did you do? Are you doing that now? Could you be?

Did your family assist you in some way (or offer to)? Did you make   **RELATIVES**
any sacrifices? Were your actions motivated by love?

Were you financially secure? Were your investments sound? Did any-   **FINANCES**
one leave you a legacy? Where did your money come from? How was
it spent? Were there any losses or frustrating out-of-pocket expenditures? Were you able to meet the cost of living?

PROBLEMS   Was there a misunderstanding between you and a friend, relative, CEO or employer? Were you having financial problems? Was there an area of your life that you were having trouble dealing with? If so, what was it? How did you handle it?

GUIDANCE   Did you feel spiritually connected? If you sought answers, did you receive them?

SUCCESS   What value did you place on money? What were your feelings about wealth and power? How did you define success? Did you think that in order to get ahead in life you had to struggle, work hard and keep your nose to the grindstone, or did you feel that all things come in time and it was more important to trust the process?

ACTION   Was there something you needed to fix, complete or resolve? What did you direct your energy toward? What action did you take to make amends, accomplish your objectives or support yourself?

• **In light of your experience, what do you believe the Ten of Pentacles signified?**

- **What did you learn from it?**

- **If you drew the Ten of Pentacles in response to a question you asked, in what way did this card answer it?**

- **Now, take another look at your card. Is there anything that stands out about it you didn't notice before?**

- **If you were to make your own Tarot card, what words, pictures or symbols would you put on it?**

SOMETHING TO REFLECT UPON

Sometimes, even when we're pursuing altruistic goals, we get so wrapped up in *doing, getting there* and *making it* we get lost and we lose our spiritual grounding; we forget that we are perfect just the way we are and that no matter where we think we *ought* to be, there is a Divine Plan and we are right where we are *supposed* to be.

Ask yourself this: If it didn't matter one way or the other, what would I do?

THE PAGE OF PENTACLES

Astrological Sign: Capricorn

Capricorn rules the tenth house and activities related to one's profession (career ambitions, qualifications, standing in the community, etc.); worldly attainments (power, affluence, prestige; things of substance); and dealings with superiors, authority figures and one's parents (particularly the father*).

Time frame: December 22–January 19

Type: Pragmatic. Conventional. Responsible. Conservative. Practical. Thoughtful. Efficient.

Thrust: Character development. Absorbing information. Usefulness. Structure and foundations. The present (that which is *being* established).

Cornerstone: To do, to achieve, to find one's self through experience.

Life lesson: Graciousness and/or social skills

Pentacles deal with tangibles and issues involving money, manifestation, values or power.

Pages are commonly referred to as messengers, children or youths, but they can also represent one's maturing self, lovers or problems.

The Page of Pentacles connotes a person who is studious, hard-working and persevering. He/she has a serious approach to life, and although this individual knows what he/she wants, the means to attain it may not yet be apparent. Traditionally, Pentacles represent a person with dark, graying or white hair but no particular eye color is specified.

Did you feel that you resembled this card type? Have you recently come in contact with someone who does?

• **What stood out the most in your experience of this card?**

In addition to your recollection, here are some other possibilities you might want to consider:

---

*Note: Some astrologers associate the mother with the tenth house. How did *you* experience it?

Was your career or professional status your chief concern? Did you **FOCUS**
want material things (furniture, clothing, luxuries, etc.)? Were you
enrolled in a school or learning a new trade? How were you relating
to your parents, teachers or boss? Were there obstacles you had to
surmount? What were you trying to accomplish, achieve, learn or become?

Were you wishing you were more successful or affluent? Did you **DESIRES**
want to better yourself or have a (more) stimulating career?

Were your friends and relatives trying to get you to go out more? Did **LOVE**
you think that dating (or being in love) would distract you from your
work or studies? Was a relationship or marriage changing? Were you
wondering what to do about a romantic involvement? Did you handle your affairs with integrity and behave in a way that made you feel
good about yourself?

Did your ambition make you bossy, insensitive or callous? Were **OTHERS**
(sales) people apathetic or unwilling to extend themselves? Did a
friend offer assistance or do something nice for you? Did your
coworkers respect you?

Was someone reluctant to come to your house or delayed in return- **HOME**
ing? Did a visitor drop by unannounced? Was your rent increased?
Did something positive occur related to your home or property?
What requirements were necessary for you to be happy at home?

TRAVEL

Did you travel for work, business or scholastic reasons? Did you discuss or go on a tour? Did you just *have* to go out or buy something?

WORK

Vocations suited for a Capricorn type are building contractor, engineer or mason; architect, designer or draftsman; real estate appraiser; buyer; osteopath; executive; banker; sculptor (marble, metal, glass or ice); making or repairing functional items.

Do any of these professions sound like something you're doing or would like to do? Did you speak to, or associate with, someone who worked in one of these trades?

Did you feel like you were in a slump? Did limited skills, information or training hinder your ability to perform or communicate effectively? Was paperwork arduous, extensive or tedious? Did you discuss business over lunch or dinner? Were your expectations realistic? Did a promising lead pan out?

BODY/MIND

Health issues associated with a Capricorn type are knees; skin; bones; joints; teeth; chills, congestion and colds; bruises; tinnitus; acidic conditions; ulcers; depression.

Have you experienced problems related to any of these areas recently? Has anyone close to you?

Was a chronic condition or habit hard to heal or break? Were you feeling heavy, pensive or gloomy? Were you tired of *trying?* Did you have trouble defining the word "fun"? Were you exhibiting symptoms of depression, stress or strain? Was your stomach bothering you? Were your ears ringing?

Did you have a symbolic dream? Were you lucky in material matters or through a union that brought in money? Did you acquire something for your home, work, diet or wardrobe that pleased you?

SPIRIT

Was a plan rejected, canceled or postponed? Did someone's behavior bring out the worst in you? Were you curt to your relatives or neglecting your family? Were you just like your father? What values did you learn from your parents or teach your children?

RELATIVES

Were you a good negotiator? Were you able to talk others into giving you the deal you wanted? Were you researching a higher/lower premium or yield? Were your investments or expenditures conservative? Did a worrisome delay soon blow over?

FINANCES

The negative characteristics of a Capricorn type are insecurity, stubbornness, callousness, self-absorption, suppressing emotions, driving oneself (or others) too hard.
   Did you see these traits in yourself or notice them in another? What troubles or disappointments were you experiencing?

PROBLEMS

Did you get the impression that if something was meant to be, it would happen of its own accord, or that it was pointless to worry over things you had no control over? Were you willing to listen to new ideas or consider alternative approaches? What special guidance were you receiving?

GUIDANCE

SUCCESS   Did success come through a business proposal or social invitation? Did a phone call clear up an error or a question of concern? Did persistence and steadfastness eventually pay off?

ACTION   If blind determination got you what you wanted, was the upshot (or what it took to get it) to your liking?

• In light of your experience, what do you believe the Page of Pentacles signified?

• What did you learn from it?

• If you drew the Page of Pentacles in response to a question you asked, in what way did this card answer it?

• Now, take another look at your card. Is there anything that stands out about it you didn't notice before?

• **If you were to make your own Tarot card, what words, pictures or symbols would you put on it?**

SOMETHING TO REFLECT UPON

Be kind to yourself. The highway to attainment is frequently under construction.

 # THE KNIGHT OF PENTACLES

Knights symbolize comings or goings, beginnings or endings and direction of thoughts or energy. When a Knight appears, long-term conditions will change.

There is no astrological or numerological correlation to the Knights.

Pentacles deal with tangibles and issues involving money, manifestation, values or power.

• **What stood out the most in your experience of this card?**

In addition to your recollection, here are some other possibilities you might want to consider:

FOCUS

Were your activities geared toward business, promotion, advertising or real estate, but your heart and mind on travel, love and the pursuit of happiness? Did your life, or something you were doing or involved in, change or go in a different direction? If your pace had been frantic, was it beginning to ease up and slow down?

DESIRES _____ Did you want to have a successful relationship, find a cure or improve an existing situation? Were you seeking the peace of mind you believed only the grace of God could bring?

LOVE _____ Were you seeing (or involved with) someone intelligent, easygoing and agreeable? Did love, or being with the person you loved, become the most important thing in life? Was your spouse/mate/lover's career, schedule or ambition getting in the way? Were you intuitively sensing what was to come?

OTHERS _____ Did people in business run hot and cold (mostly cold)?

HOME _____ Was a property matter emphasized, debated or resolved? Were you pleased with your home or surroundings? Were you more in tune with the earth and your environment?

TRAVEL _____ Did you go on a shopping spree (or plan to)? Did you discuss or buy something for an upcoming trip? Did you travel with someone you like or love?

WORK _____ Were your thoughts on your work or somewhere else? Was progress slow or at a standstill? If you had fallen behind, did you get caught up? Were conditions improving?

Were you holding back your feelings or enforcing rigid restraints? **BODY/MIND**
Did you make a decision about your health, such as quitting your
diet or treating yourself to some personal time? Were you feeling
more calm or peaceful? If so, why?

Did *things* make you happy or were you happy just *being?* Did some- **SPIRIT**
thing (or someone) turn an ordinary event into an extraordinary experience? Did you enjoy the rapport you shared with another? Was
there a spontaneous outpouring of love and affection?

Did you and your family see eye to eye? Did you want to see, talk to **RELATIVES**
or share your feelings with someone but felt you couldn't? Was there
someone in your family you could always count on?

Were you anxious about making, saving or collecting money? When **FINANCES**
you gave it more thought (or time) did you realize that you were better off than most, that your assets and earnings were actually increasing? Did awaited money finally arrive?

Were you troubled by a disconcerting awareness? Was there a chasm **PROBLEMS**
between you and what you wanted that you feared might never be
bridged? Did you feel unsupported?

Did you see, hear or read something that gave you insight into the **GUIDANCE**
root of a problem, assured you that your future was secure or vali-
dated your intuitive process? Were you shown that there are *always*

alternatives? What messages were you receiving from your Inner Teacher?

SUCCESS _____   Were your desires ultimately realized?

ACTION _____   Did you heed the dictates of your heart, hunches or gut feelings?

_____

- In light of your experience, what do you believe the Knight of Pentacles signified?

- What did you learn from it?

- If you drew the Knight of Pentacles in response to a question you asked, in what way did this card answer it?

- Now, take another look at your card. Is there anything that stands out about it you didn't notice before?

• **If you were to make your own Tarot card, what words, pictures or symbols would you put on it?**

SOMETHING TO REFLECT UPON

You may want to tape this guided meditation and play it back with your eyes closed.

Take a few deep, relaxed breaths, and for the next minute or so, experience the sounds, smells, images and vibrations of your surroundings. . . .

Now, turn your attention to your body. . . . Notice how it feels against the chair you're sitting in . . . how your clothes feel against your skin . . . the weight of your arms . . . the rise and fall of your chest . . . and any other sensation you may be experiencing. . . .

Now, bring your attention to your feelings. . . . Do not judge them or look for any meaning . . . just observe each one and then wait for the next to surface. . . .

Begin now to observe the stream of your consciousness . . . as each thought enters your mind, simply witness it and then let it go as if you were watching sticks floating down a river . . . if you find yourself getting caught up in a particular train of thought, acknowledge that also and then bring your attention back to waiting for your next thought to arise. . . .

Now take in *everything*. . . . Let *all* of the sounds, smells, sensations, thoughts and images come flooding in. . . . Feel yourself becoming one with them . . . and when you are ready, slowly open your eyes. . . .

Life is a meditation waiting patiently for us to open our spiritual eyes.

THE QUEEN OF PENTACLES

Astrological Sign: Aquarius

Aquarius rules the eleventh house and activities related to hopes, goals and aspirations; friends (or forming friendships); and advancement, knowledge and opportunity gained through social contacts, affiliations and organizations. (Note: Because the element associated with the suit of Pentacles is earth, Virgo is also attributed to this card. How did *you* experience it?)

> *Time frame:* January 20–February 19
> *Type:* Progressive. Open-minded. Altruistic. Sociable. Detached. Objective. Aspiring.
> *Thrust:* Spiritual Awakening. Inner purpose. New avenues or ideas. The unconventional.
> *Cornerstone:* To reform
> *Life lesson:* Warmth

Pentacles deal with tangibles and issues involving money, manifestation, values or power.

The Queen of Pentacles is described as eclectic, efficient and self-reliant. A multitalented person who, whether an artist, psychic, actor or executive, is able to call upon her/his many resources and channel them into bettering the lives of others and serving the needs of mankind. Traditionally, Pentacles represent a person with dark, graying or white hair but no particular eye color is specified.

Did you feel that you resembled this card type? Have you recently come in contact with someone who does?

• **What stood out the most in your experience of this card?**

In addition to your recollection, here are some other possibilities you might want to consider:

FOCUS   Were group activities highlighted? Were you evolving (or receiving benefit) through your association with others, fellowship-type meetings or counseling? Were humanitarian interests, service and tangible results more important to you?

DESIRES _____

Did you wish you could find your center, your place in the world or your true purpose? Were you looking for verification? Did you have an "impossible dream"?

LOVE _____

Were you seeking (or more comfortable with) intellectual companionship? Were you interested in someone unusual, striking or electric? Were people drawn to you? Were you weighing a relationship against your higher ideals or practical standards? Did the idea of spending *all* your time with someone make you uneasy?

OTHERS _____

Were you more concerned with the welfare of others, animal rights or social reform? Were you feeling magnanimous? Did you have many acquaintances but few friends? Were people inclined to assist you? Did others commend your skills?

HOME _____

Were you preparing for a future event? Did you like/dislike being a homemaker or spending time at home? Were there earthquakes or lightning storms?

TRAVEL _____

Were you planning a family function or vacation? Were travel plans or accommodations discussed? Did you get together with someone you've been intending to visit? Were your travels enjoyable?

WORK   Vocations suited for an Aquarian type are occultist; astrologer; palmist; New Age/metaphysical teacher, preacher or healer; radiologist; paramedic; inventor; social worker; urban developer; aviator; science fiction writer; radio announcer; actor.

Do any of these professions sound like something you're doing or would like to do? Did you speak to, or associate with, someone who worked in one of these trades?

Did you want to change your career? Were you attracted to the ministry, healing arts or metaphysics? Were you working in the entertainment industry? Did you get a call for work in the field you were contemplating or something that made better use of your talents than your current (or previous) profession?

BODY/MIND   Health issues associated with an Aquarian type are ankles, calves, shins, blood, blood poisoning, anemia, retina, pituitary gland, electric shock, nervous disorders, motor responses, circulatory problems, strange accidents.

Have you experienced problems related to any of these areas recently? Has anyone close to you?

Were you more of an observer than a participant or more mental than physical? If you were feeling moody or discouraged, did it quickly pass? Did honesty, conviction and integrity play an important role in your life? Did you want to heal another or need a spiritual infusion?

Were words, ideas or prophecies coming to light? Did you feel that **SPIRIT**
you had benefactors in both realms (spiritual and material)? Did you
enjoy helping, serving or giving to others? Was a fondest wish fulfilled?

Was family togetherness emphasized? Were you and another (a sib- **RELATIVES**
ling?) planning an outing together? Did someone need consoling?
Were you the type of person others could depend on?

Were more moneymaking opportunities available to you? Was in- **FINANCES**
come derived through something involving papers? Were financial
transactions done by mail? Were your profits increasing? Was money
coming in or freeing up? Were you feeling affluent?

The negative characteristics of an Aquarian type are unpredictability, **PROBLEMS**
indifference, rebellion, irresponsibility, erratic behavior, eccentricity.
    Did you see these traits in yourself or notice them in another?
What troubles or disappointments were you experiencing?

Did answers come when you sought them? Were you encouraged to **GUIDANCE**
keep following your star? If you needed reassurance, did something
or someone provide it?

Did a problem that looked like a mountain turn out to be a molehill? **SUCCESS**
Did you *attract* success? Were you ahead of your time?

ACTION　　　　　Did you look at obstacles as opportunities to do something different?

_____

- In light of your experience, what do you believe the Queen of Pentacles signified?

- What did you learn from it?

- If you drew the Queen of Pentacles in response to a question you asked, in what way did this card answer it?

- Now, take another look at your card. Is there anything that stands out about it you didn't notice before?

- If you were to make your own Tarot card, what words, pictures or symbols would you put on it?

SOMETHING TO REFLECT UPON

What are five goals you'd like to see materialize between now and this time next year?

1. _____

2. _____

3. _____

4. _____

5. _____

It's never too late to follow your dream.

◆ # THE KING OF PENTACLES

Astrological Sign: Gemini

Gemini rules the third house and activities related to one's communications (skills, method of expression, how one processes information, etc.); relatives (and how one relates to one's family, neighbors and surroundings); short journeys. (Note: Because the element associated with the suit of Pentacles is earth, Taurus is also attributed to this card. How did *you* experience it?)

Time frame: May 21–June 20

Type: Versatile. Inquisitive. Imaginative. Enterprising. Communicative. Clever. Charming.

Thrust: Variety. Activity. Change. Connecting. The immediate environment.

Cornerstone: To experience

Life lesson: Harnessing thoughts and energy

Pentacles deal with tangibles and issues involving money, manifestation, values or power.

The King of Pentacles is considered to be gifted, intelligent and benevolent, a person of character who, in order to achieve success and pave the way for others, may have sacrificed a great deal emotionally. This King is often described as a person of industry who has attained some measure of wealth, power or fame. Traditionally, Pentacles represent a person with dark, graying or white hair but no particular eye color is specified.

Did you feel that you resembled this card type? Have you recently come in contact with someone who does?

• **What stood out the most in your experience of this card?**

In addition to your recollection, here are some other possibilities you might want to consider:

FOCUS   Did you meet or associate with people in positions of power or authority? Were communications highlighted? Was there something you were beginning or in the process of completing? Was there anything you had to sacrifice in your pursuit of success?

DESIRES   Did you want to have more money? Were you hoping that you were moving in the right direction, or that a project would work, be accepted or well received? Was there someone you hoped to influence or get together with?

LOVE   Was someone behaving coldly, indifferently or irresponsibly? Was the give-and-take lacking? Did your career (or your partner's) interfere with the kind of relationship you wanted to have? Was there an eventual reunion or reconciliation?

Were there successful, influential or gifted people in your life? Were **OTHERS**
they mostly male? Were you involved with the public in some way? If
you felt alone, did you feel that you could reach out?

Did the hours you put into your work interfere with your home life? **HOME**
If you were involved with someone, did work or travel keep you from
spending more time together? Was there an emphasis on phone calls,
letters, communication devices or intellectual activities? Were you involved in any neighborhood projects?

Did your job entail traveling? Was commuting an issue? Were there **TRAVEL**
any pleasant schedule changes? Did you change your car insurance
policy or company? Were you contemplating a trip to the seashore?
Did you chauffeur a friend or pick up someone at the airport?

Vocations suited for a Gemini type are anything in the arts or media **WORK**
arts (motion pictures, radio, television, etc.), writer, journalist,
camera operator, technical engineer, manicurist, travel agent, transportation manager, traveling salesman, interpreter, lecturer, editor,
contract writer/negotiator, agent.

  Do any of these professions sound like something you're doing or
would like to do? Did you speak to, or associate with, someone who
worked in one of these trades?

  Were you involved with the arts, media or literary field in any way?
Did you wear many hats? Were you juggling several jobs at the same
time? Was your work admired or in demand? Did you get a commis-
sion or assignment? If so, what kind?

BODY/MIND   Health issues associated with a Gemini type are shoulders, arms or hands; trapezius muscle tension; thymus gland; diseases of the lungs, bronchial tubes or blood; respiratory or intestinal troubles; abdominal pains; anxiety attacks; speech impediments.

Have you experienced problems related to any of these areas recently? Has anyone close to you?

Was your overall health improving? Were you preoccupied with something?

SPIRIT   What activities did you most enjoy? What did you thrive on? How did you spend your time? Who or what pleased or surprised you?

RELATIVES   Were children important or problematical? Did you spend less time with your family (or more)? Did a relative give you strength or help you become a more balanced, stable person? Were you emotionally available?

FINANCES   Were your negotiations fruitful? Were you making more money or coming into money? Did you feel prosperous?

PROBLEMS   The negative characteristics of a Gemini type are restlessness, inflexibility, superficiality, insincerity, indecisiveness, dissipating energy.

Did you see these traits in yourself or notice them in another? What troubles or disappointments were you experiencing?

Did someone suggest that you needed to make a change in your life?   **GUIDANCE**
If so, did it confirm something you were inwardly feeling? What did
you feel led, directed or inspired to do?

Were your endeavors successful? Did your business or social connec-   **SUCCESS**
tions help you get where you wanted to go? Did you receive positive
acknowledgment, recognition or acclaim?

What did you need to work harder at or let go of?   **ACTION**

- **In light of your experience, what do you believe the King
  of Pentacles signified?**

- **What did you learn from it?**

- **If you drew the King of Pentacles in response to a question
  you asked, in what way did this card answer it?**

• Now, take another look at your card. Is there anything that stands out about it you didn't notice before?

• If you were to make your own Tarot card, what words, pictures or symbols would you put on it?

SOMETHING TO REFLECT UPON

When you are thinking or doing something your essence says is right, it's because it *is* right. Truth *feels* like truth . . .

How would you like to be remembered?

CHAPTER 5

Recording Your Cards

Your Card for the Week

Month _____   Month _____
1st Week _____   1st Week _____
2nd Week_____   2nd Week_____
3rd Week _____   3rd Week _____
4th Week _____   4th Week _____

Month _____   Month _____
1st Week _____   1st Week _____
2nd Week_____   2nd Week_____
3rd Week _____   3rd Week _____
4th Week _____   4th Week _____

Month _____   Month _____
1st Week _____   1st Week _____
2nd Week_____   2nd Week_____
3rd Week _____   3rd Week _____
4th Week _____   4th Week _____

Month _____   Month _____
1st Week _____   1st Week _____
2nd Week_____   2nd Week_____
3rd Week _____   3rd Week _____
4th Week _____   4th Week _____

Month _____   Month _____
1st Week _____   1st Week _____
2nd Week_____   2nd Week_____
3rd Week _____   3rd Week _____
4th Week _____   4th Week _____

Month _____   Month _____
1st Week _____   1st Week _____
2nd Week_____   2nd Week_____
3rd Week _____   3rd Week _____
4th Week _____   4th Week _____

Your Card for the Week

Month _____

1st Week _____

2nd Week_____

3rd Week _____

4th Week _____

Month _____

1st Week _____

2nd Week_____

3rd Week _____

4th Week _____

Month _____

1st Week _____

2nd Week_____

3rd Week _____

4th Week _____

Month _____

1st Week _____

2nd Week_____

3rd Week _____

4th Week _____

Month _____

1st Week _____

2nd Week_____

3rd Week _____

4th Week _____

Month _____

1st Week _____

2nd Week_____

3rd Week _____

4th Week _____

Month _____

1st Week _____

2nd Week_____

3rd Week _____

4th Week _____

Month _____

1st Week _____

2nd Week_____

3rd Week _____

4th Week _____

Month _____

1st Week _____

2nd Week_____

3rd Week _____

4th Week _____

Month _____

1st Week _____

2nd Week_____

3rd Week _____

4th Week _____

Month _____

1st Week _____

2nd Week_____

3rd Week _____

4th Week _____

Month _____

1st Week _____

2nd Week_____

3rd Week _____

4th Week _____